GASKIN

James MacVeigh

GASKIN

JONATHAN CAPE
THIRTY BEDFORD SQUARE LONDON

First published 1982
Copyright © 1982 by James MacVeigh and Graham Gaskin
Jonathan Cape Ltd, 30 Bedford Square, London WC1

MacVeigh, James
Gaskin.
1. Gaskin, Graham   2. Socially handicapped
youth – Great Britain – Biography
I. Title
305.2′3′0924   HV1441.G/
ISBN 0-224-01997-X

Printed in Great Britain by Butler & Tanner Ltd
Frome and London

To Maguy Confurgues and
to Christopher Logue
James MacVeigh

To Brenda
Graham Gaskin

Contents

1 | *Early Days*

The door snapped shut for the last time behind her, and she looked wildly up and down the street. Her husband was away and couldn't stop her, so she was determined to do it today. A few strands of hair were stuck to her cheek where she had been crying. She clutched the baby more tightly to herself and walked, sobbing, towards the main road.

'There goes Joan again,' said Mrs Dunn in the front room of number 37 as she passed their window. Her husband grunted, not looking up from his *Echo*, and blew out Woodbine smoke with an annoyed hiss. They were used to her dramas in Andrew Street.

It was a warm evening in June, which would have pleased her once. She stopped sobbing for a moment at this thought, and smiled grimly. Her stiletto heels clacked tip-tap on the pavement, rang over the manhole covers. Mrs Fitzpatrick was standing on the step of her house, number 11.

'What's the matter, love? Where're yer goin' with that baby at this time o' night?'

Not slowing her steps Joan looked back, doomed and defiant. 'To do meself in!'

Mrs Fitzpatrick's face sagged. The desperation in Joan's voice woke the baby, and he began to howl. At the corner of the street she met her mother. The old woman put her heavy shopping bag down on the pavement, folded her arms, and stood barring her path.

'Now, what the 'ell is it this time, love?'

'Out of me way, Mum.'

'What's the idea? What d'yer think that baby is, love, one o' them dolls I used to buy yer?'

Both were exhausted with these arguments. Both had had enough.

'I'm goin' to do meself in,' she repeated, desperately.

'What, love?' her mother said. 'Again?'

Joan pushed past and the old woman let her go, but her firm hands seized the baby as their bodies touched. She rocked it reassuringly as she watched her daughter sob her way across the road, then run for a bus.

An hour later Joan threw herself from the stern of a Wallasey ferry boat, and the dark, choking water sucked her in. She had been a ballroom dancer and a beauty queen. All that remains of her now is one of the sashes she won, 'Miss Scafell', and a few old-fashioned photographs.

The baby, of course, was me.

They heard the news in the middle of the night, and next morning Grandma moved into our house to look after us. My brother Robert was three, Brenda, my sister, was seven. My father could never stand his wife's family and soon, uttering threats and recriminations, Grandma was thrown out. Various friends had me for a time. None was enthusiastic about having someone else's baby, and they quickly handed me on. In September 1960, when I was nine months old, my father ran out of friends and placed me in the care of the local authority, Liverpool City Council.

When something frightened me or I needed a cuddle, she was there. Her apron was damp, and smelt of soap and vegetables. At teatime she'd stop me pushing my big car across the kitchen tiles and pop me into the high chair at the head of the table. I was a kind of king then, so high up, watching the nine or ten big munching boys who were my subjects. The mugs of tea were sweet, and the Marmite sandwiches lovely. The taste of the stuff still takes me to her.

'Mummy, Mummy!' I'd shout when I had something to show her.

She would stop what she was doing and haul me on to her knee, jiggling me around till I was comfortable. Listening to her patient explanation was like hearing a familiar fairy story, I knew the words before they came.

'Now, Graham, *I'm* not your Mummy. You know that really, don't you? I *love* you as if I was a mummy, but . . .'

Her hands trembled as she did up the buttons of my overcoat. She tugged the lapels towards her and gave me a last, hard kiss. She was crying. The lady took my hand and I followed her with little steps out to the car, not understanding. At four years old, social services had decided to move me.

That was the start of it. After that I never stopped moving. The first place was a social services house in Lordens Road, Page Moss, run by Mr and Mrs Johnson. Brenda and Robert were already there, Robert having a hard time because he was the youngest. They had sent me there to make things easier for him. Now *I* was the youngest, and had to survive the bullying.

School was still in the future, for the present I was at home all day with Mrs Johnson. A face like a cleaver and flyaway glasses. She was annoyed at having a child in the house all day, and my time was spent on out-of-the-way chairs, keeping quiet. When I was naughty she stripped me and stood me in the bath, then threw buckets of cold water over me. She knew her stuff, that lady. Later the same trick was to be used on me by the screws in Wormwood Scrubs, though by that time they had to put me in a straitjacket and a padded cell to get away with it. When she took me out of the bath Mrs Johnson rubbed me briskly with a towel like sandpaper, then made me stand naked on the landing.

'Go on, stand there. Face the wall. Little devil . . .'

For hours on end, shivering, watched by wallpaper roses. Though the worst I would have got from the woman in the first house would have been a slapped leg, it didn't occur to me that I was being ill-treated. As far as I knew my life was normal.

Before I was five I started at infants' school in Page Moss.

Used to being the smallest kid around, I suddenly found myself the biggest in the class. Goading the others was easy, and I soon gained a reputation for toughness among the tots. Though I was miserable and unsettled, other things were happening. There was truant to play, a way of being free at last. School was something the other kids endured during the daytime. When the bell rang it signalled their freedom and they went home happily to mum and dad. For me the bell was a knell of fear. Time to go back to the Johnsons.

Who eventually left, loading their stuff on to a van and disappearing forever in a puff of blue exhaust. Others came. There is nothing much to remember about them. They were strict at table. They never made me unhappy. Just the same, I was desperately miserable. In my sleep I endured endless horrors, dreamt of suffocation, woke screaming, gasping. Once they heard me, came into my room and took me to hospital. Dim uniforms and white tables, a chemical tang of ether. For a day? A week? A month? Who knows? A child's mind cannot grasp the notion of time.

At this time, too, recurrent nightmares about water. A ship on the water, watched as though on T.V. It was sailing along with the sea glass-flat beneath it and this gave me bliss, a kind of ecstasy. But the ripples would always come, replacing my peace with anxious frenzy. The water-line would suddenly jerk to an angle, like a fishtank tilted, and the ship would rush downhill. When this happened I twitched and shivered in a seizure of fear, raging, trying to control it, to make the sea go flat again. The ship rushed on, down, down, down, out of control, terrifying. The dream went on and on: after the calm, always the warning ripples and the panic-striking, sudden tilt.

When I was fourteen and discovered how my mother died, this nightmare became comprehensible. People had talked about her death in front of me, and it had filtered into my mind. At school I was forever drawing rowing boats and fishing smacks, galleons and galleys. I always began with the water, taking a ruler and drawing a line that was dead straight, rigidly horizontal. Only when I was satisfied with this would the colour go in.

It was a cold Sunday morning.

'Where're we goin', Bren?'

My sister wrapped my scarf around me. Her skin glowed. She was twelve.

'Yer'll find out soon enough,' she said smugly. My excitement at the unknown treat was immense. Robert looked at me scornfully as we went out. I chattered and skipped on the rein of Brenda's arm to the bus stop. After a long time the bus swished to a halt before us. At the Ice Rink in Prescot Road we changed buses, and caught a number 27 to Walton. When we climbed off it she told me.

'Yer goin' to see yer Dad, Graham.' Her voice was proud and lively.

'Me Dad?' I said. 'Me Dad? Who *is* me Dad, Brenda?'

His house was near, a terraced house with a rug-sized garden in front. The man who opened the door hadn't shaved yet or put his teeth in. The front ones were missing and his gums gleamed, shiny and wet. We watched him curiously. He took us into the kitchen where a fire was lit and the radio playing. There was a little yellow table and some chairs. Brenda and Robert took their coats off and made themselves at home. Swinging my legs from the chair because my feet didn't yet reach the floor, I stared while he made his curious breakfast. He put Cornflakes into a bowl, broke Shredded Wheat over the top, then poured hot milk. It made me feel queasy. When he had eaten he tossed some money on to the table for Brenda.

'Get the dinner, love.'

With that, he went out. Brenda bought as many biscuits and cakes as the money allowed and we sat in front of the telly all afternoon, cramming them in. Dad came back at half-past four. We had to be back at the Home by five. Brenda has since told me that my father used to visit us in our foster homes, and that I had seen him before this day. I believe her, but have told it like this because that is how I remember it.

On the day of our school Christmas party I was unhappy and craved attention. Someone to put their arms around me, to whisper comforts, to give me a cuddle. I refused to eat. You might call it my first hunger strike, a prelude to the later ones in prison.

'What's the matter, Graham?'

The teacher was concerned, but harassed. Too busy for a cuddle.

'I've got earache, miss.'

It was something which often troubled me. To my surprise she took me home in her car, where it was decided that I was very ill. They whisked me off to Alder Hey, the children's hospital. So much for Christmas. The date is stuck in my mind. 20th December.

Though I'm sure there was nothing wrong with me, they kept me in for six months. It was a mixed ward and for some of the time there were girls on either side of me. The doctors gave me tests and a series of terrifying injections. The word 'needle' raised goose-bumps all over me. No one visited me until the final week. The parents of other children got to know me and brought me sweets when they came. When their child was discharged they vanished forever.

One day a fat man with light-trapping spectacles came to see me. He sat on the chair at my bedside.

'Hello, Graham. How are you? Any better?'

'Yes, thank you.'

'Good. Well. I'm Mr Griffiths, and I'm a foster parent, see.' His face quivered as he smiled. 'Brenda and Robert have been with me a while, and we were wondering would you like to come too?'

'Thank you, Mr Griffiths,' I piped in my politest voice. 'Yes, please.'

Next day Brenda came. My voice shrilled down the ward as she sought my face.

'Brenda, Brenda! I'm comin' to live with yer again!'

She sat on the side of my bed.

'It's horrible there,' she said.

The house was in a mean street off West Derby Road. At first it was just a house. As it became more familiar it acquired a grim, barrack-like aspect like the entrance to a prison. Brenda, standing in the hall, pressed a gift into my hand as I passed in Mr Griffiths's wake. A little tin bus, bright red. Mrs Griffiths turned from the stove to look at me as I came in. A great, waddling, slatternly woman, as fat as her husband.

'Oh, you're the new one, are you?'

She turned back to her cooking.

They had a kid of their own, an immensely fat girl a little younger than me whom I soon came to hate. Her name was Sandra, and they doted on her. We Gaskins were pariahs in their house, nuisances they tolerated for the money we brought.

They fed us first, on the leftovers of their last night's meal, then sent us out while they ate as a family. Their food smelled delicious as we sat in the musty parlour listening to their chatter, peeping around the door sometimes to catch a glimpse of their family life.

Mr Griffiths ruled us with the strap. It was shiny and well-worn with use. They never made any attempt to be fair to us, apparently believing it right to treat us like dirt. Fat Sandra peed the bed every night, and they cooed over this as one of life's misfortunes. In all the time I was there I did it twice.

'God, you're *dirty*,' Mrs Griffiths said, patting my bed to confirm her suspicion. 'You did that on purpose, didn't you? Don't start playing those games with me, my lad. You wait till Mr Griffiths gets home.'

Both times, he gave me a tremendous whipping.

At night I used to tweak Sandra's nose while she was sleeping, and call her names.

'Bastard. Why don't yer die? Bastard. Bastard.'

If she had been awake she would have told them. Sometimes when she hit me I would hit her back. Fat arse wobbling in distress, she would waddle off to tell her Mum. When Mr Griffiths came home he would ceremoniously get out the strap, his fat face radiating beastliness while I cried at the coming pain, and Rob and Brenda glowered. Brenda, as the oldest, had all the most difficult tasks. Asking for our pocket money was one.

'Er, we still 'aven't 'ad our pocket money, Mrs Griffiths,' she would begin, wincing when the fat woman furiously turned.

'It's being saved up for you. Now go and get the brush moving in that kitchen, and stop wasting my time.'

There was a tin of sweets on a high shelf in the parlour, and she used to dole two of them out to each of us every day. The rest of the money social services gave her for our pocket money went into their bank account, or helped buy the Mars bars and bags of toffee she lavished on Sandra. She was a shrewd businesswoman, Mrs Griffiths. In the supermarket:

'Pick up as many receipts as you can, you lot. The one who collects the most gets a lolly ice.'

Dodging between the trolleys and around the tills, we would pick up as many as we could, and she'd click them into her purse with a satisfied sigh. Years later we realized the point of this game. She could select the right receipts, make up a fictitious budget, and collect the cash from social services.

'Right,' she said on Monday mornings as we finished our thin, sugarless porridge, 'dinner money.' Grudgingly she put five shillings into each of our palms.

On my way to school I'd stand on the threshold of the sweetshop, smelling the chocolate and toffee within. If I spend just *one* shillin', I thought, it'll on'y mean havin' no dinner today, and when I'm eatin' the sweets it'll be like havin' pocket money. Soon it got down to spending two shillings, then three, finally all of it. To satisfy my hunger I'd check the doorsteps as I passed them, dive down a path and snatch a bottle of milk when I saw one.

Brenda and Robert started running away. Each time they went they walked to the social services office in town. They were brought back in a car, and Mr Griffiths gave them the strap. The first time I ran away I was six. It was after school and I stood outside the gates till the other kids had all gone, and the road was empty of whoops and cries. The thought of going back to the Griffithses was unendurable.

The first bus said EDINBURGH on the front, or so I thought. It must have been AIGBURTH, the only place in Liverpool that looks remotely similar. It didn't matter to me where it was going, so long as it took me away from the Griffithses.

'Fares please.'

The sixpence was blood-warm in my palm but I didn't need it. There was a man and woman who had already paid on one seat, with their little girl on a seat across the aisle. I sat next to the girl and the conductor didn't notice me. The bus stopped in the middle of nowhere, and everyone left it. They all had places to go to. It was dark now as well as cold. The coat-deep warmth of the bus soon ebbed. The strange houses and immense sky were frightening. The wind soughing through the trees filled me with loneliness.

'Where are yer goin', love?'

She had stepped off the bus ahead of me and walked away, but she came back when she saw me standing there. The kindness in her voice precipitated my tears.

'I don't know,' I wailed. 'I'm lost.'

It was a nice house and she had a little boy like me. We had our tea together, sausages, beans and chips. I wanted to stay forever.

Instead, the policewoman was efficiently maternal.

'Now, come on, you're a big boy and you *must* know where you live. Why don't you tell me?'

Silence.

'Your name, then. What's your name? You can tell me your *name.*'

She kept it up for a long time, but I did not tell. In the end the copper who was with her had the idea of looking in my coat, and they found the label with the address on it. The Griffithses were as nice as pie to them when we arrived.

'Reg'lar little tyke, this fellow,' Mr Griffiths said, patting my head. Effusive with thanks, they smiled the police through the front door then slapped me along the hall and up to bed. One of Mrs Griffiths's harder clumps knocked my head against the banister, and they had to keep me off school next day because of the mark. After that, running away became a habit.

Summer arrived, and they took us on holiday. It was a big house in the country, and the back garden seemed a mile long. Rob and I shared a bed in the same room as Sandra. On the first night I had a nose-bleed, and when I awoke I was frightened. The pillow was wet and scarlet. Was it blood? Where had it come from? Sandra slid out of the room, and a minute later I heard her father coming up the stairs. He led me by the ear to his room, and opened a suitcase. From under his wife's tank-cover dresses and Big Top bras he pulled out the familiar strap. Nose-bleeds bothered me for years afterwards.

In two days our room was fuggy with the smell of Sandra's urine: fat, smug and treacherous. To get us away, Brenda took us for walks. There was an old church and a river where we went every day. Around the church, along the river, back around the church. Under the dripping elms, talking. Brenda was thirteen then, an age at which girls are selfconscious. Normally very proud, she actually pleaded about the baths.

'But I want a bath on me *own!*'

Mrs Griffiths put the shampoo and soap down with a bang.

'Don't start putting on airs with *me*, missy. Who'd want to look at *you*, anyway?'

We stood watching with the Griffithses while she sat in the

bath, trying to wash and to cover herself at the same time. Poor Brenda.

When we got back to Liverpool she and Robert ran away to social services again, and this time they took me with them.

'We're *not* goin' back, we're *not!*'

Her voice rose hysterically. All three of us were crying. They took us back in a car, but returned after a few days and took us to the Children's Admission Unit.

It was like a workhouse. Grey walls and cold, stone-flagged corridors. They humiliated you in little ways. On the first morning Brenda was taken into a room to have her hair put in the compulsory plaits, and came out weeping. You had to wear wellingtons all the time, even in the house: clump, scrape, clump, scrape. They said they were looking for a place to put us, but found schools for Brenda and Rob. A bad sign. No school for me, but I learned just the same. How to fight dirtier, strive harder, survive. Rob was a hard case by now and looked after me with the older kids. After three months, another journey through featureless streets, another unknown destination. Mr and Mrs Bird.

They lived three streets away from my Dad, and it gradually filtered through to us that we were going home. It was a strange house because the Birds were so remote. They never did anything bad to us, just didn't want us around. At weekends we had to stay in bed very late. The house creaked around us while we carried on whispered conversations above the sound of their breathing.

'Shut UP! Go back to SLEEP!'

Their irritated shout whenever we woke them. At eleven o'clock she'd get up and start moving about in their room. We'd lie with our mouths watering, listening to her getting dressed, dying for her to go down and make the tea and toast. Stuck in our beds, we'd hear the kettle singing and the harsh rasping, loud as an alarm clock, of a knife on burnt toast.

'Right. Breakfast's READY!'

We'd leap out of bed and blunder hastily into our clothes, then charge down.

'Quiet!' she'd shout. 'Be QUIET all of you!'

As soon as we had finished: 'Right, all of you out now and don't come back till teatime.'

Social services had pressured them into taking us. They never took any more kids after we left.

A week later Brenda went home to help Dad get everything ready. I was put in the infants' school in Rice Lane and Rob, now eleven, started at Warbreck comprehensive. Day by day our excitement mounted. A fortnight snailed past. On our last day with the Birds I grew worse by the hour. At night I played up terribly.

'That's it,' Mrs Bird said in the end, 'I can't take no more o' this. You're goin' home now, me lad.'

This scared me shitless.

'But me Dad,' I protested. 'Me Dad'll go mad.'

She dragged me round there and put me over the doorstep. Dad was out and had left Brenda in charge.

'Oh, Graham,' she rebuked me, ''ow can yer be so naughty when we're all comin' together?'

She issued me with a jam butty and a glass of milk and sent me, chastened, to bed. When I came home from school next afternoon Rob was there too. We were a family at last.

We didn't see much of Dad. He was at work when I got up, still there when I came home, and out every evening. We rarely met. When he came home for his tea we all had jobs to do. Brenda cooked the meal, Rob washed the dishes, I polished the shoes. Often he would have a woman with him. They were always posh, and talked like lady social workers or teachers. It was now deep winter, and snow began falling.

'D'yer want yer path clearin', missis?'

'Er, okay son. 'Ow much?'

'A shillin', missis.'

'Right. Give us a knock when yer've finished, an' I'll take a look.'

Making money this way was easy. I borrowed a shovel, and started to play truant in order to work. The cash flowed in and I bought sweets, mounds of them, toffees and chocolates and boxes of Quality Street. I loved sweets. They were like love to me, in most of the Homes you never saw them. When my Dad found out what was happening he confiscated my cash and gave me a hiding for staying off school. The only other time he hit me was when I told him I hated him.

My truancy didn't stop, though. When I had been at home for only two months Rice Lane school expelled me and my Dad put me in another, Northcote Road, which was better for me. It was bigger, and for a tough kid a big school is always best. There's bound to be someone there who is tougher.

A truantless week went by, then my teacher called me out of the classroom.

'Graham, it's going to be hard for you to understand this, but I want you to try. You're not going home tonight, you're going somewhere else . . .'

A bombshell. They were taking me away. Not long ago I 'acquired' my social services file, and in it this teacher is criticized for telling me. By some queer sociological process they came to the conclusion that his telling me made me feel guilty, that my being sent away was a punishment. I am grateful to him. So few people ever told me the truth that I appreciate those who did. Half an hour later two social workers arrived.

'All right, Graham. Come with us.'

They put me in their Mini and drove me away.

'Where're we goin'? What'll me Dad say?' As his betrayal dawned on me, tears flowed. 'What about me Dad? Me Dad . . . ?'

They took me to the Parkfield Children's Home in Aigburth. Brenda and Rob were not there, and stayed with my Dad from then on. Lying again in institutional sheets, I wept till the other kids in the dormitory shouted at me. I was only seven. I hated my Dad for handing his dirty work over to cold professionals.

They started me at another school, and truancy began the next day. Once I stayed off with a big girl, Sheila, who went to a comprehensive. She was thirteen. We rode the escalators in Lewis's till the store detectives threw us out then walked around town, in and out of the shops. After a time we found ourselves in a derelict area close to the city centre.

'Let's go in there,' she said, adding darkly, 'I'll show yer everythin'.'

'Okay.'

We went into a bombed house and she quickly took off her clothes. She stood in the light of the smashed windows while I stared at her budding breasts and her sparse growth of hair. Having seen bigger boys with girls on their arms, I was interested. I pulled my shorts and underpants down and rubbed up against her.

'Is this what yer do, Sheila, is this what yer do?' I demanded. She wasn't much help.

'I don't know,' she said.

At this time I started running away in earnest, though never for more than a night. Sometimes I went with another kid, but mostly it was on my own. At the back of Tesco's there was a huge heap of empty boxes where I often slept. The place was mine, and I kept it secret. In the daytime I always ended up near Parkfield, getting chased. Exasperated coppers chased me all over the Lark Lane area, through the park, over fences, hedges and walls, along alleys, across yards. I was still small enough to hide in a dustbin, and often did. After four months Parkfield had had enough of me. They sent me to New Heys Reception Centre in Allerton.

This time it lasted longer, over a year. For hours on end I would sit in a chair, a small blond boy with blue eyes and a serious face, talking to no one, rejecting all advances. There was a big garden at the back with high trees in it, and I'd climb one and look at the world from that height, that solitude. There were rabbits in a hutch, and guinea pigs. They were nice. When I was with them I didn't feel so alone. Yet what I craved was solitude. There was a woman among the staff who used to take me in her room and cuddle me. It was frightening, but nice. Once she gave me some grapes from a big bunch. They reminded me of her breasts and I couldn't eat them.

The staff were all right, featureless providers of clothes and food. No name or face has stayed in my mind. If they had been gods they could not have helped me.

A guinea pig littered, and they gave me one of the babies.

'Give the book back to Jeremy, Graham.'

Using my size as usual, I had taken it.

'No. It's mine.'

'Now, Graham.' Warningly. 'Jeremy had it first. I saw you take it, now give it back like a good boy.'

'No. Fuck off.'

Tantrum time. After hurling the book at the boy's head I'd run along, screaming, my arms held rigid at my sides, till they caught me. Or I'd pick up something hard and heavy and smash as many windows as I could before being restrained. During all the time I was at New Heys I didn't once get pocket money. It was always stopped to help pay for broken windows.

One day I overheard them talking about me.

'Graham? Oh, he's nuts. Right off his rocker. Shouldn't be in a place like this at all.'

By the way they looked at me I could tell they all thought so. Was I mad? Perhaps they were right for once, and I was. One day a social worker came out of the office with a bulky file under his arm, and caught hold of me as I ran past.

'You're going to a nut-house, young man.'

His exact words. Was it a joke? As the morning progressed it became clear that I *was* going somewhere. After my many moves it was easy to detect the signs. Finding a box, I carefully made holes in the top and put in some grass from the garden. When the social worker came to fetch me I had it tucked under my arm with my guinea pig inside. We were ready to go.

It was a long drive. All the way into town, through the Mersey Tunnel, then a long way on the other side. We arrived at a place with a fence round the outside and Nissen huts within. As we drove through the gates I read the sign that was stuck there, MOSTYN HOSPITAL. The social worker took me into one of the huts. An office with a doctor in a white coat, sitting at a desk. There was a young bloke talking to him. He was a police cadet attached to the hospital as part of his training, and was soon to become my friend.

'You can't have that in here,' the doctor said when he saw my pet. 'This is a hospital, not a zoo.'

I bawled my head off.

'I want me guinea pig, I want me fuckin' GUINEA PIG!'

The social worker who had brought me backed out with the box in his hands. The police cadet spoke reassuringly.

'Come on, kid. I'll take you down the Canteen.'

He chatted to me on the way, and I warmed to him.

'Ten Park Drive, please,' I said to the man behind the counter, dead casual. Out of the corner of my eye I saw the police cadet watching me. The fag tasted horrible, but if it made me look grown up it would be worth it.

The Nissen huts were wards, and as the nurse was taking me to mine it occurred to me that I hadn't seen any kids.

'Where's all the kids, mate?'

'Kids? There's no kids 'ere, son.'

In the ward there were all these old nutters walking around, right off their heads. Their pyjama flies flapped disgustingly open, they talked to themselves, made funny noises and flung their arms about, twitching. There was one other lad in the ward, in a little room at the end. My bed was one of a row, and the others were all occupied by raving loonies.

That night I ran away. When I was half a mile down the road I stuck my thumb out as I walked, hoping for a lift. I was only nine, and must have looked terribly conspicuous. After a time a man called out and stopped me. He motioned to the hospital.

'You're from over there, aren't you?'

'No.'

'Yes, you are.'

Without another word he took hold of my arm and dragged me back. How had they caught me so quickly? They must have agents, I thought, agents who stay in the road and watch for you. I reckoned they'd radio'd through to this one when they saw I was gone.

The Charge Nurse was very angry.

'Do that again and it's the needle for you.' He showed me a long, shiny, sharp hypodermic. 'You get this in your backside next time. We put you to sleep.'

The word 'needle' sent fear through me. The terrifying injections they had given me in Alder Hey were not forgotten. When he said he would put me to sleep I thought he meant forever, like an unwanted kitten. That night, lying in the dark ward with the nutters moaning and snuffling around me, I cried myself to sleep.

There was a snooker table and T.T. – table tennis – at the end of the ward. The police cadet used to come and play with me. He was a great bloke, the only good thing about the place at first. He used to give me menthol cigarettes, though I'm sure he knew I wasn't really smoking them. He spent a lot of time with me. The sad thing is, I can't remember his name.

After a fortnight the other lad went out and they gave me his room. On the same day, a Friday, they told me my Dad and a social worker were coming the following day.

'What time?' I asked eagerly.

'Don't know, Graham. In the afternoon, probably.'

That night I could not sleep, and nine o'clock next morning found me sitting on top of the gatepost, my eyes searching the approaching cars for signs of my father. The day trudged past.

At six o'clock they made me come in. I was crying. The following week the same thing happened. All day I sat on the bum-numbing post. It did my head in when he didn't come.

There was no school for me, so most of my time was spent playing snooker with the police cadet. Gradually I began to venture out of the ward, and soon I started to make money by taking pop bottles back. There was a hole in the fence on the main road, behind a big bush, and I used to sneak through it, nip over to the filling station opposite, get money for the bottles and buy sweets.

It was fun to climb on top of the wards and scamper about, and as the weather became warmer I spent more and more time up there, running along the rounded roofs, exploring and looking for birds' nests. There were wild cats everywhere and I carried a stick to fight them with, and stole their kittens. There were dozens of these around the bins, scavenging like me.

Swearing was another way of being grown up, and though the police cadet disapproved I swore like a sewer.

'Bastard. Cunt. Shit. Poo.'

One day they called me into the ward office.

'We've good news for you, Graham. You've been given permission to have your guinea pig after all. Your Dad and a social worker are bringing it this afternoon.'

This made me very excited. My father was coming, and bringing me company! When they arrived I flew into the office and over to the little cage. To my surprise I saw, inside, not my guinea pig but a white baby rabbit.

'There you are, Graham,' the social worker said. 'Here's your friend back. Nice little chap, isn't he?'

It wasn't my guinea pig, of that I was certain. What were they talking about? One of the nurses came in.

'We've brought Graham his guinea pig,' my Dad said.

The nurse poked his finger through the wire bars.

'Oh, a white one, eh?'

They must be right, I decided. It *must* be my guinea pig. Perhaps they were right about everything, perhaps I was even mad like they said. It did look like a rabbit, though. Frightened they would start giving me queer looks if I voiced my doubts, I kept my mouth shut. A minute later a young doctor came in.

'Whose is the baby rabbit?' he said. 'Yours, Graham?'

Who was mad, me or my Dad and the social worker? Here

they stood, telling me rabbits were guinea pigs and almost making me believe them. Years later this social worker told me that my guinea pig had littered on the way back to Liverpool, and that she and the babies had died.

There was a broom cupboard on the ward which had a door that led outside into the big circle of huts, where there was some grass.

'Can I keep me rabbit in 'ere, nurse?'

'Er, I suppose so, Graham. All right.'

It made the place its home from then on, and grew at an astonishing rate. Soon it was hopping about on its own, foraging like me. It was a pretty tough rabbit and held its own against the wild cats, turning and lashing out with its strong claws whenever it saw one. They soon learned to leave it alone, and it hopped in through the door of its bedsit each night unscathed.

Like my rabbit, I began to establish my own little domain at Mostyn. There was a patient who acted as teaboy for the ward, and when he went out I took his job over.

'Good mornin'. Two sugars you 'ave, innit?'

'Uh?'

Grunt, grunt of waking loony. Every patient gave me two shillings a week to buy tea and sugar, and I made a wholesome profit. Getting up at six, an hour before the others, I'd bustle about filling my trolley and talking quietly to the night watchman, feeling part of a community for the first time ever. As I put my life into a higher gear money came flying at me from all directions. As well as my catering concern and bottle recycling, it was my habit to pester the patients for cash.

'Give us two bob, mate.'

'Wha'? Wha'?'

'Give us two bob, will yer?'

Noses running, slobbering, afflicted with murderous twitches, they would fly at me, squawking and flapping their lunatic limbs.

'All right, a shillin' then. Just a shillin' an' I'll leave yer alone.'

Most of them paid. After all, they were nuts. My new-found wealth made life easier. I bought orange juice, cakes and biscuits, and ordered the *Beano*. In this last effort I was thwarted. A patient in another ward already took it, and as only one copy per week was delivered to the hospital I had to make do with the *Dandy*. After two months a doctor called me into the office and told me I was to be given pocket money. Pocket money! Like all kids that age, I was so adaptable that when life changed I left the old habits completely behind. Pocket money was something I had forgotten about.

'Sign here,' he said, and gave me three shillings.

During all this time I felt angry towards my father. Once he came and took me to his usual day-out place, Chester Zoo. Turning down his offer of a ride on the elephant, I looked across the cages at the captive animals, the tigers and polar bears morose in the drizzle. They were like me. Zoos still depress me. On another day he arrived with one of his girlfriends. She was dead snooty and posh, and stood with her nose in the air. He splashed out and took us to Blackpool. Though I spent most of the profits from my business ventures I did save some. I had four ten-shilling notes and some silver, a lot of money for a boy in those days. My Dad was generous.

'Do you want an ice cream, son?'

'No thanks.'

A minute later I bought one for myself.

'How about a go on the Moon Rocket, Graham?'

'Yeh! Looks good, Dad, doesn't it?'

I ran up the painted steps and paid the man while he was still digging into his pocket. It was a kind of vengeance and I kept it up all day, not letting him pay for anything. All he ever did was try to buy me off. When he saw me he would buy me a lot of things, just that one day. Afterwards, nothing. He never gave me anything of himself.

By this time I was happy at Mostyn, happier than I'd ever been. There were frightening characters amongst the loons, and once or twice when I had a New Heys-style tantrum the nurses threatened me with the needle, but I coped with these fears as I did with the horror films on T.V. The watchman let me stay up after ten o'clock when the others went to bed, and I'd hide behind an armchair while the horror movies were on, peeping out at the screen when I was brave enough. If they were too scary I'd go to bed, and try to think of something else until sleep came.

On other nights I'd visit the alcoholics and junkies in their ward, which was the next one along. They used to sit up half the night and were great company, being dead sane compared to the nutters in my ward. When the first men landed on the moon I went down there at six in the morning before I made the tea, and they were all sitting watching it on T.V. and cheering. The men in the silver spacesuits bounced up and down, taking giant leaps through the atmosphere, actually standing on the moon for the first time. It was great.

The women's ward was connected to mine by a passage like the ones that link the H-Blocks in Northern Ireland, and was another of my favourite haunts at night. They used to have panel games, and appoint judges to decide which was the best out of so many records. All the mad women in the audience would be cheering and cackling and making jokes, some being taken out when they grew too excited and pissed their chairs, or forgot where they were and started masturbating. There would be some on the panel along with a doctor and nurse and, when I could wangle them into it, me. They would play a record, sometimes classical, sometimes pop.

'Well, er, I didn't like it that much but I know that kind of music appeals to people so I'll give it four.'

When it came to my turn I used to say what the person before me had said, or a mixture of what two people had said, trying to make it sound original. At that age even pop music didn't interest me, let alone Handel and Bach. But when they played a Beatles record I'd stand up and put my arms over my head, taking the audience with me.

'It was GREAT! I LOVED it! I give it TEN!'

One night my rabbit didn't come home.

'It'll be here in the morning, Graham,' the police cadet said as I climbed into bed.

But it wasn't. Grave with worry, I set about tracking it down, trying to make sense of the patients' ill-remembered and possibly imagined statements. On the far side of the hospital in an area where I had scarcely ventured, I found a nutter who had a rabbit too, kept in a box on the grass outside his ward. Mine was there. He had pinched it to keep his company.

'I shorry, shon, I shorry. I pinch' your shrabbit, shon. I shorry.'

'Sorry? Yer will be if yer touch it again, lar. Believe me.'

Glowering and muttering threats, I tucked its warm body under my arm and we went home. This incident has become funny with time. Others have not.

It began as a promising day.

'Graham,' the police cadet said in the morning, 'you're addicted to bad language. You couldn't go a day without swearing.'

'Bullshit,' I replied. ' 'Course I could. Easy.'

'Easy?'

'Yeh, easy.'

'Right. I'll bet you five bob you swear before bedtime.'

'Yer on.'

All day I stuck to it, once or twice just biting off a swearword as it shot out from between my teeth.

'Oh, fu . .'

He would look down at me, smiling. 'We won't count that one, eh Graham? Only half a one, wasn't it?'

When the urge came on strong I'd run to the far side of a green, look at the sky, and let it out.

'FuckshitshagfannybastardcuntfartwanktitarseHOLE!'

Then trot sedately back.

At this time they were dosing me up to the eyeballs with heavy downers like epanutin and largactyl. After lunch I was walking out of the ward, mentally working out the night's snooker strategy, when a nurse pulled me into the office.

'You haven't taken your pills today, lad.'

I had.

'I 'ave, nurse. I've took 'em, honest.'

'Don't come the case with me, kid. Now take these.'

He held out his hand with two pills on it.

The argument escalated, and rage was soon gushing uncontrollably through me. In a few seconds I had swept all the things from his desk and was lashing into a cupboard with my boots. Another nurse came running, then another. Though I bit, kicked, shrieked and yelled it was futile, they were all big men and I was a little boy. One held my arms and another my legs, and they carried me to the Treatment Room where the third prepared my injection. Obscenities flowed from me like shit from a sewer. The police cadet came through the door, his face haggard with concern, and I knew that the bet was lost. It made everything worse. They held me flat on my belly and my trousers came down. The needle pricked my skin and one of them said, 'Count.'

It was like dying. The last thing I knew was the police cadet stroking my head.

'Don't worry, Graham. Don't worry, son . . .'

Part of my mind was counting. When it got to four it was thrown with the rest of me into blackness.

It was supposed to keep you out for hours, but I woke before they expected me to, feeling ill and hot as though in a fever. For a long time I was too dopey to move. After a few minutes, in search of coolness, I slipped my hand under the pillow. My fingers touched something cold. Hazily, I pulled it out. It was my promised five shillings.

Shortly afterwards the effects of my sweet-eating caught up with me, and some teeth were taken out. After they put the mask on I felt something scratching my hand, and it seemed to be that which put me out. I came to in a side ward full of slobbering nutters, all of them ranting and roaring. While under the anaesthetic I had had nightmares, and I was desperately frightened. Quickly putting my dressing gown on, I opened the window and climbed out. Dizzy and ill, I got to my ward, ran the bath, and climbed in unaware that the staff were running everywhere looking for me. After a few minutes the door burst open and a doctor frothed anger on the threshold.

'What the hell are you doing in here, you little nuisance?'

'Er, I woke up an' it was 'orrible, so I ran away . . .'

'Do this again and you get the needle. Understand?'

My gums ached as I crawled into my lonely bed and lay there shaking. When I fell asleep it was to dream of extractions, roaring loonies and sharp, shiny syringes.

People started giving me tests. They were like little puzzles and games, you had to fit this into that, that into this, and decide which way a boat would go if the water was flowing from left to right and a cable broke at one end. Mostyn had been my home for four months when my Dad and social services decided to move me. They only did so under protest. The psychologists had said I was of above average intelligence, had no serious personality disorder, and should never have been sent there in the first place.

A hospital social worker told me the news.

'You're leaving here today, Graham.'

The police cadet wasn't in that day, so I couldn't say good-bye. I drilled air-holes in a cardboard box with nine-year-old intentness, and stuffed grass inside. My Dad and a social worker arrived to drive me away. From the back seat of the car I looked at the Nissen huts with regret. My rabbit scrabbled restlessly in its box, and I stroked the smooth cardboard. We were ready for anything. Though we did not know it then, disaster loomed for us both.

2 | *Institutions Galore*

My Dad's house in Andrew Street. Would I be staying? No one told me at first. It was good to see Brenda and Rob again, they both seemed happier. Dad let me know in roundabout ways that I would soon be moving on. After a week a social worker came to take me to the new place. My Dad came along. With my rabbit again in its box on my knees I watched clean fields swish past all the way to Stroud in Gloucestershire.

We passed a garage and a little shop, then turned in at the gates of the new place, Blatchwick. The usual big house. As soon as the car stopped, fear, irrational and certain, seized me. A man was standing on the top step and came down to meet us.

'So this is the young man we've had so much trouble with, is it?'

He was Mr Lawrence, the Head. A small man who walked like a soldier and had the outlook, as well as the moustache, of a Hitler. Blatchwick was privately owned and he made a profit for his landlord. His wife, son and daughter-in-law all worked

there, so it was very much a family affair. Like the Mafia.
Another master, Mr Wood, gave me a soft hand to shake. I
tugged my Dad's sleeve, pulling his ear close.

'I don't want to stay 'ere, Dad.' My voice trembled. 'I don't
want to stay.'

He replied in his reasonable way, 'You've got to try it out
first, Graham. How can you know what it's like if you don't
try?'

My voice wobbled. Tears shot through tubes behind my eyes.
'I don't want to try. I 'ate it 'ere. I want to go 'ome with you.'

It was the first time I had ever said this. He turned away and
frowned as he looked up at the building, then at the sky and
trees. He walked up the steps, his forehead furrowed with deep
frowns, and in through the front door. I followed him inside.

'There are hutches at the back where you can put that.'

Lawrence indicated the box I was carrying. My Dad and I
went outside to find them. The house and grounds were deathly
silent, all the kids being at school. One hutch was empty. My
Dad lifted the little latch and I put the animal inside. Dry sobs
racked me.

'Dad, why don't yer take me 'ome? Don't yer want me there?'

Sob, sob. He put his hand in his pocket and gave me a two-
shilling piece. No cuddle because I kept asking him not to leave
me. We had lunch in the main hall, our echoing voices making
me more lonely than before, then my Dad and the social worker
drove away.

'Go out for a while,' Lawrence said.

After mooning about in the grounds for a time I got bored, so
went to the shop and bought my rabbit a carrot. When I
returned Lawrence was back on the top step, staring into space
almost dreamily. He did not look at me.

'Where have you been?'

'Er, to the shop, sir. I went to get . . .'

'You don't go out of here on your own,' he said, 'ever again.'

He turned and went into the house. As my rabbit was taking
its first nibble the other kids started coming back, quietly, in
subdued little groups, not catapulting past in a satchel-swinging
mob as you would expect. There were sixty boys there aged
from seven to seventeen. At nine, I was one of the youngest.

At teatime Lawrence and his family sat at a raised staff table
at the end. He had his hands pressed together as though in

prayer and tapped his teeth with his fingertips, looking here and there among the kids. I was sitting at one of the long tables getting to know people when his voice rasped.

'Gaskin.'

A hushed silence fell.

'Sir?'

'Come here, boy.'

Tap, tap of steel-tipped toes on parquet.

'Did your father give you any money?'

'Yes, sir. Two shillings.'

His hand came out, palm uppermost. There was a jingle of dropped coins.

'Where's the rest?'

His loud voice brought the sixty-odd kids into his game. A spring-tide of faces, incoming, receding.

'Er, I bought a carrot, sir. For me rabbit.'

Some kids tittered. Lawrence leaned back and roared with laughter. Upon receiving this official sanction they all joined in. Shamed, I went back to my seat. It was then that I began hating him.

Blatchwick was run like a West German prison for terrorists, and all the boys accepted it. The first thing they accustomed you to was the cane. 'You!' they'd shout. You had to go over and take it, agonizing swipes across the arse, anywhere, at any time, for anything. There were so many pointless rules that it was impossible not to break them. After meals you had to sit in silence with your arms folded, listening to Lawrence telling stories about the war. It was bed at seven for the little ones, and even the kids of sixteen had to go at nine thirty. They must have been dead soft, those big kids, putting up with his abuses. Before I was eleven he wouldn't be able to do a blind thing with me.

You weren't allowed to talk in bed. Landing Boys appointed by Lawrence sat outside the open dormitory doors, listening. If anyone spoke they ran down and told him. He came up. Swish, yell, swish, yell, swish. He caned the seven-year-olds almost as hard as the big lads.

They kept me away from school till they had knocked me into shape. Their shape. They knocked me harder and more often than I've ever been knocked since. By the time I started school I was completely in their thrall. Most other Blatchwick kids went to a big school called Moortown, but they sent me to

Wescombe. It was smaller, and I'd be easier to watch. In fact it was tiny, with only three classrooms and the same number of teachers. It was an old village school next to the church, and the pupils were posh. Mrs Lawrence took me there by car in the morning, drove me back along country lanes at night.

My first morning. We were playing football in the yard and I scored.

'Goal!' I was excited. 'Goal, goal!'

A kid pushed through the players, maddeningly authoritative. 'That didn't go in. It was miles off.'

The posh voice and Head Boy badge didn't dispose me kindly towards him.

'What are yer talkin' about, kid? That was a bloody goal.'

'Who are you calling "kid"? You're only a Third Year, aren't you?'

Slam. My knee came up and he fell squirming at my feet. It was easy.

There was only one kid bigger than me at Wescombe school, and he was a gentle soul. From that moment on I was inviolate. The school was all right, and the fact that I was good at sport and scored goals made me popular. Not a bad footballer, I was more body-hard than the others and could easily force my way through any opposition. I was best at every sport we played and could out-run, out-jump and out-swim everyone. We used to go swimming with Moortown school, and their instructor took us too. He didn't like me. I would be competition for his team at the annual Gala.

Otherwise my work was terrible. When you consider the gaps in my schooling, it's not surprising that I could not write. I could read, though. As far as I'm concerned I must have taught myself when I was little. There have been many times in my life when I've opened books as though they were doors, and fled through them. At Wescombe I realized that the other kids were better educated than I, and this hurt. But on the whole school was all right. It was Blatchwick that was hard.

The silence, the fear, the awful regimentation. You came home from school, changed, ate, and went to bed in the sound-less dormitory. On some nights Lawrence thought of diversions, and these were worse than the grinding monotony. After tea, his praying hands, tooth-tapping. His darting eyes, and the clap of his palms.

'Right, clear the tables to the sides of the room.'

A tremendous bumping and scraping while this was done.

'Tonight we'll have . . . a *boxing match*! How's that? Is everyone *keen*?' Weak smiles from the kids he looked at while his eyes sought a victim. 'You, Jones,' the big hulk of a lad grinned hugely, 'and, er, let me see . . .' his eyes swept, paralysed, swept on. Then his hand swung back to kids who had thought they were safe, and his finger fixed on a round-shouldered, ill-matched boy. 'Yes. You, Harris. It'll do you good.'

He would make them batter each other till blood, snot and tears were flying while he stood at the side, cheering, jeering.

Some weekends he used that age-old trick of the torturers, sleep deprivation. The smack of his palms at two in the morning, accompanied by his hearty shouts.

'Come on, Smith, you're going for a little walk, lad. Yes, *and* you, Gaskin. No good putting your head under, I know you're there.'

Climbing out of the warm blankets, half a dozen of us would stagger into our clothes and go downstairs, cross the cold drive-way and stumble into his car. Whistling, he'd drive us to a spot some miles away and dump us, leaving us in the charge of one of the older boys. We never got lost, but you weren't allowed into Blatchwick until nine o'clock. Lawrence always sited his dropping-place at such a distance that you'd get back at about seven, and have to wait in the road for two freezing hours. By the time you had changed and had breakfast it was eleven o'clock. You could go to bed. He woke you again at one and you spent the rest of the day tottering about, longing for sleep.

Sunday would find a line of us queuing in the main hall.

'Who's coming today, then? You, Graham? You'd better be full of beans, though. We're going over the hills to Chalford.'

His curly hair hung to his shoulders, and his name was Malcolm. He was a voluntary worker who came to the Home to take some of us out. He wore hiking boots, carried a stick and a knapsack full of goodies – chocolate bars and a Thermos of hot soup – and used to take us walking. Chalford and Slad are two of the Cotswold valleys, and he often took us to them. We loved it. Not because Malcolm was anything special but because it got us away from Lawrence for a while. Malcolm was nice to the kids, I remember him rolling in the grass with me and pulling my hair, but he sat with Lawrence at mealtimes which made us suspicious.

A new kid came to Blatchwick and started with me at Wescombe school. We called him Elephant because of his enormous ears. On his first morning in school he stood in the playground, holding forth.

'Any kids 'ere think they're 'ard? Jus' send 'em over to ole Elephant an' let 'im roll on 'em. Squash 'em flat, 'e will. Right?'

Splatt. My head thudded into his face. No one was allowed to be tougher than me. My boots pounded into him and the other kids stepped back, shocked. The incident was found out, and I was punished. Worse, it made me unpopular with the kids. After a few days it became obvious that Elephant was only a harmless idiot.

He looked normal enough, but he was a strange boy. His queer habits earned him the additional nickname of Bummer, our name for anyone we suspected of sexual abnormality. Elephant sucked ears. He would be sitting behind you when suddenly, shockingly, you'd feel his lips on your ear, his tongue moving squashily inside. Some kids went into a kind of rapture while this was going on, and sat as though hypnotized.

After the Elephant fight the Headmaster was constantly telling me off for bullying. At the same time I had my first crush. Her name was Nicola, a wisp of a girl, blonde like me but waif-like and fragile. She was a Fourth Year, and posh.

'Er, d'yer wanna take a walk over the churchyard dinner time, Nic?'

'Not today, Graham.' She would purse her lips and drop pale lids over her eyes. 'I'm with Mandy.'

Mandy's goofy smile would make me look away.

Nicola's house was opposite the school, a spacious modern bungalow with a swimming pool at the rear. Like everything about her, it was gorgeous.

At sport I continued to excel. The Stroud teams held football trials to select the Stroud Area team. Eighty kids went to the first, and the best twenty-two were chosen and made into two teams, the Possibles and the Probables. I was one, but only made the Possibles and determined to try harder. For the match they put me at right back. My size and strength made it easy for me to stop anyone getting through, and at the end of the game they put me into the Stroud Area team.

The Stroud schools' Annual Swimming Gala was held in the open air baths in Stratford Park. The day dawned sunny and bright, and by mid-morning it was hot and the grass was vibrant with insects. The Moortown swimming instructor paced up and down pep-talking his team, trying not to show his dislike when he looked at me. Normally a swimmer could only represent his team in two events, but Wescombe was so small that they had granted me a dispensation. I was taking part in four. Mr Wood was there from Blatchwick and came in while I was changing to give me some encouragement, which surprised me.

'You should be in with a chance today, eh Gaskin?'

He looked away as I squirmed into my costume.

'Yeh, Mr Wood. 'Ope so.'

With so much competition from older kids in Moortown school I went down in the first three events and had to pin my hopes on The Dash, a one-length speed race. In the semi-final I finished second, a long way behind a Moortown kid. Their instructor strutted proudly along the poolside, glancing over in triumph. I braced myself for the final.

It began with a false start, which is never good for the nerves. Mine were taut as sprung snares as I stood on the box waiting, taking deep breaths. When the pistol cracked we all went into our racing dives, and I knew in the blackness of mine that it was longer and deeper than I had ever done before. When my head shot out of the water I was neck and neck with the Moortown kid but he was already swimming, his dive not having been so good. With every gramme of my being fixed on winning, I lifted my head and hauled myself forward. The Moortown kid was a better swimmer but every bit of Graham Gaskin went into that swim, and I heaved myself to victory with nothing but brute strength. It was easy. By the time the Moortown kid touched the end I was out of the water and standing on the side, smiling at his instructor. I won that race because I was bigger and stronger. And because I wanted to beat them all.

Malcolm had picked me out as a kind of favourite.

'How would you fancy a day out on Sunday, Graham?'

'Yeh, Malcolm!' It was no use trying to conceal my pleasure. 'With you? Is anyone else comin'?'

'No, just you this time. We can go to my house again. You'd like that, wouldn't you?'

A huge mansion. There was a lake at the side of the house

with geese on it which he let me feed, and doves in a little house on a stilt outside his kitchen window. There was a big barn to play in, and he was lavish with sweets and cakes and cans of Coke. And no Lawrence, which was enough in itself.

For Blatchwick was hell. To be alive was to endure humiliation, to suffer defeat. Lawrence had to keep kids away from school because he had marked them so badly. Once, the Landing Boy told him that some boys in my dormitory were talking and he came up in a frothing rage, off duty. He came into the dormitory lashing the thin cane like a Cossack his sabre, hitting them wherever he could. The boys, terrified, jumped from their beds and fled, screaming, out of his way. This made him more angry and less accurate. When he had finished their backs as well as their arses were striped with red weals. Next day they were black and blue, and he kept them off school.

Before my tenth birthday I was ill and had to stay off school. As I was lying in my top bunk reading a *Beano* album the door opened softly, and Mr Wood walked in.

'Hello, Gaskin. Any better?'

'Er, yeh sir. Not bad.'

'Think you'll be back at school soon?'

He leaned against the bunk while he talked, resting his pale hands on the coverlet.

'I 'ope so, sir.'

This was true. Even school was better than Blatchwick.

As we chatted in this stilted fashion he slipped a hand under the sheet. I tried to ignore it, but after a minute it came into my pyjama jacket and stroked ticklingly over my belly. By now both of us had stopped talking. His hand came into my flies and took hold of the little tassel of flesh there. We remained silent while he held it.

'Penny for your thoughts,' he said.

Silence. He jiggled his fingers about softly then spoke in a babyish voice:

'Is somebody coming?' More silence while he continued with his game. 'Are you scared of somebody coming?'

No reply. He stopped fiddling and stood just holding my prick. In the end its flaccidity got through to him.

'Don't you like that?'

'No!'

He let go of me and walked out of the room.

A month or so later a coloured kid in our dormitory, Roy, made an announcement. It had to be in a whisper because of the Landing Boy, but was no less dramatic for that.

'I'm gettin' out uv 'ere.'

He sounded so sure that we were immediately envious. Lawrence had us so terrorized that even veteran escapers like myself thought we could never get away.

'You'll never get out,' one said. Then, 'How will you?'

Roy leant against a bunk, his dark face smooth with certainty. 'I'm goin' all right. I'm gettin' out uv 'ere. You just watch me.'

'How?' we whispered in unison. 'Why?'

'It's because o' Wood.'

Small shocks pulsed through me.

'Wood? What about Wood?'

' 'E took me up to 'is room last night, that's what. 'E tole me to take me clothes off an' I done it. Then 'e lay down on the bed an' tole me to sit there, undressed like. After a bit 'e tole me to put me 'and on 'is cock, like.' Roy paused. ' 'E asked me to give 'im a wank.'

There was shocked silence in the room.

'You never done it, did you?'

He looked round defiantly. 'Yeah. It'll get me out uv 'ere, won't it?'

Roy was older than me. He was ten. Other kids began to tell of incidents with Mr Wood, and I recounted what had happened to me.

Next morning Lawrence came up to me looking happy, trying to repress a smile. Nothing to do with Mr Wood, that was for sure.

'Bad news, Gaskin. A fox got in at the rabbits last night . . .'

My heart shoved squirts of panic through me as I ran out into the grey morning, wet grass licking my boots as I raced across the lawn. It was carnage at the hutches. After some probing among what was left of the rabbits, I found a hind leg which had probably belonged to mine. Its fur was as smooth as ever, its ripped end bloody and smashed. My first thought was, Lawrence has done this. He came out in the night with an axe and chopped them to pieces because one was mine. Probably it was paranoia, but even now I'm not sure. He was capable of anything.

A few days later when Mrs Lawrence collected me from

school, Lawrence was with her. Instead of taking the familiar road to Blatchwick they drove me to the police station in Stroud, and a room where a bobby in a grey suit asked me questions.

'I expect you know what this is about, don't you, Graham?'

What had I done?

'Er, no.'

He shoved a piece of paper over for me to read. It was covered from top to bottom with a child's handwriting.

'Roy Beech's statement,' he said.

It went like this. 'As far as I remember, the curtains in Mr Wood's room were blue, the carpet was brown and there was an armchair and a little table by the window ...' When I had read this much he took it back.

'Now, tell me about the day in the dormitory when you were off sick, Graham. The one you told Roy about.'

I looked at the Lawrences. They sat impassive and immovable, all eyes and ears, he stroking his Hitlerian moustache. When this was over they would take me back to Blatchwick. How could I tell?

'Well, er, I'll tell yer the truth, mister. I sort of made it up.'

Though he carried on questioning me, even taking me down a grim passage to show me a cell 'where we put liars', Mr and Mrs Lawrence did not leave us, and I stuck to this line. With them sitting there I could never have told.

By the time I moved up into the Fourth Year I was getting into a lot of trouble at school. Wescombe put a play on every Christmas, and this year they picked me to play the lead. In no time they dropped me again for swearing at a teacher, and gave me a lesser part. Rehearsals were held in the church and during one of them I had a skirmish with a lad behind the altar, and kneed him in the balls. They gave me the job of looking after the lighting. By now I was only interested in disrupting the play, and made fun of the others during rehearsals, farting at moments of high drama or grimacing at Nicola to make her laugh. They had no place for me in their play and I wanted to spoil it for the rest. In the end I didn't even see it. They rang Lawrence on Christmas Eve and told him not to send me.

At Blatchwick too, things worsened. Lawrence was caning me two or three times daily, but it only made me more rebellious. It could not go on much longer. In January there was a sponsored walk for the school, which like everything else at Wescombe had something to do with the church. In the morning I collected seven pounds and handed them to Lawrence's daughter-in-law to mind in the office. In the afternoon I was returning, tired, from the second half when I met some kids from Moortown school, also on their way to Blatchwick.

'We saw you, Gaskin. Smokin' on the sponsored walk.'

'Yeh? So what, like?'

'So we're goin' to tell Lawrence,' one of them said. 'That's what.'

'You know how ole Lawrence feels about kids who smoke,' said another.

They went on their way, laughing. I looked at the fiver I'd collected that afternoon. That was it. The gun had been loaded and the trigger squeezed. Like a bullet I shot back to Wescombe, where I had a pair of long trousers hidden in my desk. The cleaners were mopping the classroom floor as I dashed in and banged my desk lid open. In the Boys' I changed swiftly, stuffing my shorts in the bin. Then I ran hell-for-leather to Stroud and caught a bus to Gloucester.

'A single to Liverpool, please.'

'Bit young, aren't you?'

Confident in my long trousers, I pointed to a car that was pulling away outside.

'They're friends o' me Dad's. I've been stayin' with 'em an' they just dropped me.'

The ticket was just over a pound.

I sat for a long time, fear-stricken, waiting for the train to move. It pulled forward once, went only ten metres, then stopped with a squeal of brakes. Scanning the platform anxiously, I prepared to jump from the far side and leg it across the tracks should Lawrence or the police arrive. Then, with infinite slowness, it began to move. It picked up speed. At ten years old I had done the impossible, and escaped from Blatchwick.

At Birmingham station I bought a comic, some sweets, and a bag of greasy chips. An hour later I caught the Liverpool train. When I stepped out of Lime Street station into the city I had under three pounds. Where could a ten-year-old flee to? The number 32 bus went to Walton where my father lived. Two stops from Rice Lane I left it and started to walk. He would only turn me in and I'd be taken back to Lawrence, merciless

Lawrence from whom no kid had ever escaped before. I had to think of another plan. Meanwhile, the buses looked warm at least.

'Where to, kid?'

'All the way, mate.'

It was the last bus out that night and I stayed on it till the final stop. There were no houses or shops, just a long empty road, quite dark, and a sign saying, LIVERPOOL 7 MILES. I walked along with my thumb held hopefully out, but all the cars were going the other way so I crossed the road. Twenty cars swished past before one stopped. A man and woman looked with concern through their windscreen.

'Where are yer goin', love?'

'I live in Rice Lane. I've been at my friend's down there . . .' I gestured vaguely, '. . .an' missed the last bus 'ome.'

The woman got out to let me into the back.

'Where did yer say, love?'

'Er, Walton, missis. Off Rice Lane, like.'

They were suspicious, and wanted to deliver me to my door.

'Do yer parents know yer out?'

'Yeh. Me Dad'll batter me when I get 'ome.'

They smiled understandingly, but said later:

'Yer 'aven't run away, 'ave yer?'

'No, missis. I've been at me friend's, honest.'

They told me that I must never miss the bus again, that terrible things happened to children who wandered about on their own. At the time I didn't know how right they were. Nothing, anyway, could have frightened me more than the prospect of going back to Blatchwick, and Lawrence.

They dropped me at the corner of Andrew Street and I walked along it waving my thanks to them. Halfway down I dived into an alley, out of sight.

My Dad's was a nice house. He'd had an inside lavatory installed but the back one was still there, never used. I climbed the wall and got inside it to sleep. At two in the morning the cold woke me. It would have killed me if I'd stayed, so I took a walk to get warm. Ten minutes later, inevitably, I was stopped by a lone policeman.

At the police station they rang Blatchwick. Lawrence's voice crackled through the air sounding pleasant and reasonable. Afterwards, incredibly, they took me to my Dad's. He came

down in his pyjamas, rubbing his eyes, and they made him take
me in.

' 'E beats me up all the time, Dad. Honest he does.'

'Well, I'm sure you do something to deserve it, Graham.'

Next afternoon a social worker arrived in a car.

'You've got to go back, Graham,' my Dad said. 'There's no
room for you here.'

He came too, for the ride.

When we got into the office Lawrence acted as though he was
doing them a favour taking me back. My Dad saw it that way
too. Lawrence started in about how bad I'd been there.

'He's pig-headed, bloody-minded, and he thinks he knows
the lot. He's a bully and a liar and a thief.'

'I never stole nothin' 'ere,' I muttered, uncowed.

'You walked off with twelve pounds of the church's money,'
he said.

'Five,' I replied. 'I left seven with your daughter-in-law in
the mornin'.'

That money never did turn up.

The social worker went to turn his car around, and my Dad
stood up. I sobbed hopelessly.

'Dad, Dad, Daddy, don't leave me!' His face was slack and
solid. 'Please take me with yer, please Dad, PLEASE! Don't leave
me with 'IM!'

Lawrence, who had been barely controlling his temper during the interview, became incensed at this. He started to slap
my face and then crack me with the back of his hand. Screaming
and kicking, I clung to my father's legs while the heavy blows
fell. He leaned down and started working my fingers loose.

'Do you have to hit him so hard?'

That was all my Dad said. Then he walked out of the door.
I've hated him ever since that moment.

It took Lawrence and his son to carry me upstairs, biting,
scratching and yelling. Something in my mind said, That's it.
They'll never be able to hurt me after this. They put me in a
little dormitory above the front door and left me there, sobbing.
After a few minutes they came back, stripped me, took my
clothes and all but one of the beds away, and went out.
Lawrence tossed a pair of pyjamas on to the floor as he left, and
I heard them fixing a latch to the door outside.

They left me in there for three weeks, with only one book and no toys. There was one little window through which I could see the kids playing outside. They brought me my meals, and when I wanted the toilet I had to knock and they would open me up. It was good practice for my later time in prison. If I knocked too often it made them mad, and if it was Lawrence who opened I would be cuffed all the way there and back. I sat for long periods with my bladder feeling as though it were about to burst. On the last afternoon Malcolm came to see me with John Morgan, another voluntary worker.

Rattle, rattle. They opened the latch.

'We've brought you some toys, Graham,' John said. He put my box of Airfix soldiers on the bed. 'We hear you've been a naughty boy again.'

When they had gone I played happily for a couple of hours. Yanks and Tommies, Japs and Jerries fought it out on the rug, sniping at one another from behind chairlegs as the sky outside went from grey to navy. Night came, and with it, Lawrence. He was in evening dress and bow tie, on his way to a party. First he took the toys, throwing them on to the landing like so many pieces of shit, then he reached up, took the light bulb out, and went. The latch gave its gentle rasp. I lay in the dark, panting with hatred and fear.

After an hour my anger welled up and spilled over into action. Wrenching at the door with all my strength till the catch gave way, I ran out on to the landing ready for anything. The Landing Boy that night, unluckily for him, was Elephant. He was sitting at a table reading a comic, and looked up in surprise when he saw me. The sight of him enraged me further and I grabbed his big ears, screaming.

'Go on, tell on me, yer bastard, tell on me, tell on me!'

Then I flung him down the stairs. Bumpity-bump behind me as I flew along the passage to another flight of stairs. Though I was only wearing pyjamas and my feet were bare, I could not have borne another moment in the building. I ran up one flight and then another, then out on to the fire escape. My feet raced on the iron catwalk and by now there were footsteps ringing on the metal behind me. Down and into the garden I ran, throwing my head back and putting on all the speed I could muster. When I reached the trees they caught me.

They took me back to the room and stayed there with me. Eventually Mrs Lawrence came back from the party, dressed up to the nines. She and her son took me outside to the car, he holding my wrist in an iron grip. We drove through streets and dark country lanes to the mental hospital at Coney Hill.

This is my life story, and it is my wish to tell the absolute truth. I still have daydreams in which I am murdering Lawrence. If I could pay to have him assassinated, I would do it. He was a heartless sadist, and tortured me for two young years. Then I was a little boy, he a man with strong arms and a sharp, thin cane. Now, I am six feet two inches tall. I am strong. If he reads this, let him come.

They signed me in and stood arguing with the doctors while I was taken into a ward full of men watching a horror film on T.V. *The Birds*. A nurse came over to me, and she was very kind. She put her arms around me, which was what I needed. It was what I always needed, and never had. When her arms enfolded me I ceased to be frightened and was just glad to be there, wherever she was. Away from Lawrence. Outside, a discussion was going on, Mrs Lawrence and her son pressuring the doctors about me. I didn't care. Though there were bars on the windows, I was free.

'Come here, Graham.'

The nurse spoke gently, put me tenderly into the bed and sat stroking my hair. She was still doing it when I fell asleep.

The other patients were all right, and not as much off their heads as those in Mostyn had been. The nurse wheeled a trolley around, doling out pills. I played T.T. with the men in the ward and prepared myself for a long stay. Two days later a social worker arrived.

'I'm not goin' back! Don't try to make me!'

'It's all right, Graham. You're going to Liverpool.'

They took me to Parkfield, which I had left when I was seven. It was just another Home, but I was glad to be there after Blatchwick. To be able to play, to talk, to watch T.V., to go to bed without pressure. To live without fear, canings, Landing Boys and oppressive silence. To walk through the streets again, a free boy.

Cynthia was our senior social worker.

'No, Graham. You mustn't do that. Don't be silly now.'

She took my hand from her knee. Firmly. She was only about twenty-five and she was gorgeous. Though I was only eleven my attitude to women was changing, becoming tinged with sexuality. After the nurse at Coney Hill I came to see them as sources of affection and consolation. Cynthia's long legs in their smooth nylons still cross and uncross themselves in my mind. She offered what I craved. Love. At night I would stare at myself in the mirror that hung in the dormitory. My hair was pale gold and my face long and serious. The blue eyes that stared back at me had wonder in them.

Two months passed. Parkfield's holiday to the Isle of Man drew near.

'Graham, I'm afraid it's been decided that you can't come with us.'

'Why, Cynth?'

'I don't know.'

She did, and so did I. Though I had been quiet and well-behaved my past had caught up with me. They feared disruption. When everyone was packed up and standing outside waiting for the charabancs they drove me to my new Home, Fernlea.

They timed it perfectly. Fernlea was empty of kids when I got there. They had left five minutes earlier to go on the same holiday as Parkfield. Anyway, Fernlea was so exactly like Parkfield that I don't know why they bothered moving me. Unless it was because of Cynthia.

Fernlea is on the far side of the golf course from New Heys, the place that sent me to Mostyn, and I was soon in business selling golf balls. Most of them I found, but I stole some too. At this time, though, I didn't have much guts for stealing. When golfers were searching for a lost ball I'd help.

'Any sign of it over there, son?'

'No.' I'd prod it into deeper concealment with my toe. 'Can't see it.'

Not a few unlucky golfers at this time drove a shot two hundred yards down the fairway only to see a small boy scurry out from the trees, scoop up their ball with the panache of a Wimbledon ballboy, and disappear. Once, with another Fernlea lad, I broke into a car and stole a dozen brand-new balls, still in the box. New balls were worth a fortune, if they were old or cracked you got less for them. I scrounged some old clubs from somewhere and started to teach myself golf. It was sixty pence a time on the green so I didn't pay, just found a faraway hole and played there, furtively.

Fernlea was just a Home, and didn't bother me. They even sent me back to school. This time it was Clifford Holroyde, a school for backward children a couple of miles from my father's house in Walton. They had me down as educationally subnormal, or E.S.N. for short. This was because I hadn't managed to scrounge myself a teacher, books and a classroom during all the periods they had kept me away from school. The other kids really *were* backward and I learned nothing. You didn't have to.

'Can you do this?' the teacher would ask.

I'd glance at it boredly. 'No, sir. Can I do the one I did yesterday?'

There were girls in the school too, and we did cookery. All the kids were some kind of drop-outs, they wore jeans and swore a lot. There were the odd ones who would suddenly, for no reason at all, crack up.

'Aaaaaaaaaaagh! I wanna die, I wanna die, I wanna die!'

The teachers were nice, and would hurry over.

'Calm down, love, calm down. There, there, it's all right ...'

None of us cared about anything. We were all completely off our heads. On Wednesday afternoons the whole school played football against the teachers and it was great fun, the entire place turned into a gigantic football match. The dinner breaks were two hours long, and no one went mad if you came back late. We used the time for hanging around in a nearby industrial estate, stealing. Once, I swopped an electric shaver for a cat. One kid gave me the shaver and I agreed to pay him two quid for it, then another lad took me home and showed me the cat, so we swopped. I took it on the school bus to Fernlea, but they wouldn't let me keep it. They sent it from my Home to the Cats' Home to be destroyed. The only consolation was that I hadn't paid the first kid for the shaver.

Though Fernlea and school were okay, trouble lured me. Free of Lawrence at last, I became wild and wilful, headstrong and cunning. They threw me off the school bus for misbehaving, and though I no longer wanted to see my father I went to his house. He took me to the Home in his car. They wouldn't let me on the school bus after that, so Fernlea gave me a bus pass. Freedom. I began to travel all over the city.

Before my twelfth birthday many fights, a few escapes. Once I went with two girls, both teenagers. Rose was thirteen and her coloured friend fifteen. We went on the ferry to New Brighton.

'Lovely, Graham, isn't it?'

I looked at the lighthouse and the ships, down at the boat's frothy wake, up at the seagulls. Into Rosie's eyes.

'Yeh,' I said.

We hung around in the amusement arcades all day, thumping machines till money came out, stealing what we could, begging from drunks. When we made enough money we spent it on chips.

Night fell, and our last cash went on a cup of tea between the three of us. When we left the cafe it was cold, and we stood disconsolately in the street outside. Next thing, the coloured girl was speaking to two men. They were both drunk and seemed old to me, but were probably about thirty or forty. Five minutes later we were in the back of their car, lurching from side to side as they raced around corners. They had a T.V. and I watched *It's a Knockout* while the girls gave them our false names and told them our transparent story. The two men went upstairs, and a couple of minutes later called the girls. They clattered up after them.

During a commercial break I went up the dark staircase for a pee. A light was on in one of the rooms and the door was ajar. The two girls were sitting on the edge of a bed watching the man who owned the house. He was stark naked and sported an enormous erection. His hand went up and down, up and down. The coloured girl might have been doing something to him.

Later the men went to bed, dead drunk, and we slept downstairs in the front room. Rose slept with me across two pushed-together armchairs.

'Graham.'

Her voice was soft in parlour darkness.

'Hmm?'

'Come 'ere, then.'

Rosie's soft lips on mine, her tongue playfully licking. Her breasts were like eggs and her sex, unlike mine, had hairs on it. Having no idea what was really there I ran my hand over the front where the hairs grew. I was still doing it when I eventually fell asleep.

They dropped us on the promenade, gave us a ten-shilling

note, and we spent that day as we had the other. We slept that night in a house made of deckchairs. It was freezing so the following morning, a Sunday, we phoned the police and gave ourselves up.

' 'Ere y'are kids.'

The policeman gave us a bacon sandwich and a cup of tea each while we waited for the social worker to arrive. He came. As we were driving through the Mersey Tunnel he had words for us all. My turn came last.

'As for you, Graham, my orders are to take you to Menlove Avenue.'

This scared me. It was a Remand Home. What had I done that was so bad?

'Why, Mr Norris? Ah, 'ey, Mr Norris,' I began to sob, 'not Menlove Avenue, sir. Give us another chance, sir. Please don't take me.'

When we got to Fernlea the coloured girl and Rosie got out. All the way to Menlove Avenue I kept up my pleading.

'It's no good, Graham.' He was irritated by the time we arrived. 'You're going in here and that's that.'

When the car pulled up in the dreaded driveway I flung my door open and bolted. Fortunately I had my bus pass with me, and with it I returned to Fernlea and begged them to let me stay. They held a short conference.

'Graham, you'll have to go to Menlove Avenue for punishment. You can't go on running away like that. But if you're a good boy we'll see about taking you back later on.'

It was a hard place, run like a prison. You had to fold your kit into meticulous squares, wear shorts, and do exactly as you were told. After two days I was used to everything except being locked in. One of the Fernlea staff came then to see me.

'Sir, please get me out of 'ere, sir. I 'aven't committed no crime, sir, 'ave I?'

Sobbing again.

'We'll see, Graham.'

A week later he returned and took me back to Fernlea.

They put me in the Clifford Holroyde school again, but my stay in Fernlea was not to be a long one. A month later they accused me of lighting the Guy Fawkes bonfire two days before it was due to burn.

'I don't know nothin' about it, sir. Honest!'

I was telling the truth, and I carried on telling it all the way to Menlove Avenue.

This time I was there for six months. My twelfth birthday came, passed, receded. Most kids were there a week, went to court, and vanished. Not me. Day after day it was Work Party, twice a week an hour in the classroom learning nothing. Since I had committed no crime they let me go home for Christmas. My Dad brought me back after the bare six days. Six days. It was a Voluntary Care Order I was under, and he could have taken me out of there any time he chose. He came to visit me once, and shook his head when he saw I was mixing with criminals. He never lifted a finger to help me.

One day a member of staff marched into the dormitory.

'Right, Gaskin. Pack up your things.'

This time it was Redbank, the same kind of place only bigger. I escaped and got as far as Manchester, but was caught the same night. After five more weeks locked up they found a place that was willing to take me, St Vincent's, a Catholic approved school in Formby. They had started calling approved schools 'community homes' by then. They like their little joke.

The Head's name was Mr Lally.

'Well, Mr Hughes,' he said to the social worker, 'thanks for bringing him. You can go now, I think.'

For that, I liked him.

'You've had a hard time by the looks of it, boy. Whose fault's that, yours or ours?'

He seemed firm and fair, and even then I liked him. When the official talk was over he leaned back in his chair and smiled at me, his eyes twinkling.

'Be a good boy while you're here, Graham, and I'll take you to Lourdes. Not this time,' they were going a month or two later, 'but next year. All right?'

Kids told me later that he had never said this to any boy on his initial interview before. It was as if he was already my friend.

St Vincent's was strict. You had to eat up every bit of your food, or you were punished. They made you line up straight and march everywhere, and go to bed at nine. Next to the playground there was a lawn with four smooth-topped stumps where trees had been felled, and these were used for punishment.

'Get on that stump, Gaskin.'

'Ah, 'ey, sir. I was on'y ...'

'On that bloody stump.'

You had to stand there for ages, usually watching one or two kids on other stumps, their bodies slack with boredom. In spite of such ideas, St Vincent's was fair. I was only caned twice during my whole stay there, once by Mr Lally. He never would have caned me unless I had done something, in his terms, to deserve it. And I knew his terms. Without him I wouldn't have lasted a month there. As it was the place, and its Head, did something for me. It settled me down and gave me some schooling. Though I wasn't the toughest kid at the beginning, I was big and the others left me alone. From the start they called me Gazzer, the name I later sprayed, spelt GAZA, over half the subways and shopping precincts in Liverpool when I was on the run. After a year I *was* the toughest, and had peace. Mr Lally gave me his trust from the first week. There were doves at the back of the school, and I had the job of feeding and watering them all the time I was there. On some mornings he would walk round and visit me.

'Hiya, sir. 'Ey, sir, I used to go to this big mansion with this bloke at Blatchwick, sir, an' he had a little 'ouse for the birds like this one.'

'A dovecote, Graham.'

'That's it, Mr Lally. A dovecote.'

When I'd finished he would walk back with me. Cold winter mornings, and his arm around my shoulders.

The masters were, for the most part, all right. There was a points system for behaviour, and they carried points books and could give you Credit Points or Penalty Points. More than twenty Penalty Points in a week meant loss of your weekend leave. Some weeks I got forty or more. Loss of leave didn't bother me, as my Dad hardly ever came anyway.

The Deputy Head was Mr Alston, an admirable man. Mr Sweet, a master who impressed you with his sheer size, was also scrupulously fair. But there was another, The Neck, whom we hated. Some kids called him Bummer, for rumour had it that he had been sacked from another 'approvey', St Thomas More's, for interfering with one of the boys. He looked a bit that way, but had a pretty young wife and several children of his own. The Neck had a strange, stretched smile, a head like an inflated avocado, and was some kind of war hero, having lost an arm during the Normandy landings. When you did something wrong he would call you over, his soft voice threatening.

'Come 'ere, misteh. Come 'ere.'

You would walk awkwardly over.

'What d'yeh think this is, misteh? Eh? What d'yeh think this is?'

No reply was possible.

'Right.' The voice ever softer. 'Let me see that neck.'

You had to stoop forward with your head stuck out, your neck craned forward. Smack. His palm slapped down on the back of your neck. The pain was minimal. The humiliation and the ritual were what hurt.

One day, out of the blue, Mr Alston called me out of class.

'Someone's come to see you, Graham.'

'Sir? Is it me Dad?'

'No, Graham. An old friend, though. Mr Malcolm Bishop. D'you remember him?'

It was the same Malcolm who had taken me out as a little boy at Blatchwick. He was sitting with his mother in a huge silver car in front of the main door.

'Hello, Graham.'

'Er, hiya.'

'You remember Graham, don't you mother?'

'Oh, yes. I do now. Who would forget such a good-looking boy?'

They seemed all right, though I felt awkward with them. They took me for a game of putting, and I was able to show off the golfing skills I'd acquired at Fernlea. When they were going he asked me if he could write.

'Er, yeh. O' course, if yer want to.'

Weekends and holidays were the loneliest times for me. Every-one went home and I was left in the school by myself. At first my Dad used to come for me every month, then every six weeks. In the end he hardly ever came. Mr Lally would take pity on me and give me the money to go to Southport for the day. Mr Alston began to take me home with him at weekends. Both men despised my father for the way he treated me, and showed me love. One Christmas my Dad brought me back after the bare five days, and Mr Alston took me to his house. They were lovely people and made me feel wanted and welcome. I had a better time than I ever had with my father, and when it was time to go I cried.

I was very conscious of the injustice of my position. The other kids were thieves, but I wasn't. Sometimes I went berserk when The Neck hit me.

'Don't 'it me! I 'aven't done nothin'. I'm not *in* 'ere because I've done anythin' wrong. DON'T 'IT ME!'

The Neck used to take us for our nightly shower, and everything had to be just so.

'Right, undressed.'

We had to undress in unison, first the jacket, then the belt, then the pullover, and so on. If we didn't get it just as he wanted it:

'Right, dressed again.'

Sometimes he would keep it up all evening, making us miss our favourite T.V. shows. He was gullible, though, and we often made fun of him. I'd twist my arm up my own back, grab the pullover of the lad behind me, and shout as though in pain.

'Gerroff, will yer?'

The Neck would pace over and speak softly to my victim.

'Right, misteh. What d'yeh think this is? Eh?'

The rest you can imagine.

After a few months I told Mr Lally about my bad ears, and was allowed to take baths on my own rather than showers with the herd. He let me have an old bike, which no other kid in the school had ever been allowed, and I ran errands for the masters and for Matron, who was Mrs Lally. Usually they were to the Co-op down the road, which was run by Polo Mint Jackson. Polo Mint came to the approved school at night to play records for the boys, and as his name suggests he was generous with the famous mints. Mr Lally let me out on my own to play putting, and more than once took me with him for a game of grown-up golf.

The dormitories had names like St Michael's and St Matthew's. Mine was Sacred Heart and it was here that I learned, properly, the joys of sex. One time, probably the first, I remember vividly. It was during a holiday, and as usual my father had brought me back early. There was another St Vincent's kid there, Mark, and a blind kid from another school whom we were looking after. We had been playing hard all morning, and after dinner went upstairs for a rest. The blind kid climbed into his bed and fell asleep. I went for a bath, throwing myself face down on my bed when I came back, sluggish after the hot water. Mark came over and sat with me. After a minute he picked up a jar of Vaseline that was lying on top of my cupboard.

'D'yer want me to rub some o' this on yer back, Gazzer? It's nice.'

Half asleep, I did not move. Merely watched him.

'Okay.'

He put some on to his fingertips and began to circle it into my shoulders. Slowly, rhythmically, his fingers spinning slow arcs of pleasure, he worked his way down my body. The small of my back, my buttocks, thighs and calves, all came under the thrall of his gentle fingers. When he reached the soles of my feet my whole body was radiant with sensation, glowing with an enclosing tenderness. Lightly, he touched my shoulders again.

'Gazzer, turn over.'

I gave him a look of embarrassment. And fear.

'What if someone comes in, Mark? They'll think we're ...'

'Turn over,' he said again, softly.

Embarrassed still, I did so. The male body is not designed for the concealment of passion. Looking into my eyes, he worked with patience, slowness and delectable stealth over my collar bones and shoulders and down my chest, taking great time over my nipples. They have been sensitive, like a woman's, ever since. A few seconds after he reached my sex, I came. That done, I lost interest. The glow faded. I have always regretted my selfishness in not doing the same for him, for I know he wanted me to. This happened when I was thirteen. Mark was only eleven.

During the same lonely vacation, Malcolm came to see me. He took me to the beach and we stood at the water's edge skimming stones over the waves.

'Let's see if we can find some crabs, Graham.'

We scampered over the rocks, splashing through pools, laughing. Then turned stones over and nudged shy creatures with hesitant fingers. He bought me an ice cream, and a bag of sweets to take back to St Vincent's.

Though it was a Catholic school, I never went to Mass. The rest went on Friday afternoons and Sunday mornings, while I stayed in school playing snooker with the only other non-Catholic kid, or took hot baths. At the end of my first year they put me on the reserve list for Lourdes, though I was at the bottom of the Good Behaviour chart. When I had been at St Vincent's nearly two years they told me I was going. Mr Lally had kept his promise.

Three other kids were going too, Dusty, a Preston kid who was always chewing gum, Pat Moloney, a Liverpool lad and a good friend, and Andrew Denver, a Manchester boy. Andrew I remember most for the way he went down on me once in the shower room, kneeling behind the bath while I looked out for The Neck. Besides Mr Lally and Mr Sweet, Polo Mint Jackson from the Co-op was going. He went every year, and was great with the handicapped people it was our job to escort.

There was a planeload of us altogether, a hotelful when we arrived. Flying was exciting, and even the bus journey to Speke airport was tremendous.

''Ey, look at them planes, Pat. That one's takin' off, isn't it?'

At the hotel in Lourdes, Dusty and I shared a room, Pat Moloney and Andrew were on the other side of the passage. In the room next to theirs was a mentally retarded kid with his middle-class father. The boy was big, mad, and as strong as Samson.

Though kids weren't allowed on the streets of Lourdes at night, we went.

''Ow much is the cowboy 'at, mate?' Pat asked a shopkeeper.

'Quoi?'

'The 'at. 'Ow much?'

'Dix francs.'

'Did 'e say deece fronk?' Dusty chipped in. 'That's over a quid.'

Moloney took it anyway. We bought a bottle of wine and walked along drinking it. Suddenly, a gaggle of laughing French girls were dancing in a circle around us, singing. It might have been the Ave Maria they were singing, but I don't think so. It was all so foreign that we were baffled. At that moment Mr Lally came around the corner on his way back to the hotel. He was angry when he saw us and sent us back in disgrace. I felt I had let him down, though I hadn't really. We hadn't meant to get involved.

Next day he took us to the Basilica. A vast underground cavern with twenty thousand people crammed into it, filling every niche and nook. A cardinal in scarlet robes was saying the Mass, assisted by fifty priests. The scene was spectacular and splendid, and left me rapt. I had never dreamt such things existed. One of our party came over to Mr Lally and spoke into his ear. Standing nearby, I heard:

'Who's going to say the prayer?'

Mr Lally looked at me thoughtfully. Oh, no. To my horror he leaned over.

'Graham,' he said. 'Will you do it?'

My look must have been one of blank dismay.

'It would make up for last night,' he said.

Since he had put it that way, I couldn't refuse. I swallowed what felt like a cricket ball as I looked into his eyes, which were as bright and amused as ever.

'Er, all right, sir,' I said.

In the smart suit they had loaned me before we left, I walked nervously along one of the aisles and mounted the steps to the dais. Bright lights blazed upon me and the priests stood behind, swaying their incense. There were two big microphones in front of me, and beyond them a shifting, coughing multitude of twenty thousand upturned faces, staring. Flash bulbs popped off from here and there amongst them. My voice boomed alarmingly through the loudspeakers at the start of the prayer, and this frightened me. I rushed through it at the speed of an auctioneer.

The worst thing about Lourdes was the sweets. There weren't any. Just funny things that looked like coloured stones, and were as tasteless.

'Polo mint, anyone?'

He had brought four boxes with him.

'Er, yeh. Ta, Mr Jackson.'

'Anyone want to come to the pictures?'

The films were all about Bernadette discovering the water, the Virgin appearing to her standing on a rock, mistily sentimental, wearing flowing robes. Once you'd seen one you'd seen them all. Nevertheless, it was good there. We walked through the town at night in candlelit processions, singing.

'Ave, ave, ave Maria . . .'

It was beautiful to watch those slow-moving people, to hear their hymn, so peaceful. In the afternoons we pushed the paraplegics in their wheelchairs, round and round in a slow, sedate circle outside the Basilica. Every now and then a priest came out and waved his arms, blessing them.

'In nomine Patris, et Filii, et Spiritus Sancti. Aaaaaamen.'

During our week not one of them jumped out of his wheel-chair and did a cartwheel across the square.

Mr Sweet was amazing with handicapped people. The men-tally retarded kid in the room next to Andrew and Pat, endowed with great strength, was often quite frightening. His father gave him his own way in everything, as if that would make up for how he had been born. The lad was big, violent, and very spoilt. The first time he tried it on with Mr Sweet the master slapped his face, not hard, but shockingly.

'Cut that out, Geoffrey.'

A moment later his hand came on to the boy's and gave it a squeeze. He was a different lad after that as far as Mr Sweet was concerned. He never played him up again and was soon in love with him, following him everywhere and uttering the curious grunts which were his way of speaking. Mr Sweet was a good man, and loved him back. More, he actually improved the boy's manners, particularly at mealtimes, and we could all see the boy taking pride in this. When the holiday ended Geof-frey was heartbroken. His face sagged and tears streamed down his cheeks. Mr Sweet gently, firmly helped him into his father's car.

'Go on, Geoffrey. You must go, son.'

When we got back to St Vincent's there was a letter waiting for me from Malcolm Bishop. It was signed, naturally enough, 'love, Malcolm'. This embarrassed me and I tore it up quickly, scared lest the lads should see it. A week later something similar happened. Mr Lally met me as I was returning from feeding the doves.

'I've a surprise for you, Graham. I hope you like it.'

In his office, he pushed a copy of a Catholic magazine over to me. The entire front page was a picture of me saying the prayer in the Lourdes Basilica. Mr Lally was very chuffed.

'Oh, er, thanks Mr Lally. I'll keep that, sir.'

As soon as I was alone I ripped it into tiny pieces and flushed them away down the bog.

Shortly afterwards he hurt his back, and had to go into hospital. The weeks passed with no sign of him returning. This was a disaster for me, and it was then that things began to go wrong. The fact that I was in an approved school when I had done nothing wrong preyed on my mind, and drove me to rebellion. From now on, I decided, no one would hit me. If they tried, they would be the ones to be hit. I started by refusing to take any more punishment from The Neck.

It happened in the shower room.

'Come 'ere, misteh.'

His voice was as soft as ever, his manner as sure. He wasn't expecting resistance, and was visibly shocked when I picked up a mop that was leaning against the wall.

'Don't try an' fuckin' neck me, mate.'

The words were delivered in my most threatening tone, and I meant what I said. The result was a whiff of fear from The Neck. Something snapped inside me then, and I chased him around the baths and into the corridor, watched by incredulous kids ...

'It's not fair me *bein'* 'ere, Mr Alston,' I said to the Deputy Head. 'Why don't yer move me?'

'You have to stay here, Graham.' He shook his head sadly. 'No other place will take you.'

I ran away to Brenda's place in Wales. She was living with a guy, and brought me back after two days. The day she returned me I scarpered again, surprising them in the social services office in Liverpool when I walked in and told them my name.

'Look,' I said eventually, 'I'm not askin' yer to move me, I'm *tellin'* yer. I'm not a kid any more. I 'aven't committed no crime, an' I shouldn't be in no approvey. Yer *know* I'm right.'

They did, too.

'We'll see what we can do,' they said in the end, and took me back to St Vincent's to wait. A fortnight later they picked me up and drove me to a house in Croxteth.

'This is Graham, Mrs Smith. Say hello, Graham, no need to be shy.'

''Ello, Mrs Smith.'

'Hello, love. Like a cuppa?'

She was about seventy and suffered from crippling rheumatism, as did the old Alsatian which painfully followed her around. The social worker pressured her about me, and in the end she agreed to take me in.

'Not for another three weeks, though,' she said as she hobbled to the door behind us.

Two days later Mr Alston found out about something I'd done, and pulled me out of class by the ear.

'We've had all we can take of you, Gaskin.'

He put me in his car and drove me to a senior approved school, Greenfield House. It was a big place miles from anywhere.

On my first night they took us by minibus to the public baths. As we were coming out I saw a pound note on the step, picked it up quickly, and shoved it into my sock. Next day after tea I spoke to the master in charge.

'Lissen, I shouldn't be in 'ere. This is for criminals, this place. I 'aven't committed no crime, so I'm goin'.'

Not knowing about the money, he called my bluff.

'All right,' he said, forcedly casual. 'Go then.'

Half a mile along the road I caught a bus for Liverpool.

3 | *Street Life*

This time, being older, I stayed on the run longer. For a whole three weeks I stayed around Rice Lane in Walton, the area near my Dad's street where I knew some kids and could find my way about.

'Hiya, Fitzie. Remember me?'

He was a kid I'd known slightly for years, a tall lad with dark hair and green eyes. He was thicker set than I was and older, sixteen.

'Hiya, Gazz. Where've yer been, lar?'

At first I slept in boxes and derelict cars, but later I found a garage at the end of Andrew Street with a Land-Rover parked in it. I moved in and slept comfortably, curled up across the front seat. In the early morning I went out and pinched milk from doorsteps, during the rest of the day I stole biscuits and Mars bars from shops.

''Ey! 'Ey, Dunnie!'

'Oh, hiya Gazzer,' Jimmy Dunn said. 'Long time no see, eh?'

'Yeh. Lissen, can yer lend us a shillin' for a bag o' chips?'

In this way I managed to survive, but only just. Once, starving and stuck for ideas, I decided to burgle my Dad's. He had married by then, and he and his wife would both be at work. To be sure, I knocked first at the front door. To my surprise the new Mrs Gaskin opened it.

'Oh, dear. Hello, love. Are you Graham?'

'Er, yeh.'

'I thought so. Look, you're ever so naughty running away like that. Your Dad's very worried, you know.'

She asked me in and offered me something to eat. It was the one tactic I could not resist.

'Those chips all right, love? They look a bit soggy to me.'

'Yeh,' munch, munch, 'they're,' chomp, gulp, 'fine thanks.'

While this was going on the front door opened. My Dad came in, saw me, and went out again without a word. Though I knew he had gone to phone social services I carried on eating, unconcerned. Soon he came back.

'I don't know what your game is, Graham,' he said, 'but you can't carry on like this.'

Five minutes later a social worker arrived.

'Well, Graham, decided to give yourself up at last, eh? Being sensible for once, are we?'

Pleased with the good meal, I followed them out. When the social worker opened the car door to put me inside I surprised them and took off at full pelt along Andrew Street. They stood dumbfounded for a few seconds, then began to shout.

'Graham, stop! Come back here. Come back this *instant*, Graham.'

At the corner I turned to face them.

'Up yours, yer shower o' twats!'

An hour later I was sitting on a wall two streets away when my father rose out of the ground before me. His body was hard and angry as he took hold of my arms and pushed me into the back of his car. He drove ferociously for a minute without saying a word, then stopped as a traffic light got in his way. I flung the door open and ran hell for leather. In a nearby bombed house I sat trembling, getting up every couple of minutes to look through the broken windows for police. They weren't taking me back.

My best friends were Fitzie and the Dunn brothers, Stevie

and Jimmy, all of whom lived in Andrew Street. Jimmy was older than Stevie by two years, but was much smaller. In fact he was tiny, but possessed of a restless, almost creative energy when it came to stealing. It was with these three that I did my first burglary, a warehouse at the back of my father's house. We threw a chunk of concrete through the window and the big shards slipped slowly to the ground, landing with a deafening crash. Scrambling in, we grabbed the first things we saw, four suitcases, and dashed out and back over the wall with them. The Dunnies' house was nearest so we took them there.

''Ey, look at all this, lads!'

They had belonged to door-to-door salesmen, and were full of rubbishy belts, charms and trinkets.

'I'll stash mine in me Dad's yard,' I said.

'Is it safe?'

'Yeh. 'E's away somewhere.'

So I hid my share of the loot in the back toilet, keeping a few of the charms to show to people and perhaps to sell.

Though Fitzie wasn't old enough to drive, he did. He had just bought a Mini from Jake, Martin Eldon, an ex-boyfriend of my sister's. It was parked in their back so that night I climbed into it to sleep. At three in the morning another lad, Davvo, climbed over the wall.

''Ey, Gazzer. 'Ey, wake up.'

'Uh?' I rubbed my eyes sleepily. 'Hiya, Davvo. What're yer doin' 'ere?'

Davvo, a big lad six feet tall and eighteen years old, was a bit of an idiot who knocked around with us kids all the time.

'I've run away from me Mam's,' he said. 'Can I stay 'ere with yer?'

It was lonely sleeping in the old car by myself.

'Yeh,' I said. 'Okay, Davvo.'

'Great. I've got a few quid too, Gazzer. I'll pay me way all right.'

We lay talking till it grew light, then went out into the street. It was Sunday, and very quiet. We walked towards town, catching the first bus when it came along. At the Pier Head Davvo bought us tea and toast in the café.

'Come on,' he said. 'We'll go over on the ferry.'

'All right.'

We walked in Birkenhead until evening, mooching around

the docks getting into scrapes, being thrown off ships when the seamen caught us. We were nearly back at the ferry when a panda car slid to a halt beside us.

'Right, you lads. Just 'ang on there a minute.'

Two cops got out, slamming their doors behind them.

'Right, what're your names?'

At first they seemed satisfied with what we told them, but just as they looked ready to let us go one of them changed his mind.

'Let's just see if they've got anything on 'em.' He plunged his hand into my pocket and brought it out full of charms. 'Oho! What's this, then?'

At the police station Davvo cracked up immediately, like a child.

'It wasn't me that done the ware'ouse, mister. It was Gazzer. 'E done it with Fitzie an' the Dunns.'

I stared at him in disbelief. It was nothing to do with him, why didn't he just keep his mouth shut? As they questioned me it became obvious that I might as well own up, since they had part of the loot and would soon discover where it had come from.

'Yeh,' I said in the end, 'I done it. But I done it on me own.'

'Where's the rest of the stuff?'

'In a suitcase in me Dad's yard in Walton.'

Two C.I.D. men took me over to Liverpool to check this out. As they were dragging me into the entry I saw Fitzie standing outside his house and tried, through a series of ludicrous nods and winks, to tip him off. They never got him or the Dunnies for it, so they must have gone straight in and shifted their share of the loot. One of the detectives started to kick my Dad's gate.

'D'yer 'ave to do that?' I said. 'Let me climb over an' unbolt it for yer.'

He stopped. 'You're talking to a police officer now, son. We're not that stupid.'

With his next kick the gate flew open.

Davvo's mam came to the police station and bailed him out. For the first time in my life I slept in a real cell. My social worker was in court on the Monday and so was Davvo, his big mouth having let him in for a charge of dishonestly handling. The social worker put in a word for me and the magistrates granted me bail, also for the first time. The last too, so far. When we came out he took me to Mrs Smith's, the foster-gran who had agreed to have me from St Vincent's.

'Been in trouble, eh lad?' she said as she painfully opened the door. I wondered if it were the hinges I could hear creaking, or her rheumatic old joints. 'There'd better not be any more o' ' that, not while yer in this 'ouse.'

She hobbled slowly along the passage to the kitchen. She had her nephew staying with her, a nice enough kid about eleven years old, and Kevin, a guy of twenty-two who had been her foster son and stayed on. Kevin was one of those people who are born middle-aged. He wore glasses, a short back and sides and a new, old-fashioned gaberdine mac. We three slept in the same room, the boy and I in bunk beds. Kevin was shop steward in the hospital where he worked as a porter, and he was always talking about Tony Benn. Callaghan had just taken over the Labour Party leadership from Wilson, and Kevin was always giving me long, Leftist lectures about it. Mrs Smith and the dog were all right.

As soon as the social worker left I went out to see the lads, taking a bus to Aintree then walking along to Rice Lane. Fitzie and the Dunnies were standing outside the Youth Club. They were not overjoyed to see me, and shouted in unison as I walked up.

'Yer stinking' grasser . . .'

'. . . snitchin' twat . . .'

'. . . bloody grass . . .'

I couldn't believe it.

'Yer what?'

'Yer grassed us up. Davvo said . . .'

'*Davvo?* Don't be silly. It was Davvo that grassed, not me.'

After a time I convinced them and we went into the Club, a kids' disco which closed at ten. On our way to the chippie afterwards who should we bump into but Davvo.

'*You*'re the grass, *you*'re the grass,' I said loudly, so everyone could hear. 'Yer grassed me up an' yer grassed all these, too. Don't try to put the shit on me, lar. Thought I'd still be in the nick, didn't yer?'

He punched me in the mouth, sending me sprawling. Muttering, I climbed to my feet.

'Touch me again, Davvo, an' I'll go for our kid.'

Rob had a flat of his own now in Grey Street, a couple of

streets along from Andrew Street. It was just around the corner, and Davvo grew frightened and changed his tune.

'I'm sorry, Gazzer. I didn't want no trouble with the police. Me Mam'll kill me if I'm in any more.' Then, when Fitzie and the Dunns walked away, 'Yer don't wanna be a fall guy for that lot, Gazz.'

'Nobody'd *be* fallin' if yer'd kept yer mouth shut, Davvo.'

A few days later the same four of us broke into a Cash & Carry warehouse on a nearby trading estate. It was a cheeky job as there was a Group 4 Security headquarters directly opposite. The Cash & Carry had a sliding metal door across the loading bay, and we worked out that if three of us tugged at the bottom corner we could make a gap wide enough for Jimmy Dunn, the smallest, to squeeze through. We jammed our scuffed shoes against the wall and heaved with all our strength, and he wriggled inside. The rest of us hid behind a skipful of empty boxes, talking in whispers as we kept an eye on the Group 4 building across the way.

Thump, thump. Thump, thump. Thump, thump.

It was Jimmy's signal, banged on the metal door. We flitted over to it and heaved again, and some boxes shot out.

'It's sweets!' he hissed. ''Ang on there while I look for the booze.'

We threw the boxes in the skip and sat on the wall while he searched. When we peeped into our cartons they were full of Ruffles bars, 2 lb boxes of chocolates, chewing gum, and plastic Easter eggs with rubbishy gifts inside. Stevie Dunn rubbed his belly with a circular motion, rolling his eyes.

'Not bad, eh lads?'

At that moment the ring of an alarm bell lacerated the air. We flew, hearts pounding and anoraks wildly flapping, out of the trading estate and up Hartley's Hill past the jam factory. When we were halfway up Stevie Dunn remembered his brother.

'Our Jimmy!' he gasped. ''E can't gerrout without us!'

We pelted back to rescue him, but changed our minds when we saw lights and men outside Group 4. Fear was strong, and we abandoned him and turned to run the other way.

''Ey lads, lads! Lads, wait!'

We looked behind us and saw Jimmy pounding up the hill in our wake, his thin, spidery figure looking at once desperate and relieved. Resourceful as ever, he had somehow managed to wriggle free, leaving his coat behind. He sped after us up the dirt-track at the side of Hartley's Hill and into the policeless park.

Safe again, we mooched along the road at the far side. While Jimmy Dunn picked his ear and examined the wax, Stevie lifted a bottle and flung it against a tree. Fitzie booted a tin can along the gutter, then aimed a rock at a corrugated iron Scout Hut. It bounced off with a clang.

'I'm goin' 'ome for me tea,' he said.

'Me too,' said Stevie.

'Yeh,' Jimmy Dunn said, 'I'm starvin'.'

They all had homes except me. When they went in I just walked the streets until they came out again.

'I'll see yer later,' I said.

'Okay, Gazz,' Jimmy Dunn said. Then, 'Why don't yer go an' get the stuff?'

There was nothing better to do. 'Yeh, I'll take a stroll down there an' see what 'appens. Tell yer what, 'ow about meetin' somewhere, after?'

'All right. We'll meet yer in the ole coal yard.'

'Okay, seeyer.'

'Seeyer, Gazz.'

From the wall opposite Group 4 Security, the Cash & Carry looked quiet. The bell had long ago stopped ringing. After half an hour I walked over, took the boxes from the skip and quickly packed them into larger boxes, which I shoved behind a wall. There was a lot of stuff, and most of it would have to be hidden in the park. All the time I was working I had the feeling of being watched, so when I had shifted the loot I carried on and assembled a pile of empty boxes. All of a sudden the door of the Cash & Carry burst open and a guy came out. He marched over.

'What've you got in them boxes, kid?'

I had anticipated this.

'Nothin', mister. Just empty boxes. I was goin' to take 'em if that's all right, like. For me Mam.'

He nudged them with his foot to gauge their weight, then peered into them.

'Oh, er, yeh. That's okay.'

When he had gone inside and closed the door, I collected the full boxes from behind the wall and struggled up the hill with them. They were heavy, and it took me two trips to get them into the park. When I came into the coal yard, panting under the weight of what I could carry, the rest of the lads were already there. They fetched the remainder, and we sat in the little room where the workmen have their tea to divvy the loot.

'There's eight boxes o' chocs, a box o' Wriggerley's an' nineteen Ruffles bars each,' Jimmy Dunn said in his professional way. 'The stuff left over goes to Gazzer for doin' the 'ard work.'

At Mrs Smith's that night, I stuck the loot in the wardrobe and carefully covered it up.

'I'm goin' 'ome tomorrow, Gazz,' her nephew said later, as we were sitting in the bedroom, reading. Looking up from my book, I thought how strange it was that he seemed such a little boy when I was only three years older. I rummaged in the wardrobe and fished out some Ruffles bars.

''Ere y'are, kid. 'Ave a few o' these.'

'Ooh, great. Ta, Gazzer.'

As soon as I left the house next morning the little sneak told Mrs Smith of my generosity. She took a look and phoned social services, who phoned the police. The Law told her to let them know as soon as I returned.

Over in Walton with the Dunnies, I was happily unaware that all this was going on. Jimmy Dunn pinched a pack of two hundred fags, crawling on his hands and knees behind the shopkeeper while the man served sweets to me and Stevie. We sat in their parlour to smoke them.

''Ave another, Gazz.'

'Er, yeh. Ta, Jim.'

The cigarette smouldered away with terrible slowness. Every now and then I took a puff, being careful not to inhale.

It was eleven thirty when I left Rice Lane, and the street was completely deserted. My thoughts turned to Mrs Smith. She and her old dog were all right, and it was good to have her place to go to. 'I'll do the old dear a good turn,' I thought, 'an' get some meat for the dog.' There was a pet shop in the next row of shops, and through the window I located the plastic bin bags and the tins of Chappie. Taking a last look up and down the street to make sure no one was coming I heaved a brick through, dived in, and filled a bag with about fifty tins of food. Then I caught a bus home, hid the tins in the kitchen, and went upstairs.

'All right, Kev?' I said brightly, entering. He was busy writing up the minutes of the last Branch meeting, but looked up immediately.

'I was until you came to live here, Graham.'

'Eh?'

'Mrs Smith's been told to phone the police when you get in. You know why, selfish little get that you are.'

My reply was characteristic enough.

'I'm gettin' off, mate.'

He stood up.

'You're not going anywhere,' he said.

My pituitary shot spurts of adrenalin through me as I squared up to him, face flushed, skin tingling. I spoke in my most criminal tone.

'Lissen, mate. If I wanna go through that door . . .' I pointed to it, 'I *go*, right? No one lays a 'and on me without they get it broke, understand?'

He was a man of twenty-two, I was fourteen and fearless. If it had come to a fight he would probably have won it. Mrs Smith shouted up to us then and we went downstairs to talk. There was no phone in the house and they didn't look like going out that night, so I stayed. An inner alarm clock woke me very early next morning. Kevin was snoring softly. It was dark and windy outside and rain came out of the blackness to lash the windows. I very quietly retrieved the loot from the wardrobe, picked up my clothes, and crept out.

The first thing I did when I got to Walton was to stash the loot in a derelict house. Then I went home, on to the Liverpool streets. At first I slept in cars again, but later I made a little house in the yard of the Dunlop Club in Stalmine Road, stacking up beer crates and laying cardboard inside. Every morning I went out early and stole milk to fill up my belly a bit. Often I would meet one of the Dunnies on their paper round.

'Hiya, Stevie.'

'Hi, Gazz. 'Ey, put 'em in 'ere out o' sight.'

Clink, chink as I placed the bottles of milk in his newspaper bag. Both Dunns were car thieves, and had large collections of keys for this purpose. They gave me a few spares so I could join the business. Jimmy was the real expert, and he made me his protégé. Once I opened an N-reg, which made me very proud. Older cars were easier. If there is a worn barrel in the lock you just fidget the key till you feel it give. Soon I was good at it, and began selling the odd cassette or calculator to supplement my income. For the rest of the day I walked around having anything that looked have-able. When hunger encroached there were always the chippies. Night time was best.

'Er, a bag o' chips please.'

'Hokay.'

When the Chink turned to take them from the fryer I'd hastily slide open the hot-plate door, grab a handful of sausages or a pie, and belt out of the shop and away down the street. Later, in a doorway, I'd blow on the hot food as I crammed it into my mouth, burning my tongue.

One day Fitzie made a suggestion.

'Come an' live with me,' he said, 'I'll smuggle yer in.'

There was an empty room upstairs, and when he let me in through the front door I used to sneak up to it. Two armchairs stood in a corner and I crawled behind them and waited for Fitzie to throw a blanket over. As sleep came I often thought of my Dad a few houses away, snoring next to his new wife.

Our round of burglaries continued. One night we did the main G.P.O. building in Walton Park Road, breaking in through a side window. While Fitzie and the Dunns were looking through the parcels I went after the Registered Mail, but found it to be locked up separately in a little office. There was a basket of Recorded Delivery stuff outside so I went through that instead. The first envelope I opened contained a rent book with £9 in it, which I hastily stuck in my pocket before the others could see. They did this, 'sticking down' as we called it, all the time when we were thieving.

'What's that, Gazzer?' Jimmy Dunn said, quick as a flash.

'Nowt, lar.' I tossed the empty book over. 'Just a bleedin' book.'

In another envelope I found a ticket for that year's Cup Final, Liverpool versus Newcastle. Later I sold it to another kid for £10, so I missed the match. Liverpool won as usual, three goals to nil.

Fitzie was almost as daring a thief as Jimmy Dunn.

''Ow about screwin' Thompson's, Gazzer?'

'Yeh, okay. Sure.'

Thompson's was the little grocer's at the corner of our Coronation Street, and had a storeroom at the back with a sash window. We waited till the pubs were emptying to cover the noise then strolled past, lobbing a Guinness bottle through as we did so. The noise was minimal, and it made a neat hole in the glass. We went home to bed. We were going back at four in the morning, so I slept under Fitzie's bed to be sure of waking. A nightful of snores followed, then:

'Shit, lar! It's ten to six.'

We sprang up and fumbled into our clothes, then raced along the street to Thompson's. The window had not been touched. One or two people were going past on their way to the news-agent's or the bus stop, so we were vigilant as we set to work, Fitzie lifting the broken shards from their frame while I ran across the road and placed them in the alley opposite. In a minute the window was clear and Fitzie went silently in, and swiftly handed out boxes of butter and other valuable gear. As he passed them to me I ran over and hid them in the alley. Then we changed places, and carried on till we had a sizeable stack of loot, which we carried around and hid in Fitzie's back yard.

'Where'll we get rid of it, Fitz?'

Counting packs of cigarettes with miserly fervour, he looked up. 'We'll pay a call on Sammy Jones an' Jake.'

Fitzie's words were to plunge me into the adult world. Jake, Martin Eldon, had lived with my sister once, and I knew Sammy Jones. He was a giant of a man, enormously strong, and with a mad reputation. They were Rockers in their mid-twenties, and both of them had motorbikes, Jake a 650 Triumph. It was eleven o'clock when Sammy Jones opened his door to us.

'Come in, Fitzie. Hiya, kid. Are you Rob an' Brenda's brother?'

'Yeh. Er, look. We've got some stuff an' we wanna find a buyer ...'

After some discussion he told us to bring it round after dark and we did so, staggering under the weight of the boxes. Jake and another guy, Sonny Sackett, were there as well. They cast professional glances over the loot.

'Yeh, we'll flog that for yer. Give us a 'and to get it in the van.'

Half an hour later they came back.

''Ere y'are, lads, eighteen quid. Not bad, eh?'

It was a rip-off, though we didn't know it then. £9 is a lot of money when you're fourteen.

Next day I went to Sammy Jones's again. Sonny Sackett's gleaming Hog with the extended forks was parked outside, and it was he who opened the door. We talked for a while, then Sammy arrived.

'Got no place to stay, kid?'

'No.'

'Well, come round if yer like. Just be cool. Make sure no pigs see yer.'

At midnight I knocked on the door and he let me in. He and Sonny were lying on mattresses in front of the lecky fire so I got my head down on the couch. In the morning a girl, Teresa, came in from another room.

''Ello, who's this good-lookin' young man, then?'

My face turned crimson. She smiled mischievously.

'It's all right, kid,' she said, 'relax. I'm not goin' to eat yer. I know who yer are. Another Gaskin. No mistakin' that 'air, eh?'

She was nice, and had her own room in the house. After tea and toast I went out and stayed away all day, coming back after dark. But as the days passed the time I spent outside grew shorter, that in the house longer. Teresa always made sure I had something in my belly.

''Ad any scoff today, Gazzer?' she'd ask when she came in from work. 'No?' She'd shove a knife into my hand. 'Get peelin' then, while I go to Thompson's for some beans.'

A lot of other good people were introduced to me. There was Leo and his young wife, Valerie. Leo was a nice guy, and worked nights driving a delivery van for a supermarket chain.

''Ere's yer bread,' he'd say, throwing some stolen loaves on to the table, 'an' some cakes for the gannet.'

'Who's that, Lee?' I'd ask innocently, reaching for a doughnut.

Valerie was beautiful, with flowing hair and a face and body to knock you out. Though only seventeen, three years older than myself, she seemed worlds ahead. She had a baby that wasn't Leo's, and a Suzuki 250 which looked enormous when she was on it.

The big wheel of the group, and the one who impressed me most, was Barney Muscle. He had crew-cut blond hair, wore sunglasses day and night, and the lobe of one ear had been bitten off in a fight. He was the one they all looked up to, their hero.

'Yer wanna see Barney bendin' iron bars,' they would tell me in hushed tones. 'Honest, Gazzer, 'e's magic.'

I never did see him perform the feats of strength which gave him his name. Barney was a big-time crook, breaking into post offices and doing hold-ups, so he said. It might have been true.

One night they gave me a joint.

'Give 'im a blow,' someone said, 'see 'ow he reacks to that.'

They often talked about me like that, as though I was some kind of curiosity.

''Ere y'are, Gazz.' One of them handed me an enormous fag. ''Ave a go, lar, it's dead good.'

After a few drags of the dope I turned green, felt sick, and was. But I smoked again, and grew to like it.

My role in Sammy's house was that of a messenger boy, and it grew boring. One night he put the final two-pence piece into my hand.

'Go an' phone me tart, Gazz. Tell 'er I . . .'

'Ah, 'ey Sammy. *I*'m not goin'. I just got back from phonin' for Jake.'

Sammy was having trouble with his girl, and it had put him in a bad mood. 'Piss off out o' me 'ouse, then,' he said without further ado, 'an' don't come back.'

As I was opening the front door Teresa took hold of my arm. 'Come round if yer stuck, Gazzer,' she said. 'Yer can stay in me room for a while.'

Sadly, I rebuilt my beer-crate house in Dunlop's and slept on flattened boxes.

Next day, for something to do, I went to the Dole with a guy who was signing on. We met Barney Muscle.

'What's this about yer bein' chucked out, kid?'

'I got sick o' doin' things for Sammy all the time,' I said.

He pondered. 'Come an' stay the weekend with me.'

He collected his Giro, cashed it, and bought food and cans of beer on the way home. It was a nice flat, and his girlfriend was there. They told me she worked for a travel agent.

'Yeh?' I said. ''Ow's business? All right?'

They laughed as though I'd said something tremendously funny. Later I found out she was a prostitute, not a street-walker but high class. Barney made something to eat, the stereo was blaring, and I sat drinking beer and smoking the joint he had passed me. This was the life, I reflected, and better than any approved school.

On Sunday night we went to a party at Sammy Jones's, and who should come in while we were there but Rob, my brother, who was now eighteen. Later Barney Muscle took me home with him again. Next morning as we were having breakfast he took his shades off and turned to me seriously.

'Well, yer've been 'ere the weekend, Gazzer. Yer should go an' stay with yer brother now.'

'What?' I asked, incredulous. 'Our Rob? There's no way 'e'll take me in, Barney. 'E's not like that.'

'Ask 'im,' was all he said. He gave me a present, an almost new blazer with white piping around its edges, and we said goodbye.

Taking his advice, I called at Rob's flat.

'Why don't yer come an' live with me, Graham?'

'Yeh. Okay, Rob. Great.' I was surprised, until it occurred to me that Barney Muscle must have given him some heavy pressure.

Installed in my brother's flat in Grey Street, I passed a contented week. It was almost like having a home, since I was living with a relative.

'Come on,' he said on the Friday when he came home from work, 'get stuck into this lot with me, our Graham.' He plonked some bottles of cider on the table in front of me. Later, half drunk, we went round to Sammy Jones's. He was tripping on acid, and moaning.

'Me tart's left me. She's *left* me. She won't come back this time, I know she won't.'

Jake and the rest were sitting there, smiling. Suddenly Sammy smashed his glass on to the table, and his hand burst into blood. I was watching him, and knew he hadn't meant to cut himself. He had only smashed the glass to impress the others, but had done it badly and nearly chopped his hand off. Then he made out he *had* done it on purpose, to do himself in.

'I can't go on with it no more,' he wailed.

The rest of the lads dived on to him to snatch the glass, and there was a gigantic commotion.

'Let's get out of 'ere,' our kid said, and we left.

The trouble came, as always, without warning. We were standing in Dunlop's car park in Stalmine Road when some nosy person thought we were trying to steal a car, and phoned the police. They screeched up in a panda and I ran, wildly, through a maze of alleys till I lost them. After hiding for half an hour in someone's back toilet I decided to make it back to Sammy Jones's, off the street.

KnockKnockKnock. Urgently. KnockKnockKnockKnock.

The door opened and Sammy stood dopily in the doorway looking at his hand, which was wrapped in a tea towel and still bleeding.

'Oh, er, hiya Gazzer. Back already, uh?'

I sidled past him into the house just as a cop car pulled up outside. Something about 'wearing a blazer' crackled over their radio as Sammy closed the front door. A second later there was a tremendous hammering upon it, and flakes of plaster floated down from the ceiling. Teresa opened it and an argument, of which I could hear snatches, began on the step.

She was crying.

'But *why*'ve yer got to take 'im? 'E's on'y a kid.'

'He's wanted, that's why.'

My brother appeared from the street, drunk, and was soon embroiled. Suddenly the police were in the house, three of them with us in Teresa's room. Our men were all drunk, which made them think twice about grabbing me. As the discussion grew more heated I stood up, decisively.

'I'm not 'avin' this,' I announced. 'I'm goin' to ask Jake if they can do this.'

I walked out as though going only to the next room, closed the door, then tore along the passage slamming the rest of the doors behind me. Ten seconds later I was scaling the back wall.

WUFFWUFF! WUFFWUFF! WUFFWUFF!

The police dog meant what it said so I jumped back, but seeing a rush of blue uniforms coming at me leapt over again. I scaled the wall on the far side of the alley with the dog snapping the air below me, and jumped as many back walls as I could before the alley filled with flashing torches and crackling walkie-talkies. Then I lay sideways on top of a thin wall, keeping absolutely still. A minute later they found me and hauled me down.

'Come on, yer little bleeder.'

Kicking and screaming, I was dragged around to the front of the house where four prowl cars, a C.I.D. car and a dog-van were waiting. To quieten me down one of the coppers thumped me. This made Robert go berserk.

'That's me brother! That's me brother, yer can't do that!'

He jumped on to the cop's back, punching and kicking. More cops jumped on *his* back, and they all went down in a heap. As they got me into one of the cars, still yelling, Teresa popped her head through the window.

'Er, can we come up an' see 'im?' she asked.

Sammy Jones stood gigantic on his doorstep, the bloody tea towel dangling from one hand and a broken bottle clutched in the other, raving.

'BASterds! BASterds! Come ON, let's 'AVE YER!'

My brother was arrested too, and they drove us in convoy to the police station. Later they took me into his cell to see him. He had a busted lip and his face was pretty smashed, but they only charged him with being drunk and disorderly which made him, in our terms, lucky.

Now, after two years, they returned me to Menlove Avenue. Though the place and its routine were familiar, living there was hard after my recent freedom.

Sunday was visiting day, and I sat with some other lads in a hut overlooking the driveway, hoping the gang would come. When they roared in and parked their gleaming bikes on the gravel my chest tightened and a lump appeared in my throat. They were beautiful. The men, all big and powerful, climbed off their machines and ambled into the building, looking hard and unruly. Teresa and Valerie followed them. The kids watching with me were visibly impressed.

'Wow! Look at them 'Ell's Angels. 'Ave they come to see *you*, Gazzer?'

I had recovered enough to appear unmoved.

'Yeh.'

'*Je*sus!'

They looked at me with increased respect.

In court next day they remanded me in custody to Menlove Avenue. Now, at last, I was there for actually having done something. A week later they took me back to court and sentenced me for the lot, the two warehouses, the pet shop, everything. It was June 1974.

'We're putting you under a compulsory care order, Gaskin. Do you know what that means?'

'Yeh.'

It meant everything was the same, except that my Dad could no longer take me out of the place. Not that he would ever want to.

After six weeks I became eligible for Home Leave, and spent some weekends with my brother. He didn't want me either. It was a poky little flat with plywood walls, and he sent me to bed when he brought women back.

'Oh, Rob, Rob.' The bedsprings were twanging. 'Rob, again,' slop, slop, 'like that,' slop, slop. 'Oh, oh, oh.'

Leo and Valerie lived in a street opposite my Dad's, and said I could stay with them if Rob would collect me from Menlove Avenue. This happened for a couple of weekends, then one Friday Rob phoned the Remand Home to say he was going away, but Leo would pick me up.

All the kids for Home Leave were sitting in their best gear, waiting, going out one by one as their people arrived. In the end there was only me left, and no sign of Leo.

'Er, can yer lend us two pence, sir? I'll phone 'is mate.'

The phone rang for a long time before Jake answered.

'Jake? Lissen, can yer pick us up? Leo 'asn't come.'

'I can't, Gazzer. I'm babysittin', see . . .'

I sat down in one of the tatty armchairs and thought, Well, I'm a man now, this disappointment can't touch me. Then I started to cry.

'I'll give you a lift, Gaskin,' one of the staff said, which surprised me. He was one that I didn't like.

'Ta, sir.'

They called me into the office for my £1 pocket money and we set off, I more anxious than ever. This member of staff obviously didn't know about Rob's phone call, and was taking me to the flat. He was supposed to see me through the door, and Rob would not be there. We soon arrived in Grey Street.

'There's no need to come up, sir.' Rob's flat was at the back, but I pointed to a front window. 'Look, yer can see that 'is light's on.'

He seemed doubtful, as though he might follow me upstairs to make sure. An inspired thought came to my aid.

'Look, take this.' Without looking at him I shoved my pound note into his hand and got out of the car, slamming the door behind me. He drove away. To make it look good in case he was tricking me and came back, I went into the house and ran upstairs. Rob's light was on. He *was* there, the bastard just hadn't wanted me. Enraged, I ran downstairs muttering. 'I'll kill 'im one day, the twat. I should ask Barney Muscle to do 'im over.'

Leo was leaving for work when I got to his house.

'I was comin' for yer tomorrow, Gazz. I'm doin' overtime tonight, see, an' Val's not well. Yer'll 'ave to stay at Rob's tonight, but come tomorrow.'

I slept in one of my derelict cars.

A couple of Sundays later Leo and Valerie took me to the market.

'Oh, I like these, Lee, don't you?' Val picked up a set of matching pans. 'Yer can put little 'ooks behind the cooker to 'ang 'em on.'

'Yeh, love. Great.'

They were planning to settle down in a new house, soon to be vacated by her sister over by the flyover. As we were leaving Leo thrust a brown paper parcel into my hands.

''Ere y'are, Gazz.'

I opened it. A pair of snow-white training shoes.

'Ah, 'ey Lee. Thanks, lar.'

He had to go to work as usual, so I offered to keep Valerie company. She bought a bottle of cider on the way home and we sat drinking it. After a time we grew fed up with the telly and she switched it off.

'Throw a shovel o' coal on for us, will yer, love?'

The dust caught fire and blazed momentarily up the chimney. It was easy to imagine this domestic bliss was mine, not Leo's.

Half a bottle of cider had a powerful effect upon me in those days. This one gave me the courage to put my arm around Val's lovely shoulders. We talked intimately, like sister and brother.

'Graham,' she had always called me Gazzer before, 'are yer 'appy?'

''Appy?' I asked. ''Ow can I be, Val?'

She nodded, the firelight flickering warm on her face. 'Yeh,' she said, 'in that place. 'Ave yer got any girlfriends? Yer should 'ave, yer good-lookin' enough.'

'Well, yeh.' I looked away, pleased. 'One or two, like.'

''Ave yer ever . . .?' She smiled mysteriously. 'You know.'

'Yeh.' The lie came easily. 'Loads o' times.' There was a brief silence. 'Leo's a nice guy,' I said, looking at my shoes. It was true. ''E doesn't 'alf love yer. Are *you* 'appy?'

She looked into the fire, and my eyes followed hers to the flames.

'Well ...'

Next moment I felt her lips, shockingly, on my face. They moved, clung, moved on, searching for my mouth. After a few seconds she pulled me down on the couch, covering my face and hair with kisses. In no time we were naked and feeling one another. I put my finger inside and lay there, wondering what to do next. In the end her touch overpowered me, and I came. It was two in the morning when we said goodbye, Valerie giving me deep, clinging kisses up to the very last moment.

My neck was mottled with love bites, purple, yellow and black. Standing in front of Rob's mirror looking at them, I was filled with simultaneous pride and horror. She had said I was good-looking. I stared at my face, and a beach-boy baddie from an American T.V. film stared back. My heels ached guiltily in the shoes Leo had bought me and I kicked them off, and left them on the bathroom floor without looking back.

Leo was supposed to pick me up next morning, but he forgot to come. Quaking inwardly, I called for him.

'Hiya, Gazz,' he said as he opened the door, 'Jesus! Who give yer them love bites?'

My knees shook like jellies on a high speed train. 'Er, I met this bird. In the park, like ...'

Excited, he pulled me into the kitchen. 'Val, look at this. Our Gazzer's cert'nly growin' up, eh?'

I blushed to the roots of my hair as she turned to look at me.

'Yeh,' she said detachedly, and bent to pick up the baby's toys.

During all this time, freedom lured me. It took a huge effort of will to return to Menlove Avenue, and sometimes it proved too much for me. One Saturday night as I was going to Rob's from Leo's I saw some lads going through Thompson's back window. I went in too, and came out with four boxes of toothpaste. I swopped two, one for a box of Coke and the other for a carton of chocolate bars, then went to a cemetery where there was a mausoleum where I sometimes slept. I sat there for most of the night consuming the loot, and thinking. In the morning

I went round and gave Val the remaining toothpaste. That night, instead of going back, I stayed with her and Leo.

In the morning I made my voice as deep as I could, and phoned. ''Ello, er, this is Mr Robert Gaskin 'ere. I've 'ad me brother with me for the weekend, an' I wondered if 'e could stay another day? 'Is sister's comin' down from London, like.'

'Yes, Mr Gaskin,' they said immediately. 'Make sure you send him back tomorrow night, though.'

Later I found out they had known straight away that it was me. When it grew dark I rebuilt my little crate-house at Dunlop's. By next afternoon I had decided not to go back. At five o'clock Leo came along Rice Lane on his motorbike, and stopped.

'What're yer doin' 'ere, Gazz? 'Ow come yer 'aven't gone back yet?'

'I can't 'andle it, Lee. I'm not goin' back.'

'Yer'll get yerself in all kinds o' trouble if yer don't, Gazz.'

In the end he talked me into it, put me on the back of his bike, and took me there.

'Mr Robert bloody Gaskin, eh?' said the staff who opened the door, and started hitting me with Leo still standing there, which shamed me. There was a cell at Menlove Avenue and they put me into it, crying. They didn't give me any blankets so I slept on the bare boards. My misery was total as I stared at the stark, grey walls. It would be a long time before they gave me another Home Leave.

4 | *Breaks for Freedom*

Next morning they marched me into the office at Menlove
Avenue.

'Gaskin,' the Chief said, 'while you . . .'

'Sir, I . . .'

He held up a finger to silence me. 'While you were *away*,
Gaskin,' his voice was laden with sarcasm, 'a voluntary social
worker called to invite you on a three-week holiday,' he glanced
at a letter in front of him, 'Mr Malcolm Bishop. You know him?'

'Yeh, sir.' God, would they let me go? 'Known 'im a long
time, sir.'

'Hmm.' He appeared to ponder. 'If it wasn't for Mr Bishop's
kindness in offering you this chance, and for the fact that you
apparently have a well-established relationship with him,
there's no way I'd let you out of here at present. You realize
that?'

'Yeh, sir,' I waited a few seconds. 'Can I go, sir?'

He looked at me seriously. 'I'm going to put you on trust,

Gaskin.' My face wreathed in smiles. 'Against my better judgment, let me add.'

The following Sunday, the day before I was due to go, Leo
came.

''Ere y'are, Gazz.'

Habit made me crumple the note into my sock. 'Ta, Leo.'

Next day social services drove me to Malcolm's house, which
was about three miles from Blatchwick.

He tugged my hair playfully, and smiled. 'Hello, Graham.'

'Hiya, Malcolm. 'Ow are yer?'

After lunch we drove to the place at Fontwell, near Bognor
Regis. About thirty tents of different sizes stood in a field close
to a stream, and only half a mile from the village. It was called
the Boys' Aid Camp. Each year a hundred poor boys aged from
seven upwards, mostly from deprived areas of London, were
taken there in the charge of young volunteers like Malcolm.
This year I was one of the oldest as well as being, as usual, the
biggest. Malcolm introduced me to Neil, a friend who was Head
Boy at one of the public schools.

'Well,' he looked round despairingly, 'you look a bit more
grown up than these kids. How about the three of us going for
a drink later?'

To my surprise Malcolm did not object. When we had eaten
the three of us went down to the village pub.

'Lager, Graham?'

'Please, Malcolm.'

'Three pints of lager, please.'

Malcolm was twenty-nine then, more than double my age,
and Neil was years older than me and a practised drinker. I
tried to drink as quickly as they did, and was soon completely
drunk. By closing time I was stumbling into tables on my way
to the Gents, only dimly conscious of my surroundings. The
others seemed little better as we staggered, singing, along the
dark lane back to camp. Tottering into the one-man tent Malcolm and I were sharing, I stripped to my underpants, fell into
my sleeping bag, and crashed out.

When I awoke, light was creeping over the land and making
its way dimly through the thin material of the tent. Outside the
birds were stirring, their wild cries puncturing the air. Malcolm's arm was lying across my chest, and without even opening
my eyes I could tell he was awake. My body was tense as his

hand started to caress my chest, rippling with pleasure by the time he took my hard phallus in his grip. Arching my back against the sensations, I watched his head slide down my body, feeling his lips stop here and there for a kiss. He gave a little slurp of pleasure as his mouth slid over my prick. For a long time, perhaps twenty minutes, I enjoyed what he was doing. Then he stopped. His chest slipped over mine and something wet and hard tried to nudge its way between my buttocks.

'No,' I said sharply.

It was the only word which passed between us during the whole encounter, and as I spoke I gave the offending member a slap, just to let him know I meant it. When I lay on my back again his hand resumed its caress. As soon as I'd ejaculated I turned away from him and went back to sleep.

When I woke again it was to the sizzle of frying bacon, coming from outside the tent. Yawning, I pulled my jeans on and stepped outside. Malcolm turned a rasher with his clasp-knife, and looked up.

'Good morning, Graham.'

'Good morning, Malcolm.'

The day passed normally enough. That evening found us in the pub again for another massive drinking session, followed by another comatose sleep in the little tent. At dawn, as birds' cries carved the air, the same wordless sex took place between us. After that it happened every day.

The prospect of going back to Menlove Avenue grew grimmer as the awful Friday approached. Thursday brought an idea.

'Malcolm, will yer do us a favour? Ring Menlove an' ask 'em if I can stay the weekend with our Rob. They'll say yes if *you* ask 'em.'

'Yes, Graham,' he said. 'Sure thing.'

My idea worked. So on the Friday morning he gave me some money and I caught a train to Liverpool. It was late when I went to Rob's and there was no answer to my knock, so I got my head down on the floor outside his flat. He came in at two in the morning, with a girl.

'Oh, it's you, is it?'

'Yeh. Hiya, Rob.'

Monday came, and I stood watching the buses bound for

Menlove Avenue. Try as I would, I could not climb aboard one. This time my beer-crate house was more or less intact, and only needed lining with fresh cardboard. Next day I met Frankie, a lad I knew slightly.

'Hiya, Gazz. 'Ow goes it, lar?'

'Er, all right.'

'Yer 'aven't got any money, 'ave yer?'

This question is so frequent in Liverpool as to be almost a greeting.

'Nah,' I replied, 'not a carrot.'

'Hmm. Any ideas where we could rob a few bob?'

There was a pause while the inevitability of recapture stared me in the face. If I could get away, though ...

'Well, er, yeh. I '*ave* got an idea.'

Frankie knocked on the front door of my Dad's house while I watched from an alley along the street. No answer. In thirty seconds I was striding along the back entry.

The woman next door, alerted by the bang the brushpole made when I jabbed it through the window, looked out as I was climbing through. I smiled and waved to her and she smiled, a little doubtfully, back. Moments later I was letting Frankie in through the front door. He pulled a carrier bag from his pocket and set to work, scooping up every valuable he could see in the front parlour, nearly £300 worth as it later turned out.

'I know where there's a suitcase,' I hissed, and ran swiftly upstairs.

As I pulled it from on top of the wardrobe, the case opened. Jesus! It wasn't possible. Bundle after bundle of money was rolling out. Hearing Frankie's light footsteps on the stairs I hastily stuck two of them down, one of fives and one of oncers, cramming them into the back of my trousers.

'Bleedin' 'ell!' Frankie stood stock-still, his eyes spinning like the cherries on a fruit machine, then fell quickly on to his knees amid the bundles and picked one up. 'But this is no good, Gazzer. It's all foreign stuff. It might as well be Monopoly money.'

I picked one up, then another, and tossed them down again in disgust. It was true. The notes were American, all of them. As far as we knew it was worthless, and we left three hundred dollars on my Dad's bedroom carpet.

'Seeyer, Gazz.'

'Seeyer, Frankie. We didn't do so bad, eh?'

On my way to Lime Street station I bought an air pistol and four packets of slugs. When I counted what was left it came to just over £70. There was some idea at the back of my mind of going to see Malcolm, and it was this which made me choose my next destination.

''Alf single to Gloucester, please.'

It was late afternoon when I stepped off the train. With the Boys' Aid Camp still fresh in my memory I bought a tent and some camping gear, and took a bus to Stroud. I would live off the land on what I could shoot with my Webley.

''Ey! 'Ey, kid! Blondie!'

The shout went on for some time before I connected it with myself. When I looked back there was a black kid behind me who looked vaguely familiar.

'Didn't you used to be in Blatchwick?' he said.

I remembered him now, Tony Nkuma.

'Yeh,' I said. 'Hiya. 'Ow come yer out so late?'

He scratched his chin and smiled bashfully. 'I'm sixteen. I don't have to be in till ten o'clock.'

'Doin' anythin'?'

'Not really.' He offered me a Park Drive from a battered packet with two cigarettes inside. 'I'm meeting' me mate, then just hangin' about, like.'

'Come on,' I said, 'I'll take yer both to the pictures.'

It was cold when we came out after the film.

'Where're you goin' to camp?' one of them asked.

'Dunno.'

'Come with us to Blatchwick,' they said, so I did.

There was a shed at the back so I didn't use my tent. My new sleeping bag was warm and comfortable, and made me over-sleep. When I awoke it was to the sound of kids playing around the house, waiting for the school bus to Moortown. The thought of being found by Lawrence chilled me. Yet I was bigger, stronger, and carrying a hidden weapon. I bent the airgun grimly and put in a slug, then stepped outside with my gear. As I did so three big Blatchwick kids saw me. They walked over, looking like bad news.

'What are you doin' in there?' the biggest asked, threateningly.

Swinging my pack on to my shoulder, I closed my hand on the gun.

'Don't mess wit' me, lar.'

My harsh Liverpool accent was itself a weapon, and instilled fear. They stood uncertainly but showed no sign of backing off. I pulled out the airgun, shot the biggest in the face from less than a metre, and reloaded. They ran into the building and I made my escape.

On my way to the town I stashed my gear in a field. When I came back that night it had gone, so I started sleeping rough around Stroud. To help my appearance I stole some trousers and bought a pair of shoes.

'Hiya, Tone. What are yer doin' tonight?'

Naturally enough, he and his mate were always skint.

'Nothin'. What about you?'

'Let's go an' 'ave a coffee.'

One night we went to see *Clockwork Banana*, our first dirty film. We grinned in the darkness, showing each other our erections through the material of our trousers.

'See if yer can find us a good screwdriver,' I said afterwards.

'Okay. What for?'

'Me money's nearly gone. I'll 'ave to start robbin' from cars.'

Cold and hunger were again my companions, and doorstep milk kept me alive. The opportunities for theft were fewer than in Liverpool. One night, leaving Tony waiting in a coffee bar, I broke into the social services office. If I could not eat, at least I could strike at the enemy. Standing silently in the empty office with the broken glass of my entry at my feet, I waited for my eyes to adjust to the darkness. When I made out the dim shape of a typewriter I placed it quietly on the floor, put my foot on it and tugged, bending and snapping all the movable parts. After that I went systematically around the room, tearing up letters and files, destroying anything that would break in silence. Some of the filing cabinets were unlocked and I lobbed my prick over the side of about ten drawers, saving some piss for each. As a finale I went into the recess where the head social worker sat, opened his drawer, squatted on the desk above it, and dropped a long steamy turd inside. Smiling in the darkness, I closed the drawer after me. That would be a nice little surprise for him in the morning. Picking up a stapler, a dictaphone and a few odds and ends, I crept to the door and turned on the threshold.

'You BAsterds,' I hissed. 'You dirty, dirty BAsterds.'

Tony was waiting for me.

'Is that wot you got?' He was excited. 'Where'll you sell it?'

'Fuck knows.'

Putting it back inside my coat I peered into the cars we passed. After a minute I spotted something, and wielding the screwdriver with practised skill forced a quarterlight open and pulled out a camera, which I shoved carelessly into my pocket. We walked, on different sides of the road to check the occasional cars, under the shadow of trees. It was cold. A frozen wind blew off the fields.

When we were nearly at Blatchwick a car's headlights went on suddenly ahead of us, and a prowl car cruised along and stopped. We were walking together now, so did not look so suspicious. The bobby wound his window down.

'Where're you off to, lads?'

'Er, we're just goin' 'ome,' I said.

'Where's that?'

'Blatchwick,' Tony said, pointing.

The cop was observant. His hand came out and pulled the camera from my pocket.

'Where did you get this?'

'It's me own. Photography's me 'obby, like.'

The lumps in my clothing made by the dictaphone and other junk seemed to grow bigger. He turned the camera over in his hands, examining it closely.

'Expensive hobby, son. Got many Nikons, have you?'

Tony was released after a couple of hours, in the clear. I bet he got a hard time from Lawrence. They questioned me about the dictaphone till a cold light was creeping through the station windows, but I did not tell.

Allowing social services five minutes to get over their shock at seeing the vandalized office, and another five to find a phone whose wires weren't cut, it must have been gone ten past nine when my cell door was flung open and two fresh detectives awoke me from my slumber.

'Upstairs to the Interrogation Room, Gaskin.'

The dictaphone and stapler lay on the table between an overflowing ashtray and the list of stolen articles phoned in by social services.

'Right, son. Why didn't you own up last night?'

'Own up to what?'

'You know what.' Like a vicar blessing his flock, the senior cop waved his arms over the loot. 'That you burgled social services last night, and took this lot.'

There was no option but to admit to it. The pissing and shitting part seemed shameful now though, so I put my confession in the plural.

'I didn't think you'd find out we did it.'

His ears pricked up at once. 'Who was with you?' He glanced at the night cop's notes. 'Tony?'

'No, I'd on'y just met Tony, like we told yer mate last night.'

He stood up and put his hands on the desk, thrusting his face angrily forward. Behind me, the second detective quietly stirred his tea. They were probably wondering if it would be worth going into their Nice and Nasty routine.

'Who was it, then? What was his name?'

'Lissen,' I said wearily, 'don't start that all over again. Yer mates 'ave been at me all night. I'm not tellin' yer who was with me, but yer've got *me* for the job, 'aven't yer?'

He looked at his watch. Seven and a half more hours before he could get back to the wife. He sat down again and blew me a plume of smoke, smugly.

'Who was the dirty boy, then?'

'Uh?'

'The pissing and shitting. Was that you or your nameless accomplice?'

'I told 'im not to do it,' I said.

'Him that shit in the drawer, I suppose?'

'Er, yeh.'

'You did piss in some filing cabinets though, didn't you?'

Not following his line of reasoning, I nevertheless sensed that admission was in order.

'Well, one or two.'

He beamed, took a gulp of his tea, put his feet on the table, and tilted back in his chair.

'We knew there were two of you,' he said cleverly, awaiting an expression of bewilderment that wasn't long in coming.

'Eh?'

He replaced his cup, then jerked his chair suddenly forwards and shot towards me, stopping with his face inches from mine. I stared at the broken capillaries that covered his nose.

'No one can shit in one room then go and piss in another,' he said. He leaned back smiling. I stared at him incredulously. 'Think about it, son. It's physically impossible.'

They charged me, and in the afternoon social services arrived and took me back to Menlove Avenue. City police called for me next morning and charged me with burgling my Dad's. The following weekend Menlove Avenue, thinking that fear at my predicament might have settled me down, amazingly gave me Home Leave.

On Saturday afternoon I met Sammy Jones staring into a pie shop window in Rice Lane.

'Hiya, Gazzer. Got a place to stay yet?'

'Not really,' I said, 'on'y Rob's, an' I don't want to go there.'

'I'm the same,' he said. 'I got chucked out o' me 'ouse. Stay in me Dad's tonight if yer want.'

Sunday morning saw us back on the street, breakfastless.

'Can yer think of anywhere we could get some money, Gazzer?'

'Well,' I said, 'yeh. I've got an idea.'

We took the train out to Formby, and walked through quiet streets till we were near St Vincent's. My target was The Neck's house, a semi-detached in a street of garden gnomes behind neat privet hedges. When there was no answer to my knock I nodded across the road to Sammy and crept around to attack a back window. The one I tried moved, but would not give. Fear and excitement turned to anger and I tore at it until the entire frame came away, making a tremendous racket. Once inside, I picked up the remains of The Neck family's Sunday meal and hurled it nervously at the kitchen walls. No time for that. Kicking over anything I couldn't steal I raced through the rooms cramming odds and ends into my pockets. My clothes were bulging when I stepped on to the path, carrying a bagful of radios, clocks and ornaments.

The front door of the adjoining house opened immediately, and two women came out.

'What've you been doing in there? Hey? Don't start walking away ...'

As I came out of the gate a guy who was passing grabbed hold of me. He was inoffensive-looking and probably wished he could ignore the squawks of the two women who had followed me, at a safe distance, down the path. I thumped him, tried to kick him in the balls, missed, and butted him ineffectually. He held on more tightly still, each new blow making him more determined not to let me go. In the end we were in the middle of the road, he clinging to my left leg while I kicked him with my right, screaming.

'Lemme go. Lemme *go*, yer soft twat!'

The first car that came along stopped. As its occupants took hold of me I saw Sammy Jones walk swiftly around a corner out of sight.

Formby police added this charge to my list and took me back to Menlove Avenue. From there I was taken to Juvenile Court where the compulsory care order was extended, and social services were asked to find a secure establishment to contain me. Mr Clarke, a case worker, drove me to The Meadows, a senior approved school near Blackpool. It was a massive place, a farm with cows, bulls, horses and sheep. The boys lived on four wings called Houses – Windsor, Stuart, Tudor and Plantagenet. Clarke left me with the Tudor housemaster, and when our interview was over he showed me into an enormous dining hall.

I sat down. Predatory young eyes stared into mine, measuring me up.

'Give us yer pudd'n', lad.'

'Eh? No.'

Then, from two nearby tables simultaneously:

'Giz yer pudd'n', lar.'

'Mate, d'yer want yer pudd'n'?'

'Fuck off. I'm eatin' it meself, right?'

It was always like this. When you saw a new kid arriving, raw and out of place, you thought, Here's a chance.

After tea we had to play for an hour. There was one snooker table for a hundred and twenty lads, two T.T. tables with only one battered ball between them, and a T.V. that showed the action through a blizzard of interference. We spent most of our time messing about fighting, or sitting bored at the tables, talking and smoking. Everyone could smoke and buy tobacco in the Canteen though the minimum age was only fourteen. On Tuesdays and Thursdays we went to the baths, on Wednesdays to a Youth Club in Blackpool. We never had money to buy Coke or play pool so just sat there, watching the kids who were free.

When I'd been at The Meadows school for a month the teacher picked out six kids to do C.S.E.s. On Friday afternoon he read out the names of the chosen, and mine was amongst them. My hand shot into the air like a Nazi's.

'Sir, sir!'

'Gaskin?'

'I can't do 'em, sir.'

'You're doing them,' he said, 'and you'd better pass.'

In the end I passed three, a Grade One in Maths, a Two in Commercial Arithmetic and a Three in English. We spent more time at work than at school, though. They put me on Painters, splashing around in empty staff houses or on the wings.

'Gazz, 'ere a minute.'

My mate Titch, a Southport skinhead who was older than me but much smaller, would shout from the top of a ladder. I'd look up.

'What, lar?'

'Take a look at this crack up 'ere, will yer?'

Sometimes I'd fall for it. WHOOOSH! A bucket of half water, half paint flung over me. Drenched, laughing, fearful of what the master would say, I'd pick up a tin and swing it.

'Right, yer little get. Yer've 'ad it this time.'

There were thirty lads in each House, and you had to spend the night on the wing with them. Sometimes there were records. Every member of staff at The Meadows was an out-and-out bastard and so, therefore, was every boy. Most of my nights were spent in the bath. I'd lie in the hot water for hours, boredly playing with myself or reading. As I grew up I began to affect the eccentricities of adolescence, wearing ten chains around my neck and growing my hair down to my shoulders. My fifteenth birthday came, went by, and was forgotten. My hair crept slowly down my back. The other lads kept their distance, and did not bother me.

Three or four times I escaped, but each time I got to the Rice Lane area of Walton I was quickly recaptured. Once I got as far as my sister's place in London. She was angry as soon as she saw me.

'Graham! What are you doin' '*ere*? You're not stayin'.'

She dialled social services.

'What're yer doin', Bren? I'm yer brother. Yer know the kind o' place they've got me in, don't yer? Or 'ave yer forgotten already?'

She was not to be stopped. While we argued time was passing, and in the end I fled. As I was going down the steps of the house I met a copper coming up.

'Where are you rushing off to, son?'

He clasped my arms with irresistible strength.

Summer arrived. It was the night before our annual holiday, a camp on the Yorkshire moors. Everyone was looking forward to getting away from the grim regime at The Meadows, especially me since I had decided to abscond again, and this time to do it properly. As the vast hall hummed with voices the door flew open and the master in charge came in. He rapped one of the tables with his cane, and silence fell. The rest of the staff filed in and stood behind him, folding their arms. All eyes turned to the master. We could tell it was something serious.

He walked up and down between the rows of tables, his heels clacking menacingly on the concrete floor. 'Someone . . .' clack, clack, 'has stolen . . .' clack, clack, 'the shotgun . . .' he stopped to let the seriousness of this statement seep in, surveyed our faces, and clacked on, 'from the farm.' When he was back where he had started from he turned to face us squarely, his eyes trying to winkle out the culprit from our midst. 'Now even clots like you lot . . .' he paused to let us reflect upon our stupidity, 'must see how serious this is. Unless someone owns up tonight and the gun is found,' he looked sharply at the most troublesome faces, mine included, '. . . there'll be *no* holiday this year. Now we'll leave you to sort it out amongst yourselves.'

They filed out of the hall and closed the door.

We talked it over, but no one owned up. After a time lads began to guess where it might have been hidden.

'What about in the loft over the big barn?' suggested one.

'Nah,' another replied, 'they're bound to 'ave looked there.'

'I reckon it'll be in the sewer behind the school,' I said, 'under that long gratin'.'

It was the place where I would have hidden it myself.

'Whoever pinched it better own up or we're *all* stuck 'ere,' one of the soft kids, Richardson, said in a whining little voice. For once everyone agreed with him. The discussion went on, going over the same ground. Five minutes later the door burst open and the master in charge stood angrily on the threshold.

'Gaskin.'

'Sir?'

'Get to my office.'

I followed him in, and the shotgun was lying across his desk.

'Thanks for telling us where it was, Gaskin. Didn't think we'd be listening, did you?'

'Sir, I don't know nothin' about it, sir.'

'No? Funny it turning up where you said, isn't it? In the sewer behind the school.'

'I on'y said the sewer because it's a good place, sir.'

He laughed at this. As he did so a timid knock sounded at the door and he broke off angrily, paced over and threw it open. A coloured kid called Cranie and his mate, Stevie Smith, stood outside.

'Well?' barked the master.

They exchanged nervous glances.

'Er, well . . .' Smithy paused. 'You tell 'im, Cranie.'

'Er, the gun, sir,' Cranie said. 'We don't want Gazzer to get punished, sir. It was us that took it.'

Next morning as I was climbing into the charabanc chance put the same two boys in front of me. Out of the corner of my eye I could see the master of the previous evening watching us. As they disappeared into the bus he came over and gripped my arm.

'Don't think I'm stupid, Gaskin. I know you had something to do with that business last night.'

Our tents were scattered, orange, blue and red, in a valley between the little towns of Otley and Ilkley, high on the moors. They were pitched on both sides of a river and looked, from above, like a handful of confetti strewn across a silver string. We had a good time. The weather was hot and the sun soon turned us a dark, healthy brown. The incident on our last night at The Meadows threw me into the company of Cranie and Smithy, but though they were the best of mates I didn't really get on with either of them.

'Lads,' I said on our final evening, 'I'm doin' a runner from 'ere. There's no way I'm goin' back to The Meadows.'

They looked meaningfully at one another.

'What, tonight? Did yer already 'ave this planned?'

'Yeh, weeks ago.'

Cranie smiled.

'Us too,' he said.

We took our sleeping bags with us, and slept the first night in dodgem cars in the little gipsy fair at Otley. Early next morning we set off along the riverbank in the general direction of Leeds.

'Move in the shadow o' the trees,' I said. 'They'll be out in their cars lookin' for us.'

After a time we saw a house, and when we came up to it the key was in the front door.

'You stay 'ere, Smithy, an' keep a look-out.'

We went in and had a look around, but all we found were a melon and two bars of chocolate.

'Well, we won't starve anyway, eh lads?'

Laughter. Later we had a cockshrinker, a cold water swim in the freezing river. A mile or two further on we came to another fair. The men were taking the rides down and packing them up ready to go. Like seasoned carpetbaggers with our doss-bags slung over our shoulders, we approached the boss.

'Need any 'elp, mate?'

He beamed at us. 'Yes, lads. Thanks.'

We spent an hour picking litter up and putting it into sacks.

'Great, boys, great,' he said when we'd finished. 'Thanks a lot.'

He beamed at us still. We waited. He climbed into his lorry and drove away, waving. We resumed our tramp along the riverbank no richer, but without rancour. It was a warm, sunny, bird-twittering day and we were free. An hour later we came to a smart house set in a huge rockery of exotic plants, an artificial valley. It was a wonderful place with something about it that stirred my imagination, making me think of story-book castles long ago. Still, we had a living to make.

'I'll go down an' ask for a drink o' water,' I said, 'an' if no one comes we do it, right?'

'Right,' they said together.

Nobody responded to my knock and they followed me down. We spotted a weak window at the back, and I was through it in no time. On my way to let Cranie and Smithy through the front door I scooped the telephone box into my pocket. Later, as Smithy was rifling some kitchen drawers while Cranie banged about above our heads, I noticed a purse lying next to the sink. When I opened it my eyes caught the blue flash of fivers inside. At that moment Smithy looked over.

'Nope,' I said, tossing it down, 'nowt in it.'

As soon as he looked away I picked it up and shoved it under my armpit. Now I had what I needed to make good my escape.

'I'm gettin' out,' I said. 'It's not cool 'ere.'

Outside I took five crisp fivers from the purse, stuck them into my boot, and slung it into the bushes. The lads were a long time. When they emerged Cranie had a pair of binoculars hanging around his neck and his pockets had bananas and packets of cigars sticking out of them. We walked on to some railway lines nearby.

'Well, no money, lads,' Cranie said despondently. I pulled the telephone box out of my pocket and rattled it loudly.

' 'Ey, that's good, Gazzer,' he said in surprise. 'I never seen yer get that, did you, Smithy?'

We shared out the money, taking eighty pence each, and walked on until we reached a common where people were running their dogs. Cranie walked in full view of them trying out his binoculars, and some looked at him strangely. The time had come for us to part company.

'I'm gettin' off, lads. Yer not movin' fast enough for me.'

After walking around a bend in the road, I started to run. I cut across fields and headed for what looked like a bigger road, but ended up on an even smaller country lane. Soon I had the feeling of running in circles, and knew I was lost. Eventually, to my immense relief, I saw a bus stop. There were bushes behind it and I sat in them waiting. Half an hour later an old man came at a snail's pace along the road towards me.

'Er, what time's the bus, mate?'

He cackled amiably. 'Ee, lad, there's no buzz frum 'ere today. 'Appen there'll be one along in t'mornin'.'

After that I ran some more, keeping carefully to the grass verge and diving into the ditch whenever I heard a car. Soon I found myself back on the original road with Cranie and Smithy in front of me, strolling openly beside the white line in the middle. Keeping in the bushes at the side I caught them up.

'Psssst! Cranie, Smithy!'

We talked for a minute.

'Lissen, Gazz, 'ow about givin' us some more o' that telephone money? Don't tell us yer never stuck nothin' down.'

' 'Ere.' I handed them another fifty pence, secure in the

knowledge of the £25 in my boot. They probably thought I was
stupid.

'Ta ra, lads. Good luck.'

I went ahead of them, running till I was out of sight. The
road went round a bend and over the river, but before the
bridge there was a bus stop.

'What time's the bus, mate?'

A cuff shot up, revealing a work-scarred Timex and half a
tattoo. 'About fifteen minutes, son.'

I melted discreetly into the bushes. Ten minutes later Cranie
and Smithy trudged past and over the bridge. They were still in
sight when a bus with LEEDS on its front swept in and I hopped
aboard.

In Leeds I went to a café and had a slap-up meal, then took a
taxi to the station.

' 'Alf single to Liverpool, please.'

' 'Ow old are *you* supposed to be?'

'I'm fourteen, mate. Big for me age, like. Honest.'

At Lime Street station I sat in the cafeteria for some time,
debating what I should do. It would be good to see my friends,
but capture seemed certain in Rice Lane. In the end, with my
skinhead friend Titch's description of the place still fresh in my
mind, I took a train to Southport and spent the afternoon on
the fair.

'MOOON Rocket, fifteen pence, MOOON Rocket!'

'CANDYFLOSS, CANDYFLOSS, get yer lovely CANDYFLOSS!'

When the sun was going down I booked into a hotel, which
cost £3.50, then went for a couple of pints. Pubs had been part
of my social world since I was twelve and now, at fifteen, getting
served in them was easy. I sat in a corner with some old women
from Liverpool and had a good laugh, getting rather drunk.

The next night I was destitute again, and had to sleep under
the pier. A dark form next to me moaned as I settled myself into
my Meadows sleeping bag, then snored for the rest of the night.
It was a cold night for summer, and sleep evaded me.

'Come on, I can get us a cup o' coffee.'

My fellow dosser, a lad my age, took me to a flat not far from
the seafront. The door was opened by a guy of about fifty,
wearing dirty overalls, whose hands and arms were black with
oil.

'John, Phil,' he shouted, 'these look like mates o' yours.'

The two lads who came into the room, obviously straight from their beds, were brothers. They made coffee and after a while the kid who had brought me went away.

'Got no place to stay?' John, the elder, asked.

'No. Er, I'm on the run, like.'

'Approvey?'

'Yeh.'

They nodded comprehendingly. 'Yer can stay 'ere, but yer might 'ave to kip with Jeremy.' They leered briefly.

'Jeremy? Is that the ole guy in the boiler suit?'

'No, but 'e lives 'ere too. 'E's okay, 'e fixes cars an' gets a few bob that way. Jeremy's the guy whose flat this is. 'E works in a caffy down the road. Bent as arse'oles, 'e is.'

Jeremy came home in the afternoon. He was a thin middle-aged man with oiled grey hair. John and Phil Rawles took me out with them later, and when I came back after the pubs that night without them Jeremy was still there, watching T.V. After a while he jerked his head at one of the doors.

'Er, I've got a bed in there if yer've nowhere to stay, like.'

As with Malcolm I just lay there and let him do what he wanted, short of penetration. It's not hard to see why homosexuals call their lads rent boys. John, Phil and I paid for living in the flat by taking turns sleeping with Jeremy. Next night when I came home, John was in the flat-footed old waiter's bed, so I slept in front of the lecky fire. Both Rawleses also had girlfriends.

In a day or two I met a lad called Alfie Grant, a professional thief at nineteen years old, and began burgling hotels with him.

Now, too, I started to gamble, spending a lot of time in betting shops with the garage man, being instructed in the art of the $57\frac{1}{2}$ pence treble. On one occasion he gave me a betting slip and sent me to the bookies' to find out the result and collect any money he might have won. My chest tightened as I read the results chalked up on the board behind the counter. His first horse had come in at 11 to 1, and his second at 20 to 1. I glanced in the paper, feverishly. The money from those two was going on to a horse at 33 to 1. I calculated quickly. It stood to win over £600. The race came over the tinny loudspeaker and I listened with a hammering heart, the betting slip dampening in my palm. My soul groaned when it was a photo finish for first place. His donkey came in second, and won only £20.

'' 'Ere y'are,' I said, 'twenty quid.' He was lying under a car as usual, and I tossed the money on to the floor beside him. 'Yer nearly made six 'undred.'

He laughed, probably at my expecting him to believe I would have brought it, and looked up at me brightly.

'Pass me that torque wrench, will yer?'

Phil Rawles was caught shoplifting and put away, so John and I took over his turn with Jeremy. When I wanted to be alone I went to the big bus station in the town and slept on one of the buses. Dawn always woke me. I'd pause on top of the fence as I climbed out, listen for footsteps, then drop to the pavement and walk through the morning, looking in cars.

We used to go to a club at night to have a few pints, and play 3-card brag till the small hours. It was usually light when we came out, and next afternoon would find us continuing the game at the War Memorial on the seafront. My companions were mostly men, but I met the odd girl as well. One night as I was sitting in the club a girl took the place next to me at the bar, plonking her bag down as though staking a claim. She was in her mid-twenties, dark, and glitteringly attractive.

'' 'Ello, gorgeous,' she said. 'What'll yer 'ave?'

'Er, a pint o' lager,' I said, staring in confusion up the split in her skirt as she settled herself on to the stool. She called the barman.

'Two pints o' lager an' two brandies please, love.'

She knew what she wanted, and took me to her flat to get it. Kissing her and playing with her were lovely, and she was wet before I touched her. I wondered what I was supposed to do next, but was far too frightened to ask. In the end she grew tired of waiting and made me come, then turned her arse towards me. I dressed without turning the light on and crept out, wishing I hadn't met her.

Next day I was strolling along when my elbows were grabbed, suddenly, in the distinctive police way.

'Got yer, Gaskin,' barked a gruff voice.

Numb with the shock of this calamity, I turned. Titch, my skinhead mate from The Meadows, stood grinning at me.

'Ha hey! Cracked yer up that time, eh Gazz?'

Business was booming by then and Titch, in Southport on Home Leave, introduced me to other young criminals, which helped even more. Rigged out in shoplifted clothes I moved up

market and stole from high class shops, going again and again
for hand-cut crystal goblets priced at £40 each, and jade figur-
ines which cost £70. At night I stole from cars, opening them in
a matter of seconds when I saw something of value. Much of
my time was spent wheeling and dealing, getting rid of the loot
among the town's many felons.

'Let's try a 'otel,' Alfie Grant said one night.

We walked along looking into foyers till we saw one that was
empty, and crept inside. A single key hung behind the porter's
desk. Alfie reached over and took it and we tiptoed upstairs.
When there was nothing in the room we made our way
cautiously back to the street.

' 'Ere y'are, Gazz.' Alfie handed me the key. 'Keep 'old of it.
Yer can use it again, an' yer might strike lucky next time.'

One night I sold some statuettes to Terence, the bouncer in
the Glendeane Hotel. He was small for a bouncer, but very wiry
and tough, and something of a dignitary in the town's under-
world. More, he was a nice guy whom I found it easy to like.
When our deal was concluded he took me to the Dixieland for
a drink.

'Try one o' these, kid.'

His particular tipple, Pernod and Coke, was firewater to a
kid of fifteen, and I was soon very drunk. To my surprise we
ended up in his bed together, having sex. It wasn't the kind I
endured with Malcolm or Jeremy, but a shared thing which
gave both of us pleasure.

Afterwards I was embarrassed whenever I met him. What if
everyone found out? When we were playing cards by the Mon-
ument people would shout over to me from the nearby pub.

'Terence 'as got a drink on the bar for yer 'ere, Gazzer.'

Did they know? Doubts about my sexuality plagued me.
Every time I slept with a girl it was a disastrous failure. Did this
mean I was queer? Should I have been a girl? I put such fears
aside when con-merchants and rip-off men tried to take advan-
tage, and threatened them with Terence. It never failed. He
was famous for throwing men bodily through the doors of the
Glendeane. My life carried on this way until one morning in
October of that year, 1975.

SMASSHHHH! The garage man held the teapot poised in the
air, arrested in mid-pour by a long splinter that flew off the
door and landed on the kitchen table. On their second attempt

they did more than burst the door in. It was torn off its hinges and landed flat on the floor.

'Honeymoon's over, Gaskin,' the sergeant said, stepping across it to snap me into handcuffs, 'now move it.'

They dragged me downstairs and into a waiting car.

' 'Ow did yer know I was 'ere?'

They grinned. 'Your mate, John Rawles,' said one. 'Honour among thieves,' said the sergeant, laughing. At the police station they searched me and found the key Alfie Grant had given me.

'Where did you get this?'

'It's the key to the flat,' I said hopefully.

'Hmm. Funny it having Avondale Hotel stamped over it, eh?'

They charged me with theft of a key, which was all they had on me, and the court remanded me to Menlove Avenue again. On my first night I bent a gap in the bars wide enough to squeeze through, and vanished. After a few days living off doorstep milk in Rice Lane they nicked me again. This time Menlove Avenue and The Meadows both refused to take me so they sent me to the Suicide Factory, the adult remand prison at Risley.

There was uproar in Southport Magistrates' Court at my trial, with social services recommending that I be sent to a detention centre and my lawyer arguing openly with them across the court.

'For the theft of a key?' He was fuming. 'He isn't the *only* one here who has acted criminally.'

The magistrates withdrew to consider my case and were gone a long time, which usually augurs well. As they settled themselves back into their seats I was reasonably confident.

'We've considered your case carefully, Gaskin, very carefully indeed. In our opinion a short, sharp shock might make you buck your ideas up. We're sending you to a detention centre for three months ...'

5 | *D.C. to Dosshouse*

The place was a long way off, outside Swindon, and the two cops who drove me there were surprisingly kind, giving me as many fags as I could smoke.

'They'll be your last for a while, son.'

'Why? Can't yer smoke in there?'

'In D.C.?' They pulled incredulous faces, shook sage heads. 'You're in for a hard time all round, kid.' The driver guffawed. 'If they say "shit" you ask 'em for a shovel, right?'

By the time we reached the place I was really scared, and the sight of it did nothing to allay my fears. A concrete wall, enclosed by a high fence topped with rolls of barbed wire, went around to unclimbable gates. There was a sign fixed to them.

H.M. DETENTION CENTRE
(Junior)
NORTHFIELDS

All that was missing was *Arbeit Macht Frei* painted on to the lintel. The screws didn't seem at all out of place. They had an off-hand manner of speaking that was deeply insulting.

'What's yer name?'

'Gaskin.'

He gave me the look usually reserved for mouse dirt in the butter. 'Gaskin what?'

'Er, Graham Gaskin.'

'Gaskin WHAT?'

'Gaskin, sir.'

'Strip off.'

I did so. Their cold eyes looked at me.

'Turn around.'

I felt their eyes on my back. There was the sound of a rubber glove being shaken, then pulled on to a hand.

'Bend down and spread yer buttocks.'

Something slipped into my anus and probed about, searching for goodness knows what.

'In the bath, Gaskin.'

After sitting me in four inches of tepid water they put me on a chair, cut my hair almost to the scalp, and kicked the fallen locks over to me like so much litter.

'Clean that up.'

They put me into a shapeless uniform with a green tie and marched me to the Warden's office. He gave me my E.D.R., my earliest day of release which was in exactly six weeks five days' time, then one of them marched me to the dining hall.

'Lef'rightlef'right. Chest out, Gaskin, head back ...'

It was supper time. All the kids of the D.C. were sitting there, silent, their arms folded. Where you sat depended upon how long you had done and I was put at the very beginning of the big room, where other recent admissions sat at tables of four. All the kids at my end wore green ties. Those at the far end were on longer tables and had red ties, which meant they had passed their Grade. Once a kid gained his red tie his life became infinitesimally easier. Some of these kids looked over derisively when the screw brought me in, and one or two hissed:

'Lifer!'

'Lifer!'

Though I faced less than seven weeks inside I *felt* like a lifer.

'Up for yer supper, Gaskin,' the screw said. A kitchen lad handed me a rock cake and a quarter-full mug of tea, like dirty dishwater. The cake was a little boulder, and when I got back to the table I shoved it away. In a flash another kid picked it up and stuffed it into his jacket. Strange. In all my previous institutions these cakes were thrown away more often than eaten.

'Fold yer arms, Gaskin,' the screw said as soon as I had finished.

Ten silent minutes passed.

'Right,' the P.O. shouted, 'get them up to bed.'

'Two tables at a time,' shouted one of the screws. He pointed at mine. 'Stand.'

They formed us into lines and marched us out. The Gradeless kids went into the reception cells on the ground floor. It was so highly organized that the first boy in the line went into the first cell, the second into the second, and so on. The cell doors had windows of reinforced glass, making even the minimal privacy of prison impossible. In spite of this I made love with myself that evening, and every evening thereafter. All prisoners and mental patients masturbate a good deal, though it offers no real consolation for the loneliness of institution life. It is the only reassurance there is, so you are driven to trying it daily.

Six a.m.

DRRIIINNNG!BANG!BANG!BANG!DRRIIINNNG!

'Hands off yer COCKS, on to your SOCKS.'

You had to fold your kit into meticulous, pointless squares, as they do in military prisons. The pyjamas had to be squared to eight inches wide and folded with ludicrous precision along the edges of the stripes. If a millimetre of white showed the screw swept all your kit to the floor as he passed, and you had to start again. All this was done at top speed, to the accompaniment of ceaseless yelling.

'MOVE it, lad. D'yer want me STICK up yer ARSE?'

It was easier for me than for other receptions. My past life led naturally to this imprisonment, and since it was what I'd been trained for I soon settled into it. We were marched to the dining hall for breakfast. The meal was minimal, and for the first time in my life I wolfed the sugarless porridge.

'Right, line up for the Gym.'

In the echoing building with its highly polished floor they

introduced me to the Green Circuit, a round of exercises which had to be gone through three times at top speed. There were step-ups on to benches, press-ups, weights pushed from the chest, pull-ups on to a high beam and many more, and each exercise had to be done ten times on every circuit. The P.T. Instructor timed you with a stopwatch, and as you grew fitter you were moved to a harder circuit. In the Red you did each exercise fifteen times, in the Black it was twenty. My debauched life in Southport had put me out of condition, and I was sick to the point of collapse when it was over.

'Christ, lad, you look like a bloody young pouf lyin' there,' the P.T.I. said, happily. Some of the lads laughed, but stopped when I looked over. When I had recovered a bit the P.T.I. said, 'Go round again, Gaskin, once. Take your time but do each exercise perfectly.'

He followed me around, shouting encouragement.

'RIGHT down, get RIGHT down, touch the floor.'

The effort it took was enormous, but all he said was, 'Not bad. You'll do better next time.'

After Gym it was work, the Peg Shop, for the most monotonous and repetitive tasks. Everything depended upon seniority and you were started off on the worst job, putting the roughly cut tentpegs in a vice and sanding them down. You had to do two hundred every morning, a fearful amount. Lads who had been there over three weeks cut the wood at an angle to make the pegs, and the boy nearest release had the cushiest job of all, sitting at a machine punching holes in them. Most of the kids were from the west country, and seemed less aggressive than city boys. You took your finished bundles of twenty pegs to another lad, a Shop Orderly. After two days I found a way to make my life easier.

'Put down three bundles, lar.' I looked the Orderly in the eye and pushed one into his chest, hard. He glanced at the screw, then flinched as I lifted my hand to scratch my nose.

'Er, all right, Scouse.'

After that it was no trouble meeting the quota and I was able to buy shampoo, Mars bars and Spangles when they pushed the Canteen trolley round the dining hall on Thursdays.

After work it was lunch. The food was good by institutional standards but the meals were meagre, and you worked up such an appetite from the P.T. that you were permanently ravenous.

'Jesus,' I said the first day, 'do they give yer a magnifyin' glass?'

'Put your 'and over it,' the lad next to me advised, 'if they opens the door it'll blow into summun's oy'.'

After the meal they handed me a blank letter-sheet, a pen and a printed card.

''Ere's yer letter, Gaskin. Copy it out an' put in the name of yer relative, yer E.D.R. an' the rest. Gottit? Bring it to me when yer've finished.'

The printed card said something like this:

> Dear   ,
> Well, I'm here at the above address till
>   , if I learn to behave myself
> and don't lose any remission. I hope
> everything is all right at home. The
> staff are all right here and they are
> teaching me to face up to things. I
> have a job of work, too. Give my love
> to   and   .
>   Love,

After lunch, it was school. The teacher loved the sound of his own voice and spent the time telling boring stories about his days in the army. Nobody ever learned anything, and you got the impression the D.C. wouldn't have bothered if it hadn't been compulsory by law, since we were under sixteen. After school it was tea, and after that scanty meal, night classes. My subjects were English, German, Motor Mechanics and Wildlife. For two hours we had to sit there bored stiff, trying to shut our ears to what the teacher was saying. Everyone had to attend the Social Studies class, which for me was on Fridays.

''Ello, Miss Pym. You all right?'

'Fine, thank you, Jones. Hello, Gaskin.'

'Hiya, miss.'

All the kids in the class had come in during the same week, so we developed together. We had a good laugh sometimes talking about the place, and about how we felt about whatever had brought us in there.

'D'you think you'll be any different when you get out, Bates?' she'd ask.

'Oi'll be a lot tougher, miss.' A lopsided grin. 'There'll be a few 'eads crackin' in Gloucesturr.'

You could see people's opinions changing week by week, and your own changing with them. After night classes we were marched in for our supper, and then it was bed.

Some mornings an outside screw came into the Peg Shop.

'Right, four lads to carry wood. You, you, you an' you.'

Everyone wanted to escape the tedium of the shop, and sometimes there would even be a dog-end passed around outside, found where the screw had dropped it. The first time he came he took me, and I was glad when he picked me again the second time. As we were going out the P.O. came over.

'Not Gaskin, sir. 'E's Category A.'

'Right, sir.' The screw selected another boy, and went out. As I returned to my bench I asked, 'What's Category A, sir?'

'Get back to yer pegs, Gaskin.'

Category A prisoners are those who have to be kept under careful scrutiny in case they try to escape.

From the first week I had a date-card on which to cross off the days. Like everything else this was against the rules, so it had to be hidden. Erasing the days was pure joy. The yelling screws and unremitting discipline made life so hard that time became unendurably stretched, until it seemed as though a week had passed between one crossing-off and the next. Often I tried to save the days up, sticking it out until I could cross two or three off at a stroke. In a curious way it was as if I hadn't done the time till my pencil obliterated the days. When I finally struck out the little numbers the feeling was one of tremendous relief, like emptying your bladder after a long bus ride.

'Gaskin,' one of the P.T.I.s said in my second week, 'I've decided to put you in the First Team.'

'Ah, 'ey sir. Yeh, sir. Great, sir.'

The fun of the football was one thing, but it also meant being able to get out of the D.C. for the away game every second week. That Sunday we played at home, and won. Next day they called me up for my Grade Review.

'Well, Gaskin,' the Warden said, 'you've done well in all the activities here ...'

Foolishly, I smirked.

'Wipe that grin off your face. You've done well in all the activities here *except one*. Your schoolwork. The teachers report that you've made no effort whatever. What d'you say to that?'

'Well, sir, I . . .'

'D'you think we're stupid? You're a big, strong lad. P.T. and the work are easy for you. You're lazy, Gaskin, aren't you? Bone bloody idle.'

'Er, sir, I . . .'

He brought the rubber stamp down hard on my file.

'Grade refused.'

'About TURN,' yelled the screw, 'quick MARCH, lef'rightlef' . . .'

All the other kids in the First Team had their Grade. The question was, Would they throw me off it? Later, in the Gym, the P.T.I. pulled me roughly to one side.

'Keep yer nose clean, Gaskin, an' do some work at school for the next few days.'

On Saturday, the day before the game, the Warden called me over.

'The teachers tell me you've been trying harder, Gaskin, so I think it's only fair that I send you with the First Team, on trust. Don't let me down, or it'll be the worse for you.'

We played a team called Blunsdon and won by six goals to nil. Playing at centre forward for that match only, I scored three of them. After that my place on the First Team was assured.

Northfields was a time of terrible loneliness for me, which I spent locked up in a protective shell. As usual, I pushed to get what I wanted, knowing it would never otherwise be mine. At the same time I made friends, Mick Doherty from Southampton, and Dave and Steve from Bristol. They had all come in the same week as me, and were on the First Team too.

By the time we were halfway through, it was easy. One evening, as a lonely reception was brought into the dining hall for the first time, a lad kicked me under the table. When I looked over he grinned, and glanced around to make sure no screw was watching.

'Lifer!' he hissed. 'Lifer!'

My remaining time stretched before me like infinity. The trouble with the 'short, sharp shock' as far as I was concerned was that it never *seemed* short. A minute of pain or an hour of ecstasy, which is longer? My mates, having got their Grades, were put into a dormitory at the far end of the corridor from my cell. Radio One was piped into it.

'Christ, yer'll be dancin' in there,' I said. They looked away, half abashed. Even tiny concessions like that mattered.

To me, the First Team games were what fresh air would be to a trapped miner. It was like being free for five hours. We went on Sunday afternoons when everyone else had to attend Chapel. When we came back they were sitting in their cells waiting to go in, or were already in there singing reedy hymns. There was always food left over from tea, which the regime would not share out amongst the boys but threw away instead, and we could have as much as we could eat.

'Mick, Mick, it's oranges! Grab us a few, will yer?'

We shovelled it grimly into ourselves, in silence, till we could hold no more.

We were sitting in the minibus after one match, waiting for the P.T.I., when Mick leaned conspiratorially over.

''Ere, Gazz. Look what one of the opposition gave me.' He opened his hand to show me some cigarettes and loose matches. 'D'yer want one?'

'Yeh,' I said. 'Ta, Mick. I could murder a good smoke.'

After the meal I walked along the corridor to my cell, the single cigarette and match held anxiously in my fist, keeping an eye out for screws. When I was inside I opened the window as wide as the bars allowed and stood looking across at the Chapel, which formed part of the compound. Its roof and even its metallic cross were festooned with barbed wire, and two screws were standing boredly outside. The sound of tuneless singing came from within.

'... the Lord's my shepherd, I shall not want ...'

When the match flared the unaccustomed smell of sulphur was suffocating. I lit the fag and took deep, intoxicating drags at it, at the same time picking up my pillow and flapping it in the air to dispel the fumes. The end of the fag was soon hot and pointed like the end of a thermic lance, but I found that the smoke gave me no pleasure. Rebelliousness alone made me smoke it. It would have cost me an extra three days of the hellish life there had I been caught.

The P.T.I. who took us for football was great, and managed to be just like one of the boys on Sunday afternoons. He had played for some Fourth Division side when he was younger and regarded football almost as a martial art, as we shall see later. The other P.T.I. was called Perspex, a little fellow with a tremendously fit little body. His name derived from the long, ruler-like strip of the material he always carried.

'Right, Gaskin, I saw that.'

'What, sir?'

'You know what. It's perspex for you, lad. Bend over.'

WHACK!

Like The Neck's punishment at St Vincent's, it was symbolic rather than painful.

Prrrrrpp! The echoing shriek of the P.T.I.'s whistle, signalling the end of Circuits.

'Right, we've 'alf an hour to spare, lads. 'Ow about a game of Numbers?'

Expressions of glee from the rougher boys. Placing a medicine ball in the centre of the Gym floor, the P.T.I. would split the thirty lads into two equal groups, give everyone in each group a number between one and fifteen, and set us on the floor at the sides of the Gym to wait.

'Number . . .' he kept up the suspense, eyes flicking from boy to boy, '. . . SEVEN!'

The two boys with that number scuttled across the floor and strove to bring the ball back to their side, grappling till one was victorious. Often the screw called two or more numbers.

'FOUR, FOURTEEN, NINE!'

Six of us would scramble at top speed across the floor, everyone would jump on everyone else, and there would be a full-scale battle. Thump, smack, bang, bump! The ball lay forgotten while we hammered it out.

'Get that bloody BALL back,' ranted the P.T.I.

He never said anything about our being rough, though. Getting the ball to your side was all that mattered. There is something here which I still recall with pride. On every single occasion that my number was called in this game, it was I who came back with the ball. I never failed, not once, even when there were eight of us out there.

Prrrrrpp! The whistle.

'Circuits over, lads. What game shall we 'ave today, then?'

'British Bulldog, sir!'

'Yes, sir, British Bulldog!'

'British Bulldog!'

One lad, alone in the middle of the Gym, would be 'on' while the rest stood against the wallbars on either side.

Prrrrrrpp!

Everyone would dash to the wallbars on the opposite side while the lad in the middle tried to bring them down. Each kid brought to the floor was then 'on' as well, and tried to bring someone else down during the next frantic dash. In the end nearly everyone would be in the middle waiting to pounce, and the few who were not yet 'on' would have to run the gauntlet between them. This was the most enjoyable part, swerving and smashing my way through the rest. British Bulldog could get very rough, and kids often scudded across the floor with one hand clamped over a thumped eye, or with blood gushing from their nose.

By the time of my Grade refusal I was on the Black Circuit, two weeks ahead of time. Like everyone else, though, I cheated, doing twelve repetitions instead of twenty when I thought the P.T.I. wasn't looking. Perspex never caught me but the football P.T.I. did, once. I had made a huge miscalculation, and finished as everyone was starting to go round for the third time. No one could be that fast.

'Sussed you, Gaskin. Got you, lad. You did twelve reps every time you thought I wasn't looking.'

'No, sir. Honest, sir. I done twenty, sir.'

'You didn't, lad. I've been keeping my eye especially on you today. Now you've fucked everyone else up for games. They can watch you goin' round another three times instead.'

It was a form of physical torture. Gasping, the sweat dropping off me in torrents, I went through the exercises again with the P.T.I. screaming behind me.

'MOVE, Gaskin, MOVE, Gaskin. MOVE, MOVE, MOVE!'

At the end my underfed muscles were shrieking at me and oceans were heaving, lungs panting in my head. Kids sometimes vomited after this. While I lay on the floor, shivering, the P.T.I. tried to anger me to my feet.

'Up! Get UP, Gaskin! Lyin' there like a bloody virgin, what're you waitin' for? Me bloody COCK?'

When this happened to a smaller lad the others would be after him for spoiling their game, but this never bothered me. The few other heavy guys in Northfields were all my friends.

All the sport in D.C. was aggressively competitive, and football was no exception. The First Team had to play the Second

Team every Saturday afternoon, and any receptions who showed promise were put into the lower team for the match. If one was outstandingly good he immediately replaced his opposite number on the First Team. We went all out to protect our privileged positions and we did it as what we were, a team. In the changing room before the match we would plan our tactics.

'Right, lads,' Steve would whisper, slyly indicating a redhaired kid who had come in earlier that week, 'that ginger lad's s'posed to be tasty. Make sure he goes under, right?'

As far as the P.T.I. was concerned that was all right, it was the nature of the game to him. We fought like wolves during these internecine matches. The boy we regarded as a threat would have us around him whenever play allowed, shoulders ramming and boots going in. When the P.T.I. turned his back, which he did deliberately sometimes, grinning, the fists would fly. He liked this kind of natural selection. It ensured that only the strongest players entered, and stayed in, his First Team. Football was a bad man's game to him, and he rarely sent anyone off for fouling when the two D.C. teams were at war. The sight of a boy lying prone with two or three others kicking him was not uncommon.

When I had been in Northfields for about four weeks a skilful inside right came into the place, and I began to fear for my own position. He was bigger than me and a good footballer, better with his head than I was but not so fast on his feet. I spread word through the First Team before the match. Nobble him.

By the second half his prowess had me seriously worried. It was easy to imagine myself sitting in the Chapel the following Sunday while the new lad joined my friends in the dining hall for the gluttonous feast. Then my chance came. He was in the box at our end, and there was a corner coming. Falling back from my attacking position to defend this shot with the rest, I edged up close to him. I was certain that he would go for the ball with his head, and stood near him waiting for it to come over. As soon as it fell through the air I lunged towards him, and jumped at the very same moment. His cheeks were pink, his bright eyes fixed on the ball as I threw my head hard into his face. I made no effort to reach the ball myself, but crashed my skull into his cheek with every gramme of my strength. Next second he was lying at my feet. Blood poured from his nose and drenched the front of his Second Team shirt.

'Gaskin!' thundered the P.T.I. 'Come *here*!'

He knew what I had done, and knew I knew it. Quaking inside, I made my way over.

'Sir, fuckin' 'ell, sir, I never seen 'im, sir. 'E just come from nowhere, sir. I on'y went for the ball, sir, honest.'

He shook his head. 'Don't give me that bullshit, Gaskin. Go on, get back to your position.' He went over to the lad, who was lying on the bitter-cold field holding his face, and nudged him with his boot.

'Get up,' he said. The lad didn't move. 'Look at you. Big silly woman. Get up off your arse.' The lad sat up painfully. 'Hold your head back,' the P.T.I. said. He grinned. 'We'll play pat-a-ball in future, shall we?'

My life wasn't all like that, though. While I was in Northfields I wrote my first poem. It's called 'My Dad'.

> My dad needs glasses does'nt he
> he can not see what thier doing to me
> my dad's great he gives me sweets
> and takes me out on special treats
> he won't let them get away
> with hitting me every day
> and I know when he finds out
> he'll' be mad thier is no doubt
> my dad does'ent need glasses does he
> and he knows what thier doing to me
> he could'ent care less he's turned away
> he has'ent time for me today
> and the treats they were it seems
> nothing but my childish dreams

Now, in my cell at night, an exercise book across my knees and a pen in my hand, I had something to occupy my mind. It was hard to put my feelings on to paper, but deeply satisfying when I succeeded.

One weekend towards my release Frank Clarke, from Liverpool social services, came to see me.

'Hello, Graham. Want a cigarette?'

'Yer jokin'. Don't yer know we can't smoke in 'ere?'

'Oh yes, sorry. I forgot.'

Tapping the table nervously with my fingernails, I looked at him. 'So where do yer put me when I get out of 'ere?'

He put his fingertips together and leaned forward sincerely. 'There's nowhere we can send you, Graham.'

'What? Did yer forget about me? I s'pose yer thought it was a life sentence, did yer? That I'd never be comin' out.'

The screw supervising visits looked over, so I lowered my voice. It was time to lay it on the line for social services.

'Lissen,' I said, holding back my anger. 'There's no way I'm goin' to The Meadows, Menlove Avenue or anywhere like that. Not after this place. When I get out of 'ere I want *out*, man. Get me a flat or whatever, but no more institutions.'

'Look, calm down, Graham. Just calm down and we'll talk about it.' He nodded wisely. 'The problem with doing what you say is that you're only fifteen. You're a minor. You can't have a place of your own till you're sixteen.'

'Come *on*, now,' I exploded, making the screw look over again. I moderated my tone and went on with laboured reasonableness, 'Yer bein' ridiculous, Frank. I'm sixteen on 2nd December, three weeks after I get out. Three weeks!'

'That's true,' he said, 'but officially, you see, we can't . . .'

'Officially?' I glared at him. 'Officially? Don't gimme that "officially" crap, Frank. Could yer send me to a loony bin, *officially*, when there was nowt wrong with me? Could yer? Was it all right officially when yer put me in St Vinnie's for two years, for nothin'?'

'Okay, Graham,' he said finally, 'I'll see what I can do.'

Eventually I progressed in the Peg Shop from sanding the rough pegs to the cushiest job of all, sitting on a high stool working the punch that made the holes in the ends. There was no quota to fulfil and I could sit there taking my time, Bang, thump, Bang, thump, Bang, thump, watching the raw Lifers who still had six hellish weeks to do. I was my own man, and a kind of aristocrat. On my next to last night in Northfields, with a feeling of tremendous exhilaration, I crossed off the four days I had managed to save up on my date card. Too excited even to concentrate on my latest poem, I lay on my bunk with my hands behind my head, staring at the ceiling in ecstasy. Yes, tomorrow was my last day.

It was a changed day, not conforming to the rigid routine

which had been the rest of my life there, and when morning came life was easier. You had to see the Warden and the Chaplain and get all this chat, being told how well or badly you had done there. You were on licence for six months after your release, so most kids were given the address of the probation officer they'd have to visit. This didn't apply to me, as I was under social services supervision anyway. After our last tea we were given our release times.

'Hey, mine's eight o'clock,' said one lucky kid.

'Mine's not till half-past ten,' a more disconsolate voice responded.

The screw on release duty took every boy to a different bus so that lads could not meet on their way out to continue their criminal friendships. If a lot of kids were going out on your day it could take hours. The fact that you might have to wait two hours extra was unbearable, a blight on your euphoria at getting out. All of us were gate-happy by now. My release was timed for nine fifteen, halfway through, so it could have been worse.

After receiving our times we went on the last Social Studies class. All of us were elated and given to sudden bursts of laughter, and whatever differences had existed between us were now forgotten. We talked of how much we hated the screws for keeping our young spirits in tight discipline for six weeks, four days.

'Oooh,' said some, 'I'm not 'alf going' to slag that screw when he takes me to the bus in the mornin'. He's got a mouthful comin', I'll tell you.'

A lot of kids said they were going to do this, but I suspect that few actually did. Some definitely did, though. There were kids in Northfields doing what we called a 'second whack', and I had seen some of them being persecuted by a particular screw for giving him stick on their first release.

Morning. It was still pitch dark when I awoke, and as I became conscious the realization of impending freedom dawned on me. My stomach churned in fear and dread took the place of last night's euphoria. The night watchman plapped down the corridor in his old slippers and unlocked my door.

'Release today, Gaskin.'

Did he think he had to remind me? I lay unmoving in the darkness, butterflies running amok in my stomach. Later, when I sat with the others in Reception waiting for my turn to come, it wasn't too bad. At least I knew it was over. We talked, nervously, after each departure.

The screw snapped the metal gate shut behind us and we stepped into the free and freezing lane. The hedges were white with frost and I saw, immediately, a robin. Its little eye glared like a lit bead and it shrilled a stab of clear music, then flew away. I filled my lungs with clean, crisp, unimprisoned air.

'Back to Liverpool is it, Gaskin?' the screw asked.

'Yeh, mate, that's right.'

No more 'sir' for him. We walked to the bus stop and stood in silence till it swished to a halt before us. As I climbed aboard he waved.

'Good luck, Gaskin.'

'Seeyer then, mate.'

Though I hated that bastard, giving him uncalled-for stick would have been pointless. He would only have despised me for not doing it earlier, and I would have guaranteed unnecessary torment for myself if I had ever been sent back there. I was free, and that was enough for me.

'You managed to change trains and everything, Graham?' Frank Clarke asked when he met me at Lime Street. He received my most ironic look. Had he forgotten about me escaping from Blatchwick when I was only ten?

'I've found a place for you,' he went on, 'we'll settle you in there now, and tomorrow I'll be round with some money for clothes.'

'Yeh? 'Ow much?'

He consulted a folder. 'Sixty pounds, Graham.'

That sounded all right.

'What sort o' place 'ave yer got me? A room o' me own?'

'Well,' he said evasively, 'it's a sort of boarding house. You'll see in a minute, it's not far.'

The ride in his car was a trip down Memory Lane for me. The house he took me to was a common lodging house in Smithdown Lane, a few minutes' walk from Parkfield. We passed the Tesco's where I slept in boxes when I was a little boy.

'You'll like Mrs Munro,' he said as we mounted the steps, 'Rosie. She's got a heart of gold.'

We went along a dark, neglected hall. The parlour door was open, and through it I saw a lot of old men watching T.V.

through dense tobacco smoke. He knocked on a door at the back.

'How d'yer do, luv?' She quietened the dog which was barking behind her and asked us in. 'Like a cup o' tea?'

Rosie Munro was a fat, slatternly woman with breasts like medicine balls. As we shook hands I was repelled by the dirt ingrained in her wrinkles, the specks of dandruff in her hair. I have always been spotlessly clean myself. The house was one short step up from the Salvation Army, and full of old plonkies. Rosie was an alcoholic too. As soon as Clarke left she pulled a bottle of British sherry out of a cupboard.

'We'll 'ave a drop o' somethin' stronger, eh luv?' she cackled, filling chipped, greasy teacups to the brim.

Rosie had a fat son, Trevor, who was twenty-eight, and a lover called Harry, a grey, sorrowful man of about fifty who clacked his dentures thoughtfully between sips at his wine. He lived there too, between drunken rows with Rosie. Their room and kitchen were out of bounds to the rest of the residents, but not to me. Five minutes after Frank Clarke had left there were two bottles of wine and one of cider on the stained rug in front of the lecky fire.

'Show Graham 'is room, Trevor love,' Rosie said. His fat buttocks laboured up the dark stairs ahead of me and into a casbah of grimy passages. We passed bedrooms like animal hutches, all of them packed with drunken old dossers, cackling and coughing. There were eight beds in my room and on one of them a wretched-looking individual of about forty was sitting with his head in his hands, smoking. He looked up when we entered.

'Seeyer later then, Graham.' Trevor gave me a boozy grin. 'Come down if yer fancy a drop o' nectar.'

'Hiya,' said I to the wretched guy, ' 'ow goes it?'

'Oh, er, hiya. Are yer comin' to live 'ere?'

'Looks like it.'

He smiled sympathetically. 'Bit young, aren't yer?'

'Sixteen,' I lied.

'Christ.' He made another roll-up with shaking hands. 'I was the youngest till yer come.'

'Yeh?' They must all be really old then.

He laughed nervously. 'I'm twenty-seven,' he said. My look of surprise amused him. 'Thought I was older, eh?'

'Well, yeh. A bit.'

'It's the junk,' he said, offering me his hand. 'I'm Ned.'

We shook. We had been chatting for a few minutes when there came a thin moan from a far corner of the room. Surprised because I had thought we were alone, I looked over. In a bed by the window, under damp, hanging tatters of wallpaper, an old and yellowish face emerged from under a filthy sheet, groaning.

'Oooooh, aaa-aagh, ooo-oooh.'

As I watched this suffering head appear, a flung boot battered with tremendous force into the headboard at its side, and the moaning ceased momentarily.

'Shurrup, yer ole twat!' Ned snarled brutally. 'Don't start that bloody racket up again for Jesus' sake.'

'Ooooh,' groaned the old man, his naked, cadaverous form coming out slowly from under the bedclothes, 'leave me alone, will yer?' A leg, withered and skeletal, probed for a place on the floor, the white foot with its blue veins eventually coming to rest on a jam butty which looked as though it had been there some time. 'I'm in pain, yer know. Oooh, me piles, me fuckin' piles. Ooooh, 'ave some pity at least. Oooo-aagh.'

The sight of his sick old body was repulsive, and I looked away.

'Jeez, I wish yer'd 'urry up an' DIE,' Ned said cruelly, 'why don't yer, eh? 'Elp yerself an' do us a bloody favour at the same time.'

The old man made no reply, but stood shakily at his bedside and weakly pulled at his sheet with one hand. I could now see that the other was missing, and where it had been there was an unsightly stump, puckered and purplish. A line of blood ran down the inside of one of his rickety legs to below the knee. The sheet, when at last he succeeded in plucking it free, was covered in bloodstains.

Everyone hated this old fellow, and I'm ashamed to say that after two or three days at Rosie Munro's I was treating him like shit with the rest of them.

'Shurrup, yer ole basterd.'

Probably we should have felt sorry for him, but he should have been in a hospital, not at a place like Rosie's.

Frank Clarke arrived next morning as promised, but instead of handing me sixty quid in crisp fivers as I'd expected he brought a book of vouchers which could only be spent in the Army &

Navy Stores, and had to be signed in the shop by himself. I trailed disconsolately behind him while he bought me an enormous R.A.F. greatcoat, some pairs of baggy jeans and a couple of cheap pullovers, just the sort of clothes a selfconscious teenager likes to have.

'Cheer up, Graham. Beggars can't be choosers, you know.'

I chose a pair of climbing boots because the uppers looked like Doc Marten's, and the money was gone. Back to Rosie Munro's.

'Fancy a walk down town, Graham?'

'Okay, Ned. 'Ang on while I get me coat.'

He used to do what junkies call 'scrips', prescriptions, every day at Boots. They were hit-scrips too, for heavy stuff like morphine and heroin. When he had cashed his scrip Ned headed straight for the lavatory in Binns, the department store next door, and he came out high as a cloud. Though I knew he had a needle and everything, I didn't really understand what it was all about.

'Rosie, can yer give us me pocket money?'

'What, luv?'

'Me pocket money. I need it.'

'Oh, er, yeh. All right. It'll 'ave to be later on, though, when Trevor gets back from the pub.'

She was only interested in grabbing what she could to buy booze with, and a relentless struggle had to be waged in order to extract my pocket money from her. Soon I gave it up and began stealing from the stores in town instead, even buttering her up with a couple of quid when it made life easier. Most of my leisure time was spent in the bookies or with Trevor Munro. Bit by bit I moved into their scene, till I was spending more time in her private room than upstairs with the derelicts. Rosie, Harry and Trevor used to talk to me while they tanked up on V.P., giving me the benefit of their wisdom and setting the world to rights. To be sociable, I'd sometimes drink half a cup of the powerful syrupy wine with them.

'Come out for a drink, Rosie, 'Arry?'

'Oh no, luv. No thanks.' They would shake their heads, topping their cups up with sherry to reassure themselves. 'Ask our Trevor, 'e might.'

They never went out of the room if they could help it,

preferring to stay by the lecky fire and get out of their heads on plonk. Trevor usually went with me though.

' "The power lies within the wine-dark bowl to harness sorrow and to soothe thy soul," ' he would say, settling his fat arse on to a stool at the bar. 'Get us a Barley Wine will yer, Graham?'

Above all else, Trevor was an Omar Khayyám bore. That was all right in a way, because since writing the poems in Northfields I was interested in verse. Flushed with enthusiasm and cheap wine, his fat face glowing, he would read me great chunks of the ancient poet's work. Omar seemed to wax most lyrical when describing the virtues of wine, probably because Trevor was a wino and picked these parts out. Trevor was more than an Omar Khayyám expert, though. He had done everything.

'Yer should've seen me wife, Graham. Shouldn't he, Mam? Yer know Brigitte Bardot? An ole boot. Honest. Britt Ekland? The same. In comparison, like. Oh, she was luvley, Graham. Luvley. Blonde 'air, she 'ad, blue eyes, tall ... '

Tragedy had struck when she left him, probably because he was a total no-hoper who could do nothing but sit on his arse, drink, and bore everyone rigid. Trevor's beautiful wife wasn't the extent of his experience, though. He had spent two years in the Merchant Navy.

'Yes, yes, I remember it well, that first trip. I must've been on'y, oh, er, about your age, Graham. Aye, the first time we sailed through the Red Sea, standin' up in the bows bollock-o except for me sandals, brown as arse'oles, the deck bucklin' under me with the 'eat. Oh, an' the women, Graham, the women. Why, for a couple o' bob yer could ... '

He thought that because he had been two years at sea his body had done all the work it would be able to do, and that was his excuse for diving headfirst into a bottle. Harry and Rosie, too, enjoyed revelling in the myth of Trevor's superiority, and crowed of his coming greatness with masturbatory zeal.

'Oh, mark my words, Graham, our Trevor's goin' to *be* somethin' one o' these days. 'E's goin' to stand out, that lad.'

This said, they'd shake their heads solemnly in awe at his distinguished future. Proof of his mastery as a bore lies in the fact that he had talked them into believing in him.

'Yer should go out an' *do* something', Graham,' this man of destiny would often say. '*Do* somethin'. Take the world in yer 'ands an' mould it to yer own shape, like. Why, when I was yer age I'd ... '

Sometimes I'd object.

'Shit, Trev, I've done quite a bit meself.'

'What?' he'd laugh. 'You? Yer on'y a bloody whelp, Graham. A pup.'

For the most part I avoided strife and humoured him.

Social services had paid Rosie extra for my Christmas, but I couldn't get a penny out of her. As a matter of fact she still hadn't given me the money for my birthday on 2nd December. With arrears of pocket money it amounted to a tidy sum, so I decided to put my foot down.

The crunch came. On 19th December 1975 Trevor and I returned from the pub to find Harry and Rosie even more legless than usual.

'Oh, 'Arry, 'Arry.' She crawled over the floor and collapsed on to him, hugging his knees and dropping maudlin tears on to his fag-ashed trousers. ' 'Arry, 'ow could I ever 'ave 'urt yer?'

'Oh Rosie,' click, clack, 'Rosie me love.'

Moved beyond words, Harry clacked endearments in Morse with his dentures and buried his head between her pumpkins.

'Look, Rosie, are yer goin' to give me me fuckin' money, or what?' I interrupted.

She waved her arm dismissively, knocking over a bottle of Emva Cream. 'Ah, go 'way will yer? Bloody young pup.'

'Rosie,' I laboured the word, 'I'm not bleedin' jokin'. It's my money an' I want it, right? NOW 'AND IT BLOODY WELL OVER.'

Harry staggered to his feet and stood swaying before me, a dazzling knight errant.

' 'Ow dare yer speak to a lady in that churlish tone?' he demanded.

It was always like that. The biggest frustration in dealing with them was climbing the wall of fantasy behind which they lived. My temper flared.

'Look, I want me money. Me MONEY, the bread yer owe me. D'yer understand THAT? Yer should do, yer spend enough on this stuff.'

So saying, I lashed out with my boot and toppled one of their bottles. That did it. All hell immediately broke loose. Apparently I had done the unendurable. Harry snatched up a carving knife from the kitchen cabinet and lunged at me, and it was necessary for me to pick up a chair and bring it down on his puddled head. He crumpled and lay still. Rosie ran over and smacked my face with jaw-breaking ferocity, and even their slinking Alsatian nipped my arse. The only one who took no part in the attack was Trevor, whose first thought was for the bottle. When he had righted it he approached me gingerly, hands placatingly outstretched.

'Come, let's be civilized, we can discuss this. We can mull over the pros and cons. There's no need to act like barbarians.'

He had, after all, his Destiny to consider.

Shoving Rosie against the cooker I stepped over the slumped form of Harry, fetched my stuff from my room, and walked out. That night I stayed in the flat of a guy down the road, a dustman I had met in the pub, and next morning I phoned Frank Clarke.

'Frank? Graham Gaskin 'ere. Look, I've 'ad this bit o' trouble at Rosie Munro's. I've 'ad to get out ... '

He heard me out without a word, and there was a long silence. Sleet lashed the road in driven sheets as one or two people scuttled past, hunched into the cold.

'The best we can do, Graham, is to return you to Menlove Avenue.'

The moment of realization. Now that I was sixteen social services were no longer interested.

'Ah, 'ey Frank. There must be somewhere yer can send me. It's not my fault I've got nowhere. Rosie's a wino an' ... '

'There's nothing I can do for you, Graham.'

He was ready to hang up.

'Frank,' I pleaded, 'I'm on the street, it's the middle o' winter, Christmas, an' I've nowhere to go.'

There was a short silence. 'What about Malcolm Bishop?' he said. He obviously had no suspicion of Malcolm's inclinations. 'Do you think he would take you in?'

6 | *Mostly Malcolm*

It was an idea.

'Er, well, I s'pose 'e might,' I said.

'Have you got some change, Graham? I'll give you his number and you can ring up and ask.'

Malcolm was in, and answered the phone after only two rings.

'Malcolm? This is Graham 'ere. Yeh, Gaskin. Look, what's the chances o' me comin' down for Christmas? Clarke told me to ring, like.'

'Yes,' he said immediately, 'I'll be glad to see you.'

'Right, I'll be down as soon as I can, Malcolm. Today. In a few hours ...'

When I phoned Frank Clarke back he came to pick me up, gave me a fiver for which I had to sign, and took me to Lime Street station.

At Gloucester it was dark and bitterly cold. For once I was glad of my airman's overcoat. After ten minutes a gold-coloured car swept into the car park and stopped. It was low to the ground and at first I thought it was a Rolls. When the headlights flashed I recognized Malcolm behind the wheel, and walked over.

'Hiya, Malcolm. New car, eh?'

He shrugged modestly as I climbed in. 'Volvo 262DL,' he said, 'I had to have it imported specially, Graham. You can't get them over here.' He pressed a button on my door. 'Look.' The window slid down silently.

'Lecky windows, eh? Posh!'

He took me home then for something to eat.

'You haven't lost your appetite, Graham, I'll say that. Shall we go for a drink to celebrate your arrival?'

He took me to a pub some miles away, and brought me back drunk. In the morning I was woken by his hands moving in my underpants. Later he pulled them off entirely, and played and sucked in his usual way.

'The European Judo Championship's on at Crystal Palace tomorrow,' he announced at breakfast. 'Fancy seeing it, Graham?'

'*Do* I? Wow, yeh Malcolm. Great.' The idea of a trip to London in comfort, as opposed to hitching through the rain only to be brought back by the police like last time, was very appealing.

'We can go down today if you like, and stay in a hotel.'

'Can we? Really? Great!' I shot through the house getting everything we needed, and in ten minutes the Volvo was starting up on the driveway outside.

Malcolm was an international judo referee and very much into the sport. From what I saw this was because he met young boys through it, and could indulge in a lot of shower-room romps. We booked into a big hotel near Crystal Palace, then went to get a leaflet about the championship.

Afterwards he said, 'I've a surprise for you.'

We got back in the car and Malcolm threw it around corners, through roundabouts and along broad dual carriageways, whizzing from light to light with a smug, knowledgeable air.

'What, Malcolm?' I looked out of the window and marvelled at the size of the city. 'What kind o' surprise?'

'You'll just have to wait and see, won't you?' He gave way to a bus, drumming the wheel with his nails and whistling through his teeth. 'Be patient.'

We drove for a while then stopped outside a house, one of millions. He rang the doorbell. It was freezing, and I stamped my feet to keep the circulation going till she opened the door.

'Brenda!'

She stood on the step, smiling, obviously expecting us. I picked her up and spun her round in the air, laughing.

We talked for a few minutes, and it occurred to me that some of Brenda's friends were a bit Bohemian, and one or two might smoke dope. When I recalled my heady days on the stuff at Sammy Jones's I wanted to try for some, but was afraid to ask with Malcolm sitting there. He studiously ignored the hints I made to try and get him to leave the room. Poor Malcolm, he was probably scared I'd tell her about the sex.

Drring, drring. Drring, drring.

The phone was in the hall outside, and when she went to answer it I raced after her.

'Bren, Bren,' I whispered urgently, 'where can I get some dope?'

She put her hand over the mouthpiece. 'Get lost, our Graham. What d'you want that rubbish for?' She was smiling, though. 'You're too young.'

'Ah, go on, Brenda. I've 'ad it loads o' times, honest, with Barney Muscle an' all that lot.'

'No.' Her tone was final. 'I don't know where you can get it. Now pee off an' let me take me call.'

Malcolm had his camera with him, and took a photo of us sitting on Brenda's bed, surrounded by her cats. Later he drove us to the house of one of her friends, Stan Ryan, whom I had met years before while I was at St Vincent's. I pleaded with Stan secretly, as I had with Brenda, and eventually he took me for a walk and gave me a blow on a joint. Brenda didn't suspect, which was just as well. She would have gone through the roof if she'd known. Afterwards Malcolm took me back to the hotel.

''Ey, this is posh, Malcolm. Is that telly a colour one?'

It was. *Filmnight* was on, and included a preview of *Monty Python and the Holy Grail*. I sat in an armchair to watch it. Malcolm sat on the floor between my knees, stroking my thighs and trying to unzip me.

''Ang about, will yer Malcolm? I'm tryin' to watch this.'

Next morning we went over to Crystal Palace and Malcolm took me straight into the Members' Bar where the contestants and celebrities hang out. Two tall blond-haired men in polo neck sweaters and slacks were standing at the bar, and turned when they saw him coming.

'Erik, Lars, meet Graham, a *very* good friend of mine.'

They shook hands politely, and watched me with knowing eyes. Apparently they were Danes, in Britain to give their team some support. Malcolm had met them often at judo contests around Europe. After a couple of minutes we were talking to sports reporters from the big newspapers, names I had been reading for years. Some finalists were at the bar, too, smiling nervously as they sipped their orange juice. I introduced myself to some of the French team.

Afterwards we watched the contests. Malcolm, as an international referee and a contributor to *Judo*, the sport's magazine, was allowed to watch from the Press seats close to the mat, where the photographers take their pictures. The spectators' part was so packed that I watched from the top, right above their heads, which I still think is by far the best place. Neil Adams fought with masterly skill, and won the trophy for Britain in his middleweight class. I walked around to meet Malcolm with the excitement of the contest still upon me.

'Great, that, wasn't it, Malcolm? Jee-sus, that Adams was powerful, wasn't 'e? They both were.'

'You enjoyed it?' Malcolm lifted the sports bag he was carrying a fraction higher. 'Come and have a shower with them if you like.'

I was amazed. 'What, with the contestants? 'Ere? Can we?'

The finalists were under the hot water when we went in, and we congratulated them on their success. The Frenchmen I'd talked to earlier came in and one of them, a fellow as tall as me, offered to lend me a spare suit and take me out on to the mat. Malcolm's naked romp with his two Danish friends was getting a bit embarrassing by then, so I went. The French champions showed me a few useful throws, then some of the Dutch team came out and showed me some more.

When we had said goodbye to them all Malcolm and I went to our hotel to collect our things. That night we stayed with Ron Ashcroft, a friend of Malcolm's whom I had met at the Boys' Aid Camp. He was a teacher and lived with another guy. We watched T.V. As the evening went on it became obvious, from the way they sat together, that they were lovers.

'I'm thinking of holding a Boys' Aid Camp reunion, Graham,' Malcolm said next morning. 'What do you think?'

'Yer mean like a dinner?'

'No.' He shook his head. 'More than that. I could invite them down to my place for the New Year.'

The idea gained momentum in his mind and he began phoning the volunteers from Ashcroft's flat, then we drove to visit some of them.

'How many boys will you take?' asked one.

'Oh, five or six. As many as I can squeeze in the car.'

As it grew dark we drove around the poor, shabby areas the kids came from, looking for their houses. When we found them Malcolm launched into his doorstep patter.

'Good evening, Mr Taylor. Well, ah, I'm from the Boys' Aid Camp, and we were wondering if Stephen would like to come to a B.A.C. reunion we're having after Christmas? He'd have a good time, and of course all expenses would be taken care of . . . '

He had singled out these kids, all of whom were between eleven and fifteen and good-looking, and listed them mentally as potential sex material for the future. He had no intention of luring them into his bed just then, but was merely casting a net like the one at Blatchwick which had eventually landed him me. The parents, all of whom were desperately poor, were glad to be able to give their kid a treat, and every one of them agreed to hand their boy over the following week.

'Very good.' Malcolm rubbed his hands before starting the car. 'We'll give the lads a nice time, eh Graham?'

He drove us back to Gloucestershire and we spent the next few days at his house. Malcolm waited till Christmas morning before opening his cards.

'Hah! I thought he'd forgotten this year.'

'What's that, Malcolm?'

'A card from my uncle. He's a director of a plastics firm and every year, every single Christmas without fail, he sends me a card and a £10 note.' He tossed them carelessly on to the table. 'Otherwise I never hear from him.'

Later in the morning he handed me a rubber plant wrapped in festive paper. 'I got you this, Graham. To give to my mother.'

We were going to her place for Christmas Day. Malcolm's father was dead. His mother, a plump, jolly woman who had probably been pretty when she was younger, had recently married a retired Cambridge don and they had bought a three-storey villa along the road from Wescombe school. It was near the house of Nicola, the first girl I ever had a crush on. When we had been there half an hour I took a walk, and peeked in at the Wescombe playground. Nothing had changed. It made me sad to see the old place and I turned away, remembering the cries of the luckless Elephant as my boots thudded into him on his first day at the school. It seemed to have happened a long time ago, yet was still very fresh in my mind.

Malcolm's sister had come down for the holiday and was staying at the house too. She was fattish and hearty, a younger version of the mother, and a member of the Scientology movement. As far as I could make out she was even more loaded than Malcolm, really minted. Her father had credited her with having more business sense than Malcolm, so she had got most of the money when he died. Not that Malcolm was exactly poor.

'We're going to Dutch Wineberg's house,' Malcolm said later. 'Want to come?'

'Er, yeh. Okay.'

Walking between Malcolm and his sister, I muttered, 'Who is this bloke, Malcolm? This Tush Swinebeck, or whatever 'is name is?'

They stopped in their tracks to stare at me.

'What? You've never heard of him? Never heard of Dutch Wineberg?'

'Er, no. Should I 'ave?'

They told me proudly that he was an American painter who lived in the nearby village of Rannage, and that he was poised on the threshold of world recognition.

'He's trying to organize a trip to the Holy Land so he can do some paintings of Jerusalem,' said Malcolm. 'I gave a cocktail party at the house to raise money for it a while back, and that's how we met him.'

'Yeah? 'Ow much was the tickets?'

Malcolm's sister laughed patronizingly. 'Oh, a little beyond your means, Graham.'

When we got to his house he turned out to be a nice enough bloke, but who he was didn't matter a toss to me. I've never heard of him since, so perhaps his impending greatness was of the same kind as Trevor Munro's. If he had been Kevin Keegan I might have asked for his autograph.

We stayed until two o'clock talking to Dutch and Veronica, his pretty wife, and some other people who were there, then went back to Malcolm's mother's for Christmas dinner. When it was over I settled down in front of the telly to watch the film. It was a Western, and looked good. Just as I was getting into it Malcolm's mother came into the room.

'Well, after a meal like that I think we could all do with a walk in the hills. Is everyone game?'

'Quite right, dear.' Her husband stood up, went into the hall, and came back laden with umbrellas and coats. 'A spot of air'll buck us up no end.'

The last thing in the world I wanted was a walk in the fucking hills, staring at the wonders of nature up there in the freezing cold, but this is the kind of thing they do. I've never been able to make out whether they do it because they like it, or because it's what you should do when you've got money. Malcolm and his sister stood up and so, reluctantly, did I. They wanted to walk in the freezing cold so that's what we would do.

'Hah!' Malcolm's stepfather exhaled noisily and took hold of my arm. 'What a view, eh Graham? Beats your grimy old city any way you look at it.'

Looking at the rolling hills gave me a feeling akin to seasickness. Once you've seen one blade of grass you've seen the lot as far as I'm concerned.

'Er, yeh,' I said.

His wife, who had been striding in our wake, accelerated.

'Well, you've a good coat for up here, Graham,' she boomed, loud as a foghorn. 'You shan't freeze in that, shall you?'

'No,' I said glumly, 'I s'pose that's one thing.'

When we were back at her house we had tea, then Malcolm and I headed home. On the way we stopped at a pub, and he got me drunk as usual.

It was the morning of 29th December.

'Goodbye then, Graham. I should be back about four.'

'Okay, Malcolm. Seeyer. 'Ave a good trip.'

While he went off to pick up the boys for the B.A.C. reunion, I stayed in the house on my own. It was a lovely house and sumptuously furnished, with a colour T.V., a stereo with enormous speakers, and dozens of L.P.s. Malcolm always made sure I had everything I could possibly want, including unlimited alcohol. He brought bottles of Pernod especially for me, because

since my fling with Terence, the Southport bouncer, Pernod
and Coke was my tipple. As well as this he bought me packs of
two hundred Benson & Hedges, and made sure there were
always boxes of Coke in one of the fridges and plenty of good
food, T-bone steaks and the like. When I was bored I would
wander about the house, through the many empty rooms, idly
picking things up and looking at them, then putting them back
down. There were gold and silver trinkets, coins and valuable
objets d'art everywhere. When examining these grew tedious
I'd take a chocolate cake from the fridge, mix myself a drink,
turn on the telly, and sink sighing into one of the deep leather
armchairs.

In the afternoon he came back with five chattering boys in
tow, and at six o'clock the doorbell started doing overtime as
the other guests arrived.

'Ah, hel*lo*, Ron. Rupert, meet Ron Ashcroft ... '

There were about thirty of them including the boys, and
they had come to stay for the week. A few of the blokes were
queer but most weren't, and there were some girls too, which
helped.

'Graham,' Malcolm said, 'can you move your stuff into my
room? Then Janet can sleep in yours.'

Janet was ugly and grossly fat. The Matron at a community
home, she carried a faint institutional whiff about her which
repelled me. She was in love with Malcolm and wanted him to
marry her. Undignified in her desire for him, she begged him to
screw her every time she had had a few drinks. Malcolm was
scared stiff. I doubt if he had ever had sex with a woman, and
if he had decided to try it's unlikely he would have chosen Janet
for a partner.

Next door to Malcolm's room, and joined to it by a commun-
icating door, there was a big nursery. Some of the Cockney kids
were sleeping there, so our early-morning sex had to be very
muted. To be sure no one could interrupt us, Malcolm had fixed
latches inside both bedroom doors. One morning he woke me
at six o'clock, wanting it, and was lying there sucking me and
masturbating when there came a rattle on the landing door. We
froze and lay stock still, listening.

Rattle, rattle. 'Malcolm.' An urgent whisper. Rattle, rattle.
'Malcolm, it's me, Janet.' There was a short pause. 'Can I get
in with you?'

The pleading went on, punctuated by aggressive rattles, till he was forced to answer.

'Janet,' he said weakly, 'I don't want to.'

'Open the door,' she said, 'and we'll just talk about it.'

'Please go away, Jan. It's ten past six. I don't want to talk.'

His reply was a series of vigorous rattles.

'Janet. Please, love. You'll wake the boys in the nursery.'

There was a loud exhalation of breath from outside, and a moment later we heard her padding away down the corridor.

The Boys' Aid Camp kids, some of whom were only a year younger than I, were not allowed to drink. That didn't stop me. Malcolm always encouraged me, and on New Year's Eve he took me to the pub with the adults. We went in a convoy of cars and vans, and there was much shouting and honking of horns as we drove there. A lot of us were dead drunk by the end of the evening, and when we came home I spewed up repeatedly. On 6th January the guests went home, and Malcolm took the boys back to their parents. When he came back we settled down to our domestic bliss. A few days passed quietly.

'We'd better get an early night tonight,' Malcolm said one evening. 'Dutch is in court in the morning.'

'Yeh? What for?'

'Drunken driving. He's bound to lose his licence, so I thought we'd go along and give him some moral support.'

Next day we sat in the public gallery to watch the case, and sure enough Dutch was banned. He went to pay his fine then came out into the street where we were waiting.

'Come to the pub,' Malcolm said.

'No.' Dutch shook his head. 'Come back to my place. I have to be at the house this afternoon.'

'Why?'

'The papers might ring to get my views on the case.'

At his house we sat in dead silence for a long time, drinking. Eventually the phone rang. Like a man in a leaky boat grabbing a helicopter's dropped line, Dutch snatched the receiver from its cradle.

'Yes? *Who?* Oh, piss *off*. Ring back tomorrow and talk to my wife.' He slammed the phone down and sat glowering.

'Who was that, Dutch?' Malcolm ventured after a minute.

'The butcher in Stroud.' He topped up our glasses, grimly. 'Veronica hasn't paid him for the meat.'

Next day we were taking James and Angus, Dutch's two teenage sons, to watch a judo contest at a private school near Stroud, and on our way to collect them Malcolm bought a copy of the local paper, the *Citizen*. Dutch's bad news was splashed across one column halfway down page 3, under a caption which said, LOCAL ARTIST BANNED.

'Here you are, Dutch.'

Malcolm laid it out brightly on the table in front of him. Dutch, hung over, said nothing but gave Malcolm and the newspaper the same jaundiced look.

When he grew fed up with my incessant hints, Malcolm bought me a presentable pair of shoes. I promptly sold him my enormous hiking boots for a pound more than social services had paid for them. We went to different pubs every night and once or twice to a jazz club in Stroud, but despite the abundance of material things I grew discontented. After another month I decided to go back to Liverpool. Malcolm phoned social services and they put him through to Frank Clarke.

'Hello, Mr Clarke? This is Malcolm Bishop. Yes. Yes, fine. Yes, hmm. Well, he feels, we both feel that a change would be the best thing for him now.'

He listened for a minute more, then handed me the phone.

' 'Ello?'

'Graham, listen. What do you want to come back for? Why don't you stay and find a job?'

'Job? There's no jobs 'ere, Frank. We're in the middle o' the country. No, I want to come back. Today.'

'Today? Why today? What's all the hurry about?'

'There isn't no 'urry. Just the same I'll be on the train this affey.'

'We can't do anything for you tonight,' he said, 'I hope you realize that. If you *will* insist upon dashing about at short notice you'll have to look after yourself tonight.'

This lack of maternal instinct no longer surprised me. 'Okay. I'll stay with me mate tonight an' come down to yer office in the mornin'. 'Ow's that?' From the other end, silence. 'Okay?'

There was a pause. 'I suppose it'll have to be,' Frank Clarke said.

Malcolm went upstairs to fetch his car keys. As soon as he left the sitting room I crept over to his roll-top desk, took out three half-sovereigns which I knew to be there, and slipped them into my sock.

'Ready, Graham? Got everything you're taking?'

'Yeh. Everythin', thanks.'

In Liverpool I took a bus to Smithdown Road and knocked at the door of my dustman friend, the one who had let me stay when I left Rosie Munro's.

'Yeh, I'll put yer up for tonight, kid. But no longer, eh? I don't want no lodger.'

Next morning I sold the three coins in a junk shop for the rip-off price of £17, and went to meet Clarke.

'This is a good chance for you, Graham.' We were driving to the new place. 'Find a job and you'll be able to stand on your own two feet for a change.'

The house was off Prescot Road, and there were seven other young lads living there. They were all working, and paid two-thirds of their wages into the house. Kids were only getting £30 a week in those days, so it left them a tenner a week to spend. Every day I went to the Careers Office to look for a job, every night to the ice rink near the house with some of the lads. Though I did look, no job materialized. If I had found one my first move would have been to leave the house. The whole set-up was a rip-off. Three weeks passed.

It was Saturday afternoon. I'd just come in when the house woman bustled aggressively out of her quarters.

'Look, love, you've got no intention of finding a job, have you?'

'Well, I'm tryin' as 'ard as anyone can. There aren't many . . .'

'Find one by Monday or leave,' she said.

Finding a job is well nigh impossible in Liverpool at any time, but on Saturday night and Sunday where can you even look? On Monday morning Frank Clarke came and I climbed into his car, to go I knew not where.

'Thrown out again, eh Graham? Don't you *want* to settle down?'

'Well, yeh. I do. If they'd give me more time I'd 'ave found somethin'. They're on'y into takin' yer money in that 'ouse, Frank.'

I glanced out of the window, and suddenly realized we were in Norris Green.

'Yer not takin' me to Mrs Smith's, are yer? *She* won't 'ave me.'

'If she won't,' he said, 'who will? Any ideas?'

He left me in his car and went inside to talk to her. How he managed it I don't know, but he did. The last time she had seen me she had had the C.I.D. there, but he convinced her somehow that I was now a changed boy. I'm sorry to say it wasn't true. Crime was my way of life by then.

'Er, 'ello, Mrs Smith.'

''Ello, Graham. Goin' to be'ave yerself this time?'

Living there was all right, I got on okay with the old lady. Kevin was still there but she gave me a room of my own this time, and though we regarded each other with distaste we maintained a polite neutrality in the house. She gave me my £1 pocket money every week, and once a fortnight social services gave her £5 towards my clothes which she generously handed over. I went to the bookies every day and gambled what I had, winning or losing. Since cash was short I cadged a bunch of car keys from a mate in Rice Lane and began to go thieving at night. When I came in I used to sneak through the front door, close it quietly, creep upstairs to my room and hide whatever I had, then tiptoe down and open the door again, banging it shut behind me.

SLAM!

'That you, Graham?'

'Yeh. 'Ow are yer, love?'

Not far from her house there was a rugby club with a lot of cars outside, an ideal place for stealing. It was quiet in the sense of being out of the way, but noisy enough to cover up the sound of my work. One night when I was rifling someone's glove compartment my hand fell upon a little plastic bag. As soon as I touched it I knew it was a wad of notes. My heart was thudding with excitement as I crept into some bushes and breathlessly opened it. It was a packet of Durex. Another time I opened the boot of a car and found a guitar inside in a case. I dragged it out and scuttled off with it in the direction of Mrs Smith's, but on the way it occurred to me that the guitar seemed very light, and I went into a playing-field to open the case. Four plastic swords and a blonde wig fell out. I left the swords where they had fallen and took the wig back to Mrs Smith's. Even that was a mistake.

'Whose are all these blonde 'airs, Graham?' she asked next day, holding one aloft.

'Er, they must be mine.'

'They're too long to be yours, Graham.' She paused artfully. 'Yer 'aven't 'ad a woman in 'ere, I 'ope?'

That night I slung the wig over a backyard wall.

Mrs Smith's young nephew still came to see her, and I went once or twice to stay at his house. His mother was crippled with arthritis, even worse than Mrs Smith's rheumatism. It took her hours to move from one room to another, and was painful to watch. Once, a bible puncher came while I was there. As soon as he saw my new face in the room he flung his arm in the air, like a Zulu raising his spear.

'Hah! Are you SAVED?' He glared at me with neon eyes, waiting for an answer.

'Er, well. Not really, like.'

He sat triumphantly in the chair opposite mine and stayed for two hours, evangelizing. I had to sit there bored stiff, unable to move because their ferocious Alsatian would not allow it. It must have known the bible puncher, because it ignored him completely and concentrated entirely upon me. Once you were in that house you had to sit absolutely still, or it would go for you. Even when you sat as though frozen it circled your feet, whimpering at not being allowed to get you. If you wanted to go to the toilet she had to put it in the hall before you stood up, and when the time came for you to leave you had to make a dash for the door, and slam it shut behind you as the dog flung itself baying at the other side.

'Yer friend's 'ere,' Mrs Smith said one day.

'Friend? What friend's that, love?'

'The posh one,' she said.

Malcolm took me out for the day, and wrote the following week asking me to go on holiday with him. I agreed, and the date was set. It was arranged that he would pick me up from Mr Clarke at social services.

When the morning came I packed a holdall and walked down to the office in Norris Green, not far from the house. Malcolm arrived a few minutes after me, and Clarke came out to see us off. He looked a bit put out when he saw that the back seat of Malcolm's Volvo was stacked to the roof with cases of lager, and fastened his eyes on them.

'Oh. You're going to have a good drink, by the looks of it.'

Malcolm's reply was as smooth as a jar of salmon spread.

'We're going to a party on the way,' he said, 'and you can't go empty-handed, can you?'

One of his uncles owned a hotel in a village near Lincoln, and that was where we went. The place was being modernized and Malcolm's cousin was there on his own looking after the place. We camped in a field half a mile away, next to a wide, fast-flowing river. There were woods there and pheasants strutting about, and for as far as you could see in the distance gentle slopes and wide, free fields. If Malcolm hadn't been there it would have been lovely. We ate at the hotel and had baths there, and went out drinking with the cousin at night. As usual, Malcolm began to get on my nerves after a few days.

'Sorry, fellows,' the cousin said one night, 'you'll have to go on your own this evening. I'm expecting a phone call.'

Two hours alone in the pub with Malcolm made me more irritated still, which in turn made me drink more heavily. Back in the tent, I precipitated the crisis which was to mark a turning point in our relations. I did it by mentioning the sex. Incredibly, it was the first time either of us had ever spoken about it. Propped up against the bag of gear I was using as a pillow, with my arms folded across my chest, I looked along my body to where Malcolm's head was bobbing rhythmically up and down, up and down on my prick. My tone was contemptuous and at the same time curious.

'Do yer like doin' that, Malcolm?'

He withdrew his mouth and my prick hit my belly with a slap. As he shifted around to look at me he wiped away a thin drool of spittle that shone at the side of his mouth.

'Well,' he said, 'do *you* like it?'

'It's okay,' I replied.

He moved to the far end of my sleeping bag, and faced me. 'Well, why don't you ever do anything to me?'

'I don't want to, Malcolm.' I took a cigarette from my packet and searched around for the matches. 'I don't mind yer doin' it, if it turns yer on. It's nice. But I on'y do it because *you* like it. That's the on'y reason it 'appens, yer know that.'

A note of accusation crept into his voice.

'But *you* like it too.'

'Yeh.' I lit the fag and blew smoke into the air. 'Yer can suck my cock any time yer like, man.'

His voice took on a whining tone. 'I want you to do something

to me, though. You admit that you like it, so why won't you?
You're just selfish, Graham. That's what it is. You're utterly
selfish.'

My anger welled up at this. 'Yer've got a cheek, Malcolm,
accusin' *me* o' bein' selfish. Lissen, if that's the way yer want
it just don't ever touch me again, right? If yer think for one
minute that we 'ave sex because *I* want it, yer wrong, pal.
We do it because *you* want it an' *you* like it an' that's the way
it's always been. We wouldn't be 'ere if I didn't let yer, would
we?' He stared fixedly at a far corner of the tent. 'Would we,
Malcolm?'

He touched my shoulder then in a conciliatory way, but I
shook him off.

'Don't touch me, Malcolm.' Stubbing my fag out on top of a
tin, I turned over and went to sleep.

When I awoke next morning Malcolm was running his hands
over my chest and along my flanks. The physical sensations
were nice but I was determined that this time, at any rate, I
would have none of it. I sat up. He began massaging my back
to get me to lie down again.

'What are yer doin', Malcolm? 'Ave yer forgotten last night?
I'm not goin' to.'

Though neither of us knew it then, Malcolm had touched me
for the last time. Our association, though, was far from over.
When next our paths crossed Malcolm would be the used, and
I the user. For the rest of the holiday he left me alone in my
sleeping bag, smiling to myself in the darkness when the sound
of masturbation reached my ears.

Back at Mrs Smith's my life ran on in its settled course of
gambling by day, thieving at night. The day which was to
change everything arrived like any other, taking on significance
only gradually. It started with me looking in the paper and
seeing a horse I fancied strongly. A dead cert, and there was I
without a penny. Sitting in the kitchen with a cup of tea, I
racked my brain for ways of securing the necessary capital.
Footsteps came down the stairs and Kevin popped his head
around the door.

'See you tonight, then.'

'Off to work, Kev? Seeyer.'

As soon as he had gone I took a look in his room. His wallet
was lying on the bedside table, and when I looked in it there

was £27 inside. This made me begin some serious rationalization. It was only a case of borrowing, after all. Not all of it at that, only a couple of quid for the bet. It would be all right, I'd put it back when my horse had won and still have something for myself. When I had finished talking myself into it I picked the wallet up and took it out with me.

It was too early for the race, so I decided to have something to eat to pass the time. I could pay it back out of my winnings. I jumped a bus into town, placed the bet there, and went to a café.

'Sausage, egg an' chips, please mate. Tea, bread an' butter.'

It was still too early for the race when I'd finished, so I did some other bets to pass the time. Every one of them went down. Now I had only £18 left, and was getting more nervous with every minute that passed. It would have been agony to listen to the race so I went for a pint while it was on. When I came back it was over. My horse had won. I counted my money and it came to just over £28.

Putting Kevin's share back in his wallet, I bought a few cream cakes and a can of Coke and caught a bus to Mrs Smith's. After replacing the wallet I settled myself in front of the telly to wait for Kevin's return. He usually came home before five thirty.

At six o'clock he still hadn't come, and the urge was becoming unbearable. In a way, I was thinking, that money's mine. I looked at the stairs and crossed my legs for the twentieth time, like a ten-year-old who wants a pee. After all, I did win it, didn't I? By six thirty I was pacing the room like a caged puma, and Mrs Smith's tuneless humming was sending waves of irritation through me. At ten to seven I crept upstairs, assembled my few possessions, pocketed the wallet and left the place for good. I was bored to death with living there anyway and glad to be back on the street.

'All right, Sammy? 'Ow goes it, lar?'

'Er, okay Gazz.'

'Yer 'aven't got a place I can kip, 'ave yer?'

Usually now I slept in someone's house, and did not have to resort to derelict cars or shantytown houses built in secluded yards. Most of my daylight hours were spent selling what I had stolen during the night. No one could have called me prosperous, but at least I no longer starved.

One sunny Monday morning, after a weekend with Leo and Valerie, I was walking past the G.P.O. building in Walton Park Road, the same one Fitzie and the Dunns burgled with me as a boy, when I noticed that one of the vans outside had a bag of letters on the passenger seat. That's Registered Mail, I thought immediately. It looked too easy to miss, and fate had placed a housebrick on the pavement almost at my feet. I picked it up and took a last look round. The street was empty. The window burst into beads of glass and I snatched the bag and ran. Further down the road there's a place we call the wreck, a patch of waste ground behind Jacob's biscuit factory, and I clambered over the fence into it, pausing at the top to look down Walton Park Road. It was quiet. No one had seen me. I dropped to the far side and sidled in among the polluted trees.

'Bloody *'ell*! Shit! What's 'appened to me luck?'

There wasn't a penny in any of the letters, not even a cheque. They weren't Registered Mail at all but were all from one firm, their envelopes marked with its motif. The postman must have been delivering them by hand. Shoving the bag into a tree I climbed out of the wreck and clumped despondently along the first little street I came to, wondering what to do next. Less than an hour had passed since the job. There was a police van parked over the road but it didn't worry me. It was only the traffic police, a white Transit with a red stripe along its sides, what we call a jamrag or a jam butty. The cop beckoned.

'Come here a minute, son.'

Still not really worried, I crossed over.

'Yeah? What can I do for yer?'

He opened the door. 'Here, sit inside for a minute.'

Fear trickled into me, but it was too late to do anything else. He was asking me my name when a guy walked quickly around the corner from Walton Park Road.

'Yes, that's him, officer.' This drastic turn of events made me feel that liquid ice was being poured down my throat. 'That's definitely the lad I saw.'

'And this is the letter he dropped?' The cop drew one of the familiar envelopes from under his seat.

'Yes,' said the witness.

'Right.' Without another word the cop began the drive to the police station, through streets whose sunshine looked extra beautiful now that I was leaving it. Mentally I cursed the letter which he now had tucked under his leg, and which I must have dropped as I was climbing into the wreck.

After two hours in the Interrogation Room, though, things began to look up.

'Look, 'ow many times do I 'ave to tell yer? I wasn't nowhere near Walton at nine o'clock. I'd just got off the bus when the traffic cop pulled me.'

Except for fretful denials of this sort I hadn't said a word. In the end the soft cop and the hard cop had been questioning me for so long without shaking my story that they began to think it was true. Their act lost its conviction. As they relaxed I began to feel more confident.

'We can't just let you go like that, son. You realize that? We'll have to put you on police bail while we make further enquiries.'

Relief flooded through me. It was to be short-lived.

'Bail?' the desk sergeant said. 'Have we put his name through the telex yet? No? Better do it, then.'

He went away. When he came back he handed the senior detective a piece of paper.

'Well well well. Fancy that.' He gave the paper to his colleague, and turned to me. 'Tell us about Kevin then, Graham.'

'Who?'

'Kevin. The man with the mobile wallet.'

They charged me with both offences and the court remanded me in custody, which meant Risley again. I trudged the barren exercise yard with no hope at all of regaining my freedom. On 22nd June 1976 I went up to Liverpool Crown Court, pleading guilty on both counts.

7 | *Borstal and Escape*

'Apparently you think you're a law unto yourself, Gaskin,' the judge said. 'Detention Centre didn't change you, so I've no alternative but to send you for Borstal training.'

They took me back to Risley for the night, and next day I was taken with a busload of other Borstal fledglings to Strangeways prison in Manchester, the allocation nick for Borstal boys. There was a special Reception for us and the lads working on it were young prisoners, Y.P.s. Most of them had done at least one Borstal.

'Why are yer lookin' so down, kid? Borstal? It's nowt, lad. Dead cushy, honest.'

'Yeh?'

'Yeh,' said another. 'Yer do yer time same as anywhere else, an' that's all. Yer can do it easy or 'ard, same as yer always can.'

Carrying a pisspot each and a pillowcase of prison clothing, we were taken to the Threepenny Bit, an octagonal metal floor in the centre of the jail, and allocated a cell each on one of the

Borstal wings, G, H or I. I-wing also housed Beasts, sex cases
and grasses on protection, so I was glad when they put me on
H.

There was Association two nights a week when you could
play T.T. with the other lads or just watch telly, and for the rest
of the week you were banged up in your cell. As I adjusted to
being back inside my anguish went from black to grey, and I
started work on some new poems. After two days they made me
a Landing Cleaner, which meant I had to lend a hand serving
the food at mealtimes. This was good. We were given a very
meagre tobacco allowance, and the job gave scope for my
entrepreneurial spirit.

''Ey, mate. Are yer interested in buyin' some sugar?'

The Y.P. gave me a shrewd glance and went back to examining his nails. 'Could be.' He turned his hand to the light. ''Ow
much?'

'Two pound for a quarter ounce o' tobacco.'

'Yeh,' he said, 'that's sound. Bring it along to me cell after
tea.'

After five weeks they sent me to Hindley, the maximum
security Borstal near Wigan. They call it a Borstal, but really it
is a high security jail. From outside you could see nothing but
blank, featureless walls covered with barbed wire, and inside it
was only locked corridors with steel gates every few metres along
them, and locked cells. The thought of spending up to two years
there was grim indeed.

By this time a vague hope was forming in my mind, and
self-interest began to shape this hope into a plan. My immediate
need was to get out of Hindley. From the many interviews I had
had at Strangeways it was apparent that the Borstal authority
knew very little about my past. My Category A status at Northfields was either forgotten or had never officially existed, so I
kept my mouth shut about it. Hindley took its inmates entirely
from the North-West, and I hoped this might furnish me with
the means of escape. The reception interview took place on my
first day there.

'Going back to Liverpool after your release, Gaskin?'

This was the first question everyone was asked, and the screw
expected an affirmative reply.

'Liverpool?' I said incredulously. 'Why Liverpool? I'll be
goin' 'ome when I get out, back to London.'

'Eh?' He looked at my file. 'It was Liverpool Crown that sentenced you, wasn't it?'

'Yeh, but I don't live there. I 'aven't lived there for years. I was on'y down for that week when I done the job.'

He put down his pen. 'Look, this can't be right. What was your address in London?'

'Yer've got it there,' I said, pointing to Brenda's address on a typed sheet, which I had fortuitously spotted.

'You were living with your sister?'

'Yeh.'

'And that's where you're going when you get out? Where are your parents?'

'I 'aven't got none. I grew up in care.'

There was a glum, thoughtful silence.

'Another bloody cock-up,' said the screw. 'Will your sister want to visit you?'

'Yeah. O' course.'

'Hmm.'

A week later they called me into the wing office to see an Assistant Governor.

'You've been sent here by mistake,' the A.G. said. 'We're returning you to Strangeways for reallocation.'

'When, sir?'

'Tomorrow.'

As the van turned out of the gates next morning I turned to look at the rows of barred windows, lifted my handcuffed wrists in salute, and smiled. At the time I thought I'd been very clever.

In Strangeways they put me on G-wing this time, and while I was there I stuck to my story of living in London, and harped on how difficult it would be for Brenda to visit me up north. Five days later they sent me, exultant, with a busload of southerners to Wormwood Scrubs.

It was very sophisticated compared to the northern nicks. There was closed circuit T.V. everywhere, a prefabricated office on every landing, and an intercom system. When they called your name it could be heard over the entire wing.

'Officer on the Fours,' it would boom. 'We want a body, sir. It's Gaskin, G., from Four Two Four, please.'

The screw came then and took you down. In the interviews they gave me I was humble and polite, discreet about the past, and kept my ears open. It worked. In the end they allocated me to Huntercombe, a semi-open Borstal near High Wycombe. A fortnight later they took me there with four others.

When we were near the place we saw a regatta on the Thames. There were girls in fluffy dresses, rowing teams in dark blazers and white slacks, Rolls-Royces parked off-handedly on the grass, and marquees festooned with bunting.

'Them people don't 'ave bad lives, eh?' the kid next to me said.

'Well,' I rattled our handcuff, looked out at the August sunshine, and thought of Hindley's grim façade. A vague glow of happiness filled me. 'Ours *could* be worse, lar.'

A few minutes later our new home came into view. There was so much barbed wire that you could hardly see the squat, ugly buildings beneath it. Even so, it was an improvement on Hindley. On outside working party escape would be just possible, and escape was what I had in mind, as usual.

They put us on B, the reception wing, then took us to the dining hall to eat. The lads from C-wing who had done longer trooped in from work, and I got talking to one of them.

'Lissen,' he said, 'put yer name down for the Motor Mechanics' course, Scouse. It ain't a bad number. If they put yer on it yer'll be sent to an open Borstal.'

'Yeah?' Hope brightened. 'Truly? Ta, lar. Thanks for the tip.'

Afterwards we went to Reception for our prison kit, then it was time for our interviews with the Governor.

'Good afternoon, sir.'

The words were uttered in my politest possible tone. He waved me into a chair. There was a young woman at his side taking notes, probably some sort of trainee. A tremor ran through me at seeing a female after so long. She might have looked like an old dog, but she seemed gorgeous to me.

'Well, Gaskin,' the Governor looked at my list of offences, then at me. 'You're going to have to shape up while you're here, boy, unless you want to do the whole two years. We don't let a lad out of Huntercombe till we're convinced he's decided to mend his ways.'

'Yeh, sir. I realize that.'

Answering his questions, I felt relaxed and confident. Most of the lads in Borstal are pretty thick and cannot express themselves. Meeting someone who could would be a welcome change for the Governor, and I deliberately threw in a couple of mediumly long words when the opportunity arose. He waffled on, and after a while I felt him warming towards me.

'Ever abscond from anywhere, Gaskin?'

This was the crucial moment in our talk. How much information on me did he really have in that file?

'No, sir,' I replied firmly. 'Never.'

To my relief he didn't glance at the file, but carried on blithely. 'What kind of work were you doing outside?'

'Er, I worked in a garage, sir.' I looked modestly at my feet. 'I'd done a year o' me apprenticeship when I got in trouble.'

'Hmmm.' He paused, and struck a match to light his pipe. The trainee bent over her notes and I strained to see down her V-neck as her breasts shifted heavily forward. 'We're taking applications for a Motor Mechanics' course,' he said, 'you should put your name down for that.'

My eyes looked into his. 'I don't think I'd stand much chance o' that, sir, would I?'

'You might.' He jotted a note on my file. 'Why not give it a try?'

On B-wing I had another interview, this time with the A.G. He was all right, a little bald-headed fellow, dead nice. Assistant Governors are often better, they are usually unambitious and long-termers themselves in a way.

'You'll be on the wing for the first two weeks, Gaskin, then we'll put you on outside work party. If you try to abscond it'll set your Discharge Grade back by at least four months. Remember that.'

It astonished me that anyone had ever escaped from the place, but they had. They must have been supermen to reach the high fence and climb it before the screws caught up with them.

'I'm not into that, sir. Just want to do me time an' get out.'

'Good. I hope you're telling the truth. Here's your E.D.R.'

He handed me a piece of paper with the following typed on it: 24th February 1977. Seven more months. To me they seemed like seven centuries.

A day or two later the Motor Mechanics' application form appeared on the wing notice-board, and I put my name down. For the next fortnight I settled into the monotony of the routine there. Though my remaining time made me feel a rush of something like nausea when I thought about it, I now had the hope of escape. The only times in my life so far when I had felt really free had been when I was on the run, and I looked forward to doing it again. They put me on wing cleaners and it was breakfast, work, dinner, Gym, work, tea, Association sometimes, then back to your cell for bed. That was the day. When my fortnight was up the A.G. called me into his office.

'No outside work party for you, Gaskin,' he barked, then laughed at my crestfallen expression. 'You're going on the Motor Mechanics' course.'

'What, sir? Honest? Yer not jokin', are yer?'

'We're not that cruel, son. You leave for Finnimore Wood on 23rd September.'

Outside his office again, even the wing looked good. The stairs received the most thorough cleaning they had ever had. I was exultant. By plotting and scheming I had worked my way from the highest security Borstal in Britain to the point where, in four weeks' time, I'd be going to an open institution where I'd be able to walk out whenever I chose. What was more, I'd be able to take my time over it and life would still be bearable. The Motor Mechanics' course was a first-time experiment. The lads on it would be going out every day, without supervision, to study at the Technical College in the nearest town, Henley. The only fly in the ointment was that my February release date would no longer apply. Release would depend on how I did at the course.

The day arrived and the five of us who had been chosen were driven to Finnimore Wood in a minibus, without handcuffs. The place actually *was* a wood, the trees almost surrounding the collection of Nissen huts and huge, barn-like buildings that was the Borstal. It had been a P.O.W. camp during the war and had accommodated first Germans, then Russians. These were some of the Russians forcibly repatriated by the British government and murdered by Stalin. As you went through the gates and down the drive you saw the dining hall, the recreation hall with its inevitable T.V. and T.T., a little office, and behind it the three Nissen huts that were used as dormitories. They had steps going up to them and balconies along their fronts, just as P.O.W. camps are depicted in the movies. A screw showed us ours and we saw that it was partitioned off into cell-sized boxes.

The partitions only went up to shoulder height, so anyone could look over. Afterwards we were left with the Matron.

'Well, dearie, which one are you? Gaskin? Here's your reception letter, then. You come here for your pay on Fridays.'

She was the usual fat, professionally maternal woman some institutions stock to improve their image.

It is rare for fate to sit you next to a friend on your first day anywhere, but it happened that day.

'Er, all right, lar? What's yer name?'

He was a skinny-looking guy, even taller than me.

'Well,' he said, 'Fritz, I suppose. It isn't, but that's what everyone calls me. My parents are German, you see.'

He was a well-spoken lad, and had been reading a book till I interrupted. I looked at the title. *War and Peace.*

'Er, I'm Graham. Not bad 'ere, eh?'

'Better than most Borstals,' he said, 'sure.'

'What are yer in for, Fritz? Yer don't seem the usual type for Borstal, if yer don't mind me sayin' so.'

He smiled. 'It's a long story, Graham. Want to hear it?'

'Yeh, go 'ead. One thing I've got is plenty o' time, eh?'

We both laughed. Fritz put a fagpaper in his book and closed it.

'Well,' he said, 'first of all, I'm a member of the Communist Party.'

'Yeh? A Red, eh?'

He nodded. 'As red as our common blood, Graham. And that's why I'm in here.'

'They can't do yer for it, can they?'

'Well,' he said, 'not openly. The actual charge was assaulting a cop, occasioning him actual bodily harm.'

This surprised me. Fritz didn't look as though he could knock the skin off a rice pudding. My face must have given me away because he went on, 'Don't let appearances fool you, Graham. We're not all what we seem, are we? We Communists have a philosophy which tells us how and when to apply force, and that's why we win so often.' He laughed. 'My case is one of the exceptions. Well, on the day of my downfall I was delivering leaflets with other comrades and we had split up, taking so many streets each. It was a nice sunny morning in spring, the kind of day that puts bounce into your step. Know what I mean?'

'Yeh. The kind o' day that makes yer feel like screwin' every chick yer set eyes on.'

'Exactly. Well, I turned the corner at the end of my second street and there it was. Wham. Disaster.'

'What?'

'There, sprawled face down in the gutter, was Arthur Evans, a middle-aged comrade who had been twenty-five years in the Party. Two heavies were kicking the shit out of him, and I knew one of them by sight.' Fritz paused. 'A big noise in the local National Front.'

'Yeh? 'Eavy, man. So what did yer do?'

Fritz smiled, as at a sentimental memory. 'There are times, Graham, when I'd almost like to believe in God. Some great Force, anyway, must have put that shovel there, leaning against the wall of the corner house.' His eyes twinkled. 'It must have been the dialectic of History.'

'Yeh.' He was a funny guy, and I laughed. 'Can't reelly 'ave been anythin' else, when yer think about it.'

'It was a big, heavy, brand new shovel,' he went on, 'a Kango, the kind they use on building sites. I hit the first Nazi on the back of the head with it, and he dropped like a sack of coal. The second pulled a chain from inside his coat but didn't have a chance to use it. My first blow hit him in the kneecap, my second hacked into his side and he collapsed like a paper house in a hurricane.'

''Ey, Fritz. Bit of a ruthless bastard on the quiet, aren't yer?'

'When necessary, Graham. Well, they were on the ground and I was still holding the shovel when a police car screeched around the corner and pulled up at the side of the road. I dropped the shovel and went over to explain what had happened, but as they got out of the car they pulled their truncheons and laid into me and Arthur, who was only just getting up out of the gutter. They arrested us both, and let the two Nazis walk away. In court they produced the shovel as evidence, and said I'd attacked them with it. So that's how I come to be in Borstal.'

'Well, yer know what justice is about now, eh Fritz? The only thing that baffles me is why they sent yer to a cushy place like this. Yer don't usually get in 'em when yer done for violence.'

'You're joking, Graham.' He laughed again. 'I only came

here the day before yesterday, with four months left to do. I did the rest of my time in the Scrubs and Feltham.'

'Feltham? The queers' Borstal? 'Ow come?'

'Well, they send the gay boys and the junkies there, and anyone they think may be a bit of a loony. You see, when they got me from court to Reception in the Scrubs I refused to wear the prison clothing. "I'm in for a political offence," I said, "I'm not a criminal."'

'Yeah? That must 'ave pleased 'em. What did they do?'

'They took me down to the Block wrapped in a blanket. It was quite funny, all the guys on the wing were cheering as we went through. Then they decided I was nuts, and sent me to Feltham.'

'I'm not surprised,' I said.

'No? I was, then. Nothing they could do would surprise me now. At Feltham they're ready with the largactyl, the padded cells and the straitjackets, so I gave in. No choice. If I'd carried on I'd have ended up in Broadmoor or Rampton, certified, and had to do years and years, or maybe never got out. So I started using my time constructively instead.'

'Constructively? In nick? I'm not with yer, Fritz.'

'I passed two A levels in Feltham, and I've done most of the work for a third which I take when I get out.'

After meeting Fritz I started to get into Communism. It was a rebellion thing, I didn't like always being the one who had nothing and thought it might be the answer. It wasn't. Anyway, I lacked Fritz's dedication. My sole contribution to the proletarian struggle while at Finnimore Wood was to have a hammer and sickle tattooed on my chest by one of the lads. Life wasn't too bad there, but it was still an institution and I felt as cramped and claustrophobic as I always had in such places. When I asked them for a new E.D.R. they answered vaguely, and this made me hunger even more for freedom.

Monday morning. The screw swung the minibus into the gates of Henley Tech and stopped.

'Right, here it is. Better than the Scrubs, eh lads?'

We stepped out, conspicuous in our brand new Borstal gear. The normal uniform was blue jacket and grey trousers but they gave us green jackets and black trousers for our course at the Tech. It was strange walking around as though free and being able to talk to girls. A lot of the Tech kids were well-spoken and even posh, and there was a Students' Union with T.T. and a pinball machine. We had been sitting in there for five minutes when the Principal came in to talk to us.

'How do you do, boys?' He shook hands all round. 'Welcome to Henley Technical College, and let's hope you all do well here. First, I'm afraid, a pep talk. It's not my idea, please understand that. I've been asked to give it by your Governor. Well ... ' He rubbed his hands together and looked around awkwardly. 'The first thing is that there mustn't be any trouble, none at all, and in the event of there being any, even if one of you misses a single lesson, I have to contact Finnimore Wood. Now I hope you don't think I'm discriminating. The Borstal, sorry, Finnimore Wood have asked me ... '

It was a replica, in content if not in form, of our Governor's speech before we left that morning.

In spite of Big Brother it was good there, and better than being inside. I spent a lot of time in the Union talking to girls, and went out to a café at lunchtimes. The café belonged to the College and we had vouchers to spend on food.

' 'Ow about a pint, lads?'

'Think we can chance it, Scouse? In this get-up?'

'Yeh. We'll tell 'em we're in the R.A.F. or somethin'.'

We chose a pub some distance away, and it went off smoothly. After a couple of weeks I copped off with a girl, Lesley. She was nice, with long brown hair and gentle eyes, but I never did more than kiss her. There was never anywhere to take her, or enough time.

The Borstal seldom searched us going in or out, so I started posting letters for the lads inside. At first they paid me for it in the prison currency, tobacco. Later, when things improved, I did it for nothing.

'Lesley, is it all right if I 'ave a letter sent to yer 'ouse? On'y from me sister, like.'

'Yes, Graham, of course.'

Brenda replied by return, enclosing what money she could. Lesley handed me the letter in the morning before lessons, and at the ten o'clock break I changed a quid into ten-pence pieces and found a phone box.

' 'Ello, Malcolm. 'Ow are yer? Yeh, me again. Eh? Bad what? Penny? I'm not with yer.'

In a very few words I told him the score.

'Listen, Malcolm, why not come down an' see me?'

'Yes,' he said immediately, 'I'll come this afternoon.'

When I came out for lunch there was his familiar Volvo, sleek, golden, expensive.

'Hello, Graham. How are you, love? This is Jurgen.'

'Er, not 'ere, Malcolm. Drive round the corner an' I'll walk round an' meet yer.'

What was he playing at, calling me 'love'? He had never done that before. The Volvo was a two-door, half sports car as well as half limousine, and his friend clambered into the back so I could jump in the seat next to Malcolm.

'Where to, love? Nearest pub?'

'No, go a bit further away, Malcolm, where they won't know this crappy uniform.'

The guy he had brought with him was really strange. He was some kind of foreigner, and kept staring into a far corner of the car, replying with grimaces whenever we spoke to him. It occurred to me that Malcolm had been telling him all the way from Stroud about the lovely blond boyfriend he had, and that that was why he kept calling me 'love'. He was showing off.

'This looks all right, babe,' he said at last, pulling into a pub car park. He bought me some food and a couple of pints, and gave me an ounce of tobacco to take back with me. His silly game in front of his friend, with me cast in the role of the little wife, was only a mild annoyance and I prudently kept my mouth shut about it. After all, he had driven all the way from Gloucestershire in a morning to see me. So far so good. I had plans for Malcolm.

''Bye, love.'

'Goodbye, Malcolm. Till next time.'

At two o'clock, exactly on time, I stepped back into my class.

As usual they chose me to play in the institution football team, and a couple of weeks after Malcolm's visit we went to play Feltham. It was a big square building with bars, fences, barbed wire and little else, worse than Huntercombe. For some reason the sight of it filled me with a terrible loathing.

'Jeez,' I said to Fritz, our goalie, 'this is one place I 'ope they never send me. I'm reportin' sick if we 'ave to play 'ere again.'

The match was so funny that it changed all that. The Feltham P.T.I. appointed himself referee, and the trouble came with his first ruling.

Prrrrrrpp! The whistle dropped from his lips and bobbed on its cord as he ran over, arm in the air. 'Penalty!'

It was for his side, of course. Our P.T.I. marched over and started to argue.

'What are you on about, penalty? Where did you learn to play football, in the Girl bloody Guides?'

'Uh? What the ... ? You just lissen, wher*ever* I learnt, they taught me to abide by the referee's decision!'

'Referee's what? Not much good you playin' at bein' the ref, is there, when you can't tell a penalty from a free kick. That was outside the area, a blind man could've seen it. Bloody barnpot!'

'What? What did you ... ?'

Next thing they were thumping seven kinds out of one another, going at it hammer and tongs in the middle of the goal mouth. In a matter of seconds it spread to the boys, and there was chaos till other Feltham staff ran out and stopped it. After extended arguments we drove away with our angry screw revving the engine and blasting the horn. Grinning, I looked back at the place. The gaunt building crouched like a monstrous predator behind its fences, waiting.

The work at the Tech was easy enough so I merely carried on, unable to decide whether or not to escape. It hardly seemed worth it. Life was bearable, perhaps I should stick it out and do my time. But when would they let me out? The days passed with deadening slowness. Autumn died, the weather grew colder, December arrived. In its first few days something happened which forced me to make up my mind.

One job I hated at Finnimore Wood was helping to wash the minibus, and I seemed to be landed with it every Saturday. The screw who drove it was an irritating perfectionist and made the job last for hours, with four of us obeying his every instruction. He never did a stroke himself, but superintended with maddening thoroughness, pointing into out of the way corners.

'Look, isn't that a grain of dust in there?'

'Where?'

'There, Gaskin, there. Get it out. Use the pencil torch and tweezers.'

Well, he was almost that bad. This day we had been rinsing the damn thing for a good half hour, and had thrown about forty buckets of water over it from a tap which was miles away. He couldn't have chosen a worse moment to give me the final order. In my imagination Lesley had been persuaded to follow me into the Gents at Henley Tech, and we had locked the cubicle door. I was pulling the gusset of her spotless white knickers aside when he said:

'Fetch another two buckets, Gaskin.'

Irritation boiled through me, and I responded without thinking about it.

'Send someone else,' I said.

'What?' He came round the van and bore down on me, red-faced. 'What did you say? Where d'you think you are, Gaskin? Butlins? Now go on. Two more buckets.'

The other lads stopped work, and stood around watching.

'Send someone else,' I said again, 'if yer can find anyone daft enough. I'm 'appy as I am, doin' fuck all.'

He spluttered with rage. 'This is the last time I'm telling you, Gaskin.' As he spoke he wagged his finger in my face, and there is nothing I hate more. 'Now go and get that bloody water.' There was one full and one empty bucket at the side of the van, and he kicked the empty one towards me. 'MOVE.'

I bent to lift it, and before I knew what was happening had thrown the full one over him. He stood for a moment dripping, then bellowed as he shoved me along the driveway. At the Borstal they locked me in the cell and later that day, to my horror, snapped handcuffs on to me and drove me back to Huntercombe.

That was on Saturday. They stuck me back on B-wing and I sat awake in my cell for half the night, worrying. They wouldn't want their Motor Mechanics' course to appear a flop at the Home Office, and if they threw me out it would be a bad statistic for them. Surely they'd send me back. Wouldn't they? Probably they'd leave me worrying till Sunday afternoon and tell me then. At one point I found myself biting my nails for the first time in my life. They were certainly succeeding.

By Sunday afternoon I was thinking, Evening. It'll be evening when they tell me. Association finished and they locked me up with the rest. I lay on my bed hearing the prison grow quiet around me, my chest tight with despair. That was it. They never would have let me have a day off. On Monday morning they put me back on wing cleaners. The clank of the steel buckets and the smell of the polish induced feelings of illness in me. In the afternoon the Governor sent for me. I stood rigidly at attention before him.

'Well, Gaskin, you're a bit of an idiot, aren't you? Throwing away a cushy number like that?'

'Yeh, sir. An' a good chance for the rest of me life, sir. Been a reg'lar moron, sir.'

He nodded gravely and drummed his fingers on the desk. It was raining outside, and a sudden gust of wind rattled the windows. A full minute passed before he smiled. 'Relax, Gaskin. We're giving you another chance. You can finish your course at Henley.'

'Ah, great, sir! Thanks, sir! It's dead good, that, sir!'

He silenced me with a lifted finger. 'Watch your step this time, though. One slip, just one, and your feet won't touch.' He glared at me. 'And you won't be my favourite inmate, do I make myself clear?'

On the drive back to Finnimore Wood I did some serious thinking. The time had come. I was bound to get in trouble again, and next time would find me stuck in Huntercombe for the duration. Besides, it was getting near Christmas. College closed for the holiday on the 18th, and if I didn't get away before then I'd be stuck in the Borstal till January, with God knew how many months still to do. Now that my decision was made, even the silent screw at the wheel and the van itself began to get to me. I longed for freedom.

Over the next week I had some serious telephone conversations with Malcolm. On the next to last Friday I rang him.

'Malcolm? Yeh, not bad. Lissen, you know what we talked about last time? Yeh. Well, I've decided. We break up a week today.'

There was silence for a long time. Was he having second thoughts?

'Today's Friday, isn't it?' he said at last.

'Yeh.'

'I'll see you on Tuesday,' he said. 'Same time and place.'

The weekend dragged past. At break-time on the Monday morning I phoned again to make sure he was still coming. It rang for a long time, and when he answered it an extended yawn greeted my ear.

'Eeeeeeeeeeeeuh. Sorry, Graham, what was that?'

'Er, did I wake yer up, Malcolm? Just ringin' to confirm our little arrangement, like.'

'I can't come tomorrow,' he said. 'Dutch has decided to come back from Israel, and I'm taking Veronica and the boys to Heathrow in the morning to pick him up.'

'Ah, 'ey Malcolm. Yer can't leave me stuck 'ere like this. It's agony, sittin' 'ere just waitin'.'

'I've *got* to take them,' he said. 'Dutch has been a good friend to me.'

'Can yer come today, then?'

'Eeeeeeeeeeeeah.' He must have been dying to go back to sleep, and cursing me mentally. 'All right. I'll see you in the same place as last time, at two o'clock.'

My first feeling was one of sadness that I wouldn't be able to say goodbye to Fritz. Otherwise, now that escape was imminent, a kind of peace settled upon me.

'Lesley. Come 'ere, love.' Glancing up and down the corridor to make sure no one could overhear, I lowered my voice. 'The time's come. I'm gettin' off at dinner time.'

She and a couple of other good friends took me for a farewell drink, and when we came back at five minutes to two Malcolm's Volvo was there, parked discreetly where we had arranged.

'Ta ra, everyone.'

After giving Lesley a long, wet kiss I jumped in the car and lay down in the back. Malcolm flung a coat over me and drove off, leaving me alone with the sound of the engine.

'It's safe to come in the front now,' he said after a while. I clambered over. 'Well, what's it like to be free again, Graham?'

'Great, Malcolm. Great.'

It was. The fields seemed greener, the air cleaner now that I was at liberty. We drove to Gloucestershire, where Malcolm made us a huge meal and opened some cans of beer.

'I'll have to leave you soon, Graham. I'm taking Veronica to a judo contest tonight, then staying with her so as to get up early and take them to Heathrow.'

'Okay, Malcolm. Give 'er me love, will yer? Oh no, better not, eh?'

He put his palms together and leaned forward, like a parson about to deliver his sermon. 'My mother's coming round to feed the cat tomorrow, so remember to keep the lights off during the day.'

I nodded. The cat was like a farm cat, and never came into the house. Her dish was on the back step.

'She shouldn't come in,' he went on, 'but if she does for any reason, go in one of the rooms upstairs and keep quiet.'

'Okay.' He was already irritating me. What did he think I was going to do, come out in my Borstal clothes and enquire after the plant I'd given her the previous year? He was acting as though the K.G.B. were hot on my trail.

'Don't answer the phone unless it's me,' he said. 'I'll dial twice, and stop after one ring. The third time, answer.'

'Okay, Malcolm.'

Eventually he went. I watched his car nosing its way along the drive and through the gates. What a relief. After luxuriating in the bath to wash the prison smell away I came down naked, the hated uniform left on the bathroom floor. For a while I sat with a few cans of beer on the arm of the chair making phone calls, running up Malcolm's bill. He could afford it. I rang friends in different parts of the country and played them tracks of L.P.s to pass the time, then watched telly until bedtime. In bed I lay for a long time, worrying. What would I do now? How would I survive without stealing, and perhaps ending up in even more trouble?

The next day was spent in the same way. Still naked, I phoned the call box at Henley Tech and spoke to my Borstal mates. Two screws had come from Finnimore Wood the previous afternoon to sniff around, and later the police had arrived and asked the students, a class at a time, if they had seen me go.

Lesley came to the phone.

'Graham? Oh, hello love. How *are* you? I've been thinking about you all the time since you went.'

'Yeh?'

'Yes, and I'm missing you terribly. Already. It's only a day since I *saw* you. Graham,' her voice went very shy and soft, 'I think . . . Well, I think I love you.'

'Ah, babe, that's lovely, that is. Little darlin'.'

At that moment a car crunched its way along the gravel outside.

'Lissen, babe, I'll 'ave to ring off now. I'll try an' ring yer later.'

I turned the stereo down and mellowed the lights, then

watched Malcolm's mother get out of her car and go round the house. As she went I followed, inside, checking her through different windows. I watched through the net curtains in the kitchen as she emptied a bag of scraps into the little dish, then went away again.

Malcolm phoned later.

'I can't make it today, Graham. The plane's been delayed and we'll have to stay here till morning.'

'Yeh? That's a pity, eh?'

It was all right by me.

Next afternoon he phoned again, this time from Dutch's house in Rannage. Reluctantly, I put my Borstal clothes back on. What a nuisance it was that Malcolm's things were all too small for me. He came back, and we had our usual complement of beer. There were any number of rooms I could have slept in but we were talking so I put a sleeping bag next to Malcolm's bed. He made no attempt to touch me and I had a peaceful night's sleep.

We were going to see another judo contest. It was the next afternoon.

'D'yer think I'll be all right in this clobber, Malcolm?'

'Oh yes.' His eyes took on the old look for a moment. 'You look very nice, actually.'

As with most of Malcolm's ventures into the world of sport, this one involved some teenage boys. There were two of them, and we picked them up from the private school where we had taken James and Angus Wineberg the day after Dutch's court case. After the contest Malcolm brought them home with us, as we were taking them to another in Birmingham the next day, in which they were competing. Malcolm cooked a meal and loaded the table with bottles of wine, and we all got quite pissed. The two boys, who were the same age as me but obviously unused to alcohol, were practically insensible at the end. The four of us staggered upstairs and slept in the same room, crashed out on mattresses still there from the B.A.C. reunion.

When I awoke next morning the others had gone downstairs. The house and the world outside seemed eerily quiet. Even the birds were silent. I went over to the window and looked out. The trees, hedges and lawns of Malcolm's little mansion were covered in thick snow. Sober, I saw my predicament with frightening clarity. Staying there would not be possible unless I started to sleep with Malcolm again. The thought sent a rush of loathing through me, and my skin tingled as it does before I fight. One fact loomed huge in my mind, dwarfing the considerations of ease and convenience which cropped up around it. I was *not* going to do it.

'Ah,' he said when I came into the kitchen, 'Graham. I was about to come up for you. You've just got time for breakfast before we set off.'

By now, everything he said was getting on my nerves, even banalities like this one. I watched him casting covert glances at the two boys, realizing again how much I hated him. The worst thing about him was his patience. The gentle insistence with which he now waited for me to yield to his pressure would later be expressed in his hands, caressing, always demanding more. Not that he was going to get them on to me. Making sure they all went out before me, I searched the room frantically for an answer to my problem. It came in the shape of a gold £5 piece six centimetres across, solid, heavy and thick. I tucked it into my shoe and clattered down the steps after them.

'Come on, Graham. We're going to be late.'

'Er, sorry. I forgot somethin'.'

He looked at his watch. 'This snow will delay us, but we should make it in time.'

We picked a third kid up from his house in Bisley, the village nearest to Malcolm's house, and I liked him better. He was a working class kid and more straightforward than the other two. With four of us in the car Malcolm was in high spirits.

'We're certainly doing some travelling, Graham, you and I.'

'Yeh.'

He grimaced as we slid on a bend. 'I'm going to London the day after tomorrow. Fancy coming along?'

'Okay. Can we see Brenda again?'

We arrived at the sports centre in Birmingham five minutes before the Bisley kid was due to compete. When he came on to the mat he was the only one who didn't have a proper kit. All the others had dead smart, snow-white kits, and this kid was dressed in a suit his mother had made out of old sheets. A rip opened up under one arm as he bowed to his opponent. I felt sorry for him.

In competition judo the contest lasts for six swift minutes.

You can win by the equivalent of a knock-out, which is called Ippon, or on points. Our scruffy friend did badly, and with five minutes gone his opponent was at Waza-ari, leading seven points to nil. The Bisley kid was in the worst position you can reach without actually losing. At that point he came back with a Keikoku, which is equivalent to Waza-ari and made them even. It seemed to be a personal challenge to him, and his speed was uncompromising, his accuracy frightening from then on. With eight seconds to go he executed a perfect Uchi-mata, an inner thigh throw which floored his opponent totally. The referee's arm shot up and he stepped forward.

'Ippon!'

A knock-out. It reminded me of the day I won the swim at Stroud and I was made up for him, and yelled and clapped louder than anyone else.

We had lunch upstairs in the bar, the two schoolboys, who had yet to compete, wisely sticking to Coke.

'Have a drink to celebrate,' Malcolm said to the Bisley kid.

'No thanks.'

So it was left to me to help him drink the bottle of wine he had bought. I ate leisurely, savouring the food, and the schoolboys went off to change before I'd finished. It would be two hours before the competition ended.

'Malcolm, shall I get some chocolates for us to eat while we're watchin'?'

'Hmm? Yes, all right.'

'Er, can yer give us . . . ?'

'Yes, I've got a pound somewhere.' He searched through his pockets. 'No, only a fiver, you'll have to take that.'

I gave him a carefree wave as I went out, then trod the streets grimly till I found an antique shop.

'What'll yer give us for this, mate?'

'Let's see it?' The heavy coin shone on his palm. 'Oh, yes. Hmmm.' He brought out a scales and weighed it. 'Yes, not bad. I'll give you, oh, seventy pounds cash.'

'Whaaat? Are yer jokin'? Give us a 'undred an' fifty an' yer'll still be makin' a 'andsome profit.'

After some haggling we agreed on £100 and he started opening different cupboards and drawers, taking a tenner from one, some ones from another till there was a heap of money on his desk, which he counted.

'I haven't that much cash. You'll have to come back tomorrow.'

'Come on, man,' I said. 'Yer can get it. Try a bit 'arder.'

He locked me out of the shop while he went off to borrow. When he came back he had £86 in cash.

'Look, will you take this ring for the remainder? It's worth fourteen.'

Uncomfortable in my Borstal gear and wanting to get away, there was nothing I could do but agree.

'Go on, then. It's a deal.'

Later I found out that the coin had been worth £300.

My next move was to jump a bus into the city centre. In the bus station I felt conspicuous in my uniform, but easier in my mind now that I had money. After twenty minutes I caught a bus to Reading where I booked into a smart hotel. Henley and Finnimore Wood were now only a few miles away.

Drring, drring. Drring, drring. Drr . . .

'Hello?'

'Lesley. Lesley it's me, Graham.'

'Graham! God, where are you? Are you all right?'

In an hour she was with me. We exchanged feverish kisses at the bus stop then sat in a quiet pub, holding hands and talking. Later I took her for a meal, and when it was over we walked slowly through the town, I with my arm round her shoulders. After a few silent minutes I pulled her into a doorway.

'Lesley,' I breathed, nibbling the lobe of her ear, 'oh, Lesley.' As chance would have it it was a jeweller's doorway we had chosen, and my eyes fell upon rings, watches, and heavy gold chains. 'Was it true what you told me over the phone? That you love me?'

She looked at me moistly. 'Oh yes, Graham. Yes.'

'Well,' as my lips touched her neck my eyes noted the alarm wires in the window-corners, and I wondered with professional curiosity whether the armoured glass would withstand a properly flung chunk of concrete, 'will you come to my room and stay the night?'

'Oh, Graham.' She looked at me shyly, and buried her face in my shirtfront. 'You know I can't do that. If you love me you'll wait.'

She was a frightened little virgin and stalwartly took the bus home.

Next morning I took a train to London and stayed with my sister and her boyfriend at their flat in Clapham. They did not make me welcome. On the Monday, nearly destitute again and still wearing my Borstal uniform, I went back to Reading. With four pounds left I went to a cinema to keep warm, then tramped the streets in the freezing cold.

Eventually I came across a mountain of cardboard boxes, and crept into one. I soon went to sleep but was woken during the night by a tremendous thumping and rustling as someone, another dosser I presumed, tried to climb into my box.

'All right, mate,' I said angrily. 'D'yer 'ave to make such a racket? Yer've woke me up.'

I struck a match and saw, to my astonishment, that my co-boxee was dressed entirely in black leather. Gloves, jacket, waistcoat, T-shirt, trousers, socks and shoes, all uniformly black and shiny. Weird. He looked away when my match flared and began acting strangely, jumping about like a monkey. In a minute he left my box and scuttled across the others, then ran along an arcade of shops, dodging in and out of the doorways.

'Happy Christmas!' he shouted from the corner.

For an hour after he went I paced nervously up and down, keeping an eye open for his return, or the arrival of the police. That madman might have murdered me in my box. When nothing happened I found a new place and went back to sleep.

Very early in the morning I awoke and found myself outside a huge market, all the doors of which were open. There was no one in it that I could see so I ran in, grabbed the first thing which came to hand, a pineapple, and ran out again with it tucked underneath my arm. There must have been all sorts of stuff in there, but I had a bad feeling about the place. Fear of the police and recapture were uppermost in my mind.

Malcolm would now be in London, this I knew. Otherwise short on ideas, I decided to head back to Gloucestershire. From Reading I went to Oxford, walking with my thumb held out hopefully. It took me all that day and half the night, and no car stopped. With what little money I had left I bought chips, then crisps. When I saw milk I stole it. Six miles from Oxford a car picked me up and took me into the town. I stood in doorways, sat cramped in fridge-like phone booths till morning. Then I started hitching again, and my luck changed at once.

'Where are you headin' for, kid?'

'Stroud, mate, in Gloucestershire.'

The door of the lorry swung open. 'Jump in. I go right through it.'

On foot again I made it to Bisley, a couple of miles from Malcolm's house. As I turned into the lane that led to it I saw, with a shock that sent me reeling back round the corner out of sight, his mother. When I peeped through the hedge I could tell she hadn't seen me. She and her husband were both there, in separate cars, dropping their charlady off at her house. After some conversation the mother drove off towards Stroud and her husband went the other way, presumably to Malcolm's to feed the moggy. When his Range Rover had rounded the first bend and was out of sight I followed. The lane was deathly quiet. Every time a vehicle approached I went quickly into cover.

When I was halfway to the house Malcolm's stepfather came back. From the safety of the ditch I watched his car flash by, saw his face staring at the road ahead. Then I walked more quickly till I turned into the driveway of Malcolm's house, which I approached openly, not bothering to knock at the door since I knew the place was empty. Blatt! A neat hole appeared in the kitchen window and glass tinkled into the sink. No one would hear it here, miles from anywhere. Once in, I took a carrier bag from the drawer where he kept them and scooped up all the gold and silver I could find. The only cash I came across was a measly four quid, and I knew this would cause me headaches later on.

'Oh yeah, *yeah*!' I smacked my palm with my fist. Malcolm's uncle, the one who sent him ten quid every Christmas, it should be there! I ran to the front door and feverishly opened the letters and cards that lay there. No, it hadn't come yet.

I drooped disappointedly back to the kitchen and made a quick meal, dropped some cans into my carrier bag for the journey, and left Malcolm's house for the last time, wiping my mouth on the curtain before I stepped out of the door. Though I felt far from relaxed in my Borstal uniform it gave me no trouble, even policemen didn't seem to look twice at me.

'Gloucester, please.'

As the bus roared away from the stop I re-examined the loot. It was impressive. There was a very old and very heavy gold coin which I think was Roman, and some lesser coins, also gold, and some silver ornaments and chains. The best thing was a solid gold, square box. It was about three times the size of a snuffbox, so it's hard to say what it had originally been used for. It had a false bottom which pulled out, and behind this was an old photograph. It showed a woman lying on her back across a farm-cart, her Victorian dress pulled up over her waist, her anus and cunt visible. Next to her stood a labourer in smock and rustic hat, holding an enormous erection and leering. All in all the loot must have been worth £1,000, perhaps a great deal more.

With my remaining three pounds I tried to find a hotel in Gloucester. None would take me.

'Sorry.' She started to close the door. 'A room's £4.50.'

'Er, look. Take this.'

'What is it?'

'A gold coin. It's worth twenty quid.'

'No, we don't take anything like that. You've no luggage either, have you? Sorry.'

So I had a few pints, stayed in the pub till the last possible moment, then slept in the cab of a lorry. Next morning I'd sell the gear and go once more to London. Brenda might help me find a room, and I could get a job and stay away from crime. No sooner had the plan been formulated than doubts set in. My past failures came back to me, and I wondered if I would ever manage to lead a normal life. When I had been worrying for about an hour I drifted off to sleep.

The sound of the cab door opening woke me. It was broad daylight, and I found myself staring into the face of an angry lorrydriver.

'Uh? What are *yow* doin' in there? Eh? That's my bloody lorry, that is, not a 'ome for layabouts. Come on, out of it. Right now.'

'Er, sorry mate. I 'ad a few last night, like an' ... '

'Clear off. Go on. Clear off or I phone the police.'

With my remaining pound I went to a café to wait for nine o'clock. When the shops opened I trudged through the town looking for an antique shop, eyeing police cars anxiously as they passed. I soon found a shop, though it looked a bit posher than those I usually tried.

Bling! An old-fashioned bell jangled as I opened the door. I watched its vibrations till a woman came out of the back. Her face was stuccoed with make-up, glasses hung on a cord around her neck, and she had about a kilo of old gold on her, rings, chains, and charms. She eyed me suspiciously.

'Yes?'

'Er, I wondered if yer'd like to buy some stuff, like.'

'I might.' She seemed dubious. 'Let's see it, then.'

I tipped the contents of the carrier bag on to one of her antique tables and she clawed through it, briefly.

'Three hundred pounds,' she said.

'Ah, 'ey, be sensible, eh? There's no way I'm takin' less than five.'

She scooped everything back into the bag, shoved it into my hand and steered me towards the door.

'Er, all right.' Her grip on my elbow relaxed. 'Three 'undred, then. Cash.'

She went in the back and returned a minute later with a sheaf of tenners and twenties, pushed it into my hand and bundled me on to the street. When I counted it in a phone box nearby it was exactly right.

'Single to London, please.'

It was a relief to leave Gloucester behind me. As soon as I reached London I headed for Brenda's, but she wasn't in. I jumped immediately to the conclusion that she was away somewhere, though it turned out later that she had only been at the shops. For a time I stood outside her house, looking at her street and thinking of the thousands of streets beyond it. Everyone in London seemed to know where they were going, and their intentness on their aims made me even more of an outsider here than in Liverpool. Though I knew I would probably regret it, I decided to go back home.

One thing I liked about having money in London was taking taxis. It was like being in a film, stopping them with a raised arm and then diving in.

'Paddington, mate.'

When I'd bought shoes, jeans, a pullover and a jacket and booked into a hotel, I went for a few pints to celebrate my success as a Borstal escapee. Next morning they told me the Liverpool trains leave from Euston, so I took a taxi over there and caught one.

Still flush with money, I went up to Smithdown Lane and stayed the night with my dustman friend. Next afternoon I called on Rosie Munro.

'Hiya, Rosie. Just thought I'd come round, like. Sort o' to say I'm sorry about ... Yer know.'

'Oh, don't worry about that, luv.' Her medicine balls backed out of the doorway and she waved me into the room. 'These things 'appen, yer know. D'yer fancy a drop o' somethin' while yer 'ere?'

She had forgiven me in the 'bygones be bygones' way of a veteran wino. As I lifted my cup the door opened and a fat face popped round it.

' "Come raise the goblet now, for yesterday has passed, to-morrow never may be born ... " '

'Oh, hiya, Trev.' My pleasure at seeing the boozy sage was genuine. ''Ow are yer, lar? Look,' I dug into the pocket of my new jeans and extracted a note, 'why don't we get a couple o' bottles, like?'

After that I alternated between staying with the dustman and Rosie. On Christmas Day Brenda arrived, and took me to spend the afternoon with Jake's family up in Rice Lane.

My money was soon gone, and I began to steal again. There was nothing else I could do, and Rosie and the dustman liked me better when I had cash. Often I went out to Formby and broke into houses. There was a derelict garage there next to the council offices, and I made a little den in it from a settee and two armchairs someone had dumped, and started sleeping there sometimes. The place was good for storing my loot, and I hid some spare clothes in a tool cupboard.

My speciality as a burglar was my method of entry. Many kitchen and bathroom windows that cannot be opened have a narrow ventilation flap at the top, held open with a metal bar. People often leave these open, thinking them too small and difficult, or too high up for anyone to climb through. It was through these narrow gaps that I entered my victims' houses.

One typical day was a Sunday. I woke early, crept out of my garage and trod the streets warily, looking for a place to rob. My attention was eventually attracted to a big, detached house with five days' milk on its doorstep. I rang the bell as usual, waited, then paced around to the back. On the first floor there was a bathroom window with its ventilation flap unlocked. Good. After shinning up the drainpipe I leant over and opened it. It was fearfully narrow, and a sickening drop yawned below as I wriggled through, face down. My hips took time to squeeze through and at the last moment I lost my balance and fell headlong, headfirst into the toilet. My trapped legs slowed my fall and I managed to grab the sides of the pan before it broke my neck. My finger was cut and my hair wet with toilet water. I wrapped a towel round the wound and stepped softly down the stairs, dripping blood on to the Axminster.

There was a stereo system and I went first for that, unplugging the speakers and the amplifier. In two minutes I had almost tied myself into a knot with the wires, so I gave up and filled a suitcase with L.P.s instead. In a drawer I found a Cashcard in a plastic envelope, with a paper that gave this warning: 'Always keep this paper separate from your Cashcard in case of loss or theft.' The Cashcard number was on it. With my suitcase of records and some other bits and pieces I left the house by the front door, and went to a park to sort everything out. In my haste I threw away the paper with the vital number on it, and had to go back and chase it over the grass till the wind let me have it.

Southport was the nearest place where I could use the card, and I had no money for the train. I stood outside the station and beyond the view of the ticket office till the train came in, then when the whistle shrieked that it was leaving I pelted through the barrier and jumped on board. It was picking up speed as I slammed the door behind me. There was only one person in the carriage, an old woman. She cackled good-naturedly.

'On'y just made it, eh lad?'

'Er, yeh.' I mopped my brow and rubbed my arm, which had almost been jerked out of its socket by the heavy case.

'Great to be young, eh?' she said.

There was an old ticket on the floor by my seat and I picked it up. The ticket collector at Southport spotted it, though, and gave chase.

'Hey! Hey! Where's yer ticket? Hey, stop!'

The suitcase was nearly tearing my arm off as I ran out of earshot.

Natwest. The machine spat a ten-pound note at me but kept the card. A one-off affair, then. In a pub near the station I met a hustler from my old days in Southport.

'All right, Gazzer? Long time, eh?'

'Yeh.' I gulped at my lager. 'Lissen, are yer interested in some L.P.s?'

He laughed heartily. 'Well, yer've grown a bit, Gazz, but yer 'aven't changed otherwise, 'ave yer?'

He bought the lot for £30. I strolled back to the station and buttonholed the ticket man who had chased me earlier.

'Er, I 'ad no money, pal, so I 'ad to run 'ome an' get it, like.'

He was chuffed. 'Yer the first runner that ever come back to me, son. Twenty-three years I've been doin' this job.' I smiled modestly. His elation subsided when, after settling up with him, I bought a ticket for Liverpool.

'Oh. That's why yer come back, is it? Typical. Bloody typical.'

That night I slept for the last time in Rosie Munro's. The place was such a dosshouse and she was so good at worming money out of me that I left for good, preferring to live on the streets.

A month passed. February 1977. All thoughts of finding a job and a room and trying to blend into society like a normal person had faded from my mind. The daily struggle to find money and keep food in my belly left no time for idle dreams. That kind of life wasn't possible for me. I slept rough more and more often.

One night I was coming home to my garage in Formby when my suspicions were aroused by a car parked nearby. It was so plain, so unmarked, so anonymous that I felt a presentiment about it. Sure enough, when I made as if to turn into the cul-de-sac where my garage was its lights went on, and its engine whirred into life. I was already running. The car was level with me in seconds, its engine screaming. It was so close that I could stare into the face of its driver, a police inspector. A wall appeared in front of me and I half-ran, half-climbed over it.

'We'll have you, Gaskin,' he shouted as I disappeared over the top, 'don't worry about that.'

So they knew who I was. At top speed I traversed the town and pounded along the beach till I reached the spot where Malcolm and I had looked for crabs the first time he came to St Vincent's. The town was now behind me but I continued to run, forcing myself to maintain speed though my legs were dying, my lungs snatching air in desperate gasps. Far beyond the town, when I could run no more, I threw myself into a ditch in a field away from the road. It was five minutes before I recovered enough to stand up, my shirt soaked with perspiration. As I plodded up a hill to survey the land I became aware of the cold again.

The country lanes were dark and quiet, and it was easy to see the two points where police cars were blocking them. Both traps were behind me. They had underestimated me again. Keeping strictly in cover I walked two stations down the line towards Liverpool, a distance of several miles. For the rest of the night I crouched in a railwayman's hut at the line-side, and next morning I caught the first train into the city.

'Hiya, Jake. 'Ow goes it, lar?'

'Can't complain. You?'

'Oh, er survivin'. Scrapin' along.'

Formby had not seen the last of me, though. At the end of February I went back at night and burgled St Vincent's. They had built a block of flatlets at the side for the staff and I entered in my usual way, through a tiny window. A locked door in front of me almost proved a match for my powers. I had to hammer and jemmy at it for ages.

'Jeez!' Bang, thump. 'Give, will yer?' Wrench, bang. 'Bastard.'

In the end I got through, and found myself in a bedroom. It was pitch dark and I had no torch. After some thought I flashed the light on for just one split second, hoping that no one outside would see it and it would give me some idea of the room. It did. I pulled a bag of change from under the bed and left immediately, nervous about my brief splash of light. In a phone box I saw that the bag had '£100' written on it in felt tip. It was a disappointment when I counted the ten- and fifty-pence pieces in the station toilet and they came to only £50.

In this way I managed to survive, like a wolf or a fox, always alert for pursuers, starved for most of the time, gorging myself after a kill. This was the life for which I had been trained, and it was the only life I knew. I was aware, dimly, that to be trapped in such a life was itself a form of imprisonment, and I knew it would put me inside again and again, each time for longer than the time before. Yet I could see no way out.

Things went on this way until the middle of March. At four forty-five one afternoon I broke into the St Something's Parishioners' Club in Edge Lane. The place had nothing really to do with the church, but was just a boozing joint like many others. The wall around the car park in the front was not high enough to hide me from prying eyes across the road, but hunger and cold drove me to take the risk.

SMASHHHCLANNNG! A jangle of kicked shards, and I was in. There was a payphone there so I headed first for that, as they are easy to open. This one soon gave in to a combined can-opener and steel comb. Working with feverish haste, I poured coins into my pockets and got out, trembling, not stopping to pick up the money I had dropped. No bell had gone off, but though I was sad at leaving the cash in the juke box and pool table it was near opening time, and I feared the barmaids' arrival. When I counted my haul later it came to only £12.

'A pint o' lager, please mate, an' three o' them steak an' kidney pies.'

'Three? Did yer say three?'

'Yeh.'

'Growin' lad, eh?'

'Just give us 'em, will yer?'

At midnight I was back in Edge Lane to collect what I'd left behind. The broken window had been boarded up but the flimsy plywood soon yielded to my boot. My first target was the cashbox in the cigarette machine. Five minutes' wrenching convinced me that it was thief-proof, so I smashed the glass and started to take out the fags. To get a more direct angle of work, I moved my foot.

DRRRIIINN-NN-NNN-NNNN-NNNNG! The alarm bell yelled one long, shrill, piercing note like a person in sustained agony. In the afternoon I had either been lucky, or the alarm system had been switched off because it was near opening time. Now I had trodden a pressure-pad under the beer-slopped carpet. Grabbing as many cigarettes as I could without a bag, I shot through the fire door and over the wall into the garden of the place next door, an Old Folks' Home. When I had stashed my haul in a bush I ran back to the wall and looked over. High on adrenalin, I felt invincible, vulnerable, terrified and daring. Perhaps wanting more danger, perhaps to be gripped in society's fist, I ran into the club again, tore my jacket off, laid it on the floor and cascaded a river of fags into it. Gasping, desperate, my heart hammering as fast as the yelling alarm, I cleared the wall to safety only seconds before a police car swerved into the club driveway, its doors flying open as it screeched to a halt. For five minutes I lay trembling in the wet grass, then I hid the fags with the others and made my escape. That night I slept in a hut on some nearby allotments. When I went back next morning for my cigarettes they had gone.

8 | *Resistance*

For the rest of that day I wandered about in town, had a meal in Lewis's cafeteria and a few pints in the pubs by the Pier Head. At eleven o'clock I caught a bus to Old Swan and slept in a lorry parked near my Dad's building firm. The following night I went back there, but at two in the morning the cold woke me. Moving only to keep warm, I walked along Prescot Road and stopped outside the Police Social Club. Those bastards. How I hated them. If I could crack that place it would hurt them and be some kind of gesture against them, if only because it made people laugh. More than anything else, though, it was the cold that made me try it. The building was flat-roofed and I shinned up a drainpipe on to it.

From the top I could see yellow-lit highways and street after street of houses, all with people tucked up in bed inside them, warm, relaxed, snoring. Why wasn't this possible for me? There were plastic skylights every few metres across, and I kicked at one till it came away and I could pull it open. There was a fridge underneath and I dropped on to it, knocking something over as I landed. When my feet touched the floor I found I was in a kitchen, standing next to a huge broken jar of treacle.

I made a point of treading both feet into it to spread the mess over the plush carpets in the bar. All the time I was thinking, I'm goin' to be caught 'ere, why am I doing this? Standing nervously on the threshold of the lounge, I looked in. Little red bulbs were burning silently high in the ceiling, filling the place with an eerie glow to make you visible from outside. The room looked alive with alarms. The gadget-crazed police knew people hated them and would love to hit at them. They would have to be mad not to have their own club super-bugged.

'Payphone first, then the machines.'

My words dropped into the air like corpses into a mass grave. If I had time later I might rip the protective grille from the bar and get a few bottles. As it was I was less than halfway across the floor when a panda swept into the drive at the front, its headlights on and its blue light flashing. Probably I had tripped an alarm as soon as I kicked the fanlight. A cop climbed out of the car, turned a flashlight on and started to circle the building, examining windows. I stood block-still behind a post, out of sight. As soon as his light reached the frosted kitchen window I rocketed in there, climbed with treacled feet through the sharded fanlight, and raced across the roof.

Two cars pulled up as I ran, and all their occupants saw me. I dropped to the ground at the back of the building, then raced through undergrowth to the street. As I reached the pavement a panda came hurtling along and stopped just by me. I ran back through the sparse trees and nearly collided with a cop. He was an arm's length away as I halted my run, but was staring along the street and didn't see me. This gave me a chance to jump a fence into a front garden. Leaping over fences and racing across walls like an Olympic hurdler, I crossed as many gardens as was possible before they closed in. The crackle of radios and the incessant blue flashes alerted people to the excitement, and lights were switched on, windows nosily opened. In the third or fourth garden along I tried to climb into a bin, ridiculous the straws fear makes you clutch at, but it was full and too small and impossible anyway, so I had to hide behind it. Police were crashing all around me and I could see their dark forms lit in the intermittent flashes which seared the walls, lawns and trees. After a minute a cop, the same one who had failed to see me earlier, stumbled on to me.

'Got yer, lad. Don't try anythin'.'

He wrenched my arm up my back with socket-popping force and grabbed my collar. A button shot away and landed 'ping' on the binlid as he forced my head down.

'What the 'ell's goin' on?' I was half strangled. 'What 'ave I done? What am I s'posed to 'ave done, like?'

There were two more there by that time and they pushed me against a wall and began a contemptuous search of my person, tearing my shirt to look inside and leaving the lining of my pockets hanging out. I was wearing two pairs of trousers because of the cold, and they pulled the outer ones down to my ankles so I couldn't run away, then made me walk to the van like that. They hooted with laughter as I shuffled along.

'What's up, son? Shit yer pants?'

'Must 'ave been when he saw us comin', Bill!'

Guffaws.

'Look, I on'y went in that garden to sleep, mate.'

They laughed at me then, and gave me stick all the way to the station.

'Little cunt.'

'Shithouse.'

'Screw our club, would yer?' Jab, poke. 'That's where I take me WIFE. Little bastard.'

The C.I.D. questioned me, put me in a cell, took me out and questioned me again.

'I dunno what yer on about,' I protested. 'Honest. I was just sleepin' in that garden because I 'ad no place to go.'

'Where's your mates? Who was with you?'

It was the usual thing, and I was used to it by now. Eventually they found out I was a Borstal escapee, charged me with doing the club, and took me to Formby.

'They can't wait to meet you out there,' the detective laughed as a uniformed cop snapped me into handcuffs.

'Hmm.' The Formby cop looked through his list of recent break-ins. 'Here's another Unsolved, St Vincent's.' He read a little further, then looked at me the way fools do when they think they're being clever. 'No, that wouldn't be you. Not your M.O.'

'Not me what?'

'Your *modus operandi*, lad. Bit o' Latin. Means your style.'

Other places I'd done were mentioned, but all they got me for was the big house where I found the Cashcard.

Liverpool magistrates could not send me to Risley because I was convicted, so they sent me to Walton Jail, my first time in there. There were a couple of cells underground on the first floor, the Ones on B-wing where the Y.P.s are housed, put aside for Borstal boys passing through, and they gave me one. I worked on the servery, right outside my cell. My feelings about being back inside were mixed. It hadn't been easy living on the run, but I found the life in prison as stifling as ever. When I thought of the new court case that was looming, and the three-year Y.P. sentence I would probably get, fear saturated me. Otherwise I was more or less numb, and settled into a sullen acceptance of my situation. There was nothing else to do, anyway.

One day I was called up for a Special Visit, and found three Gloucestershire C.I.D. men waiting to see me.

'Hello, Graham.' They always use your first name like that, without even knowing you. 'We've come to see you about some gold coins and other property stolen from a Mr Malcolm Bishop ... '

They let me read Malcolm's statement, as they are obliged to, and I saw that there were no lies whatever in it. On the other hand, there were so many glaring omissions that even the detectives sensed there was something wrong. They seemed, for once, to have little confidence in their case. He said that I'd turned up on his doorstep on 14th December, the day he had driven me down from Henley. He told them about the judo contests and my subsequent disappearance, but gave no hint as to our real relationship. They started asking me questions.

'Er, no, sorry mate.' I stood up and motioned through the window to the screw in the corridor outside. 'I don't know nothin' about no gear bein' stolen.' The screw unlocked the door to let me out. 'The visit's over,' I told him.

They never came back.

One day an unexpected letter and parcel of books arrived from Fritz, my Communist pal. He was out now, and by writing to different places had traced me to Walton. It was good to know someone out there cared and I wrote back, and even read some of the left wing books. The same day they caught me with stolen milk in my cell and booted me off the servery into a cell on the Fours. A few days afterwards something happened which seemed insignificant at first, but which was to shake me out of my numb state and give me something to fight for again. As it went on it would escalate into war between the prison author-ities and myself. The trouble came, as usual, without a hint of warning.

My lawyer had been to see me, and I was crossing the yard on my way back to the wing with two screws for company. The solicitor had been pessimistic about what sentence I should expect and I was disconsolate, my hands shoved resignedly into my pockets, my shoes scuffing the concrete, my shoulders hunched. As we neared the wing two screws came out of it, a big fellow with a reputation for brutality in the nick and a little chap who had to wear thick-soled boots to reach the minimum height for the service. He wore them still, earning himself the nickname of Boots. As they drew level this pigmy barked in a bright, stentorian voice:

'Hands out o' pockets, lad.'

As if things weren't bad enough, here was another irritation to endure. I ignored him.

'YOU!' All four screws stopped in their tracks, and so did I. I looked palely at Boots. 'Get them HANDS out,' he said.

'What the fuck?' My nerves were jangling. 'Yer not even with us, are yer? Why don't yer just leave us alone, an' do whatever yer s'posed to be doin'?'

He stepped forward, livid with anger. His words seethed like a bucket of wasps. 'Don't be bloody cheeky. Now get them fuckin' hands out. Right NOW!'

His anger was out of proportion to the incident, yet my own grew to meet it. 'Yer not even with us,' I said again. 'Let these officers get on with what they're doin'.'

He stepped nearer still. 'You little bastard.'

'Don't call me bastard,' I said unhesitatingly. 'Cunt.'

He was so close now that I could see his cheeks, which were blue with five o'clock shadow, trembling with rage. In a flash I knew he was going to hit me, so I grabbed his shoulders and thrust my face up to his.

'Don't fuckin' try it, mate,' my body tingled on the edge of action, 'cos I'll fuckin' BURST yer. Tell yer what ... me name's

Gaskin, GASKIN! I'm on the Fours, number twelve, pay me a call when yer feel SUICIDAL!'

At times in this speech I was screaming. The two escorting screws grabbed me from behind, and Boots clutched my sleeve and led the procession into the wing. The big screw did not move, but stood there watching. They hauled me up to where the P.O. was standing at his desk.

'This one's nicked, sir.'

Next morning they took me out of my cell and put me in the Block, which was down on the Ones again, at the far end. The Governor told me I was charged with assaulting the little screw and would have to go up in front of the Visiting Committee, the magistrates who visit the prison to deal with offences too serious for the internal disciplinary machine to handle. The V.C. sat the same afternoon.

'What do you say to this charge, Gaskin?'

'I'm not guilty.'

Boots came in and gave an account of how I'd launched an unprovoked attack on him, pushing him violently and trying to punch him until restrained by other officers. The V.C. sat there bored stiff, not appearing to listen. Their spokesman looked at me remotely over half-moon glasses.

'Do you know where you are, Gaskin?' I didn't bother to answer. His mouth fluttered like a trapped moth. 'Prison.' He pronounced the word with relish, trilling the 'r'. 'We find you guilty of this charge,' he went on, 'and let me tell you that attacks of this kind will not be tolerated. You will be severely punished. Twenty-eight days' restricted location ... ' that meant the Block, 'twenty-eight days' loss of privileges and a recommended loss of thirty days' remission. Take him out.'

Loss of privileges meant I would not be able to spend my weekly allowance, and therefore smoke, but the recommendation that I lose thirty days was more or less meaningless. Only the Borstal authority had the power to assign me a release date. It would have made no difference to me if the recommendation had been a direct loss of time. With the possibility of a three-year Y.P. sentence hanging over me, the loss of a month wouldn't have worried me.

So it was back to the Block. They took your bed and bed-clothes out all day to stop you getting comfortable, and none of the lads outside was able to pass you a fag. There was another

door, locked and with no spyhole, a foot or so in front of the cell
door to make communication impossible. The cell had a rough
brick floor and a hard board for a bed. On the other side of the
landing there were cells for the Beasts, the sex cases and in-
formers on Rule 43. These cells had only one door so the Beasts
were better off. The only time you came out of the Block cell
was to get your food, slop out, or have your hour's exercise.
Even here they cheated you. Often the screw would open the
outer door and say:

'No exercise today, Gaskin.'

'Why not?'

'Rain.'

I'd look out of the window. Though the sky was depressingly
grey as usual, no rain was actually falling.

'Rain? There ain't no rain.'

From beyond the two doors, silence. The screw had gone.

When you did go on exercise you were not allowed to talk to
the other Block lads but had to walk round alone, so many
metres apart from your neighbour.

On my second afternoon they unlocked me to slop out. I had
returned to my emotional numbness by then, and didn't really
care where I was so long as they left me alone. The Twos and
Threes were slopping out half a landing at a time above me as
I walked, quickly with my brimming pisspot, to the recess and
emptied it down the hole, turning my head to one side to avoid
the stench as I did so. I washed the pot with lashings of cold
water, though this never seemed to do anything for the smell,
then took a piss. As I was buttoning my flies I heard a sound
behind me, and spun round. The big screw who had been on
the yard that day was standing right behind me, and grasped
me by the throat.

'Ooh,' he said. 'I'd love to do you, lad.'

When another screw appeared outside fear ran through me.
I wrenched myself free of the big one's grip.

'What the fuck are yer doin', man?'

My shout died on the cold tiles. The second screw sauntered
in, turning a tap on as he passed it. The water poured hard and
loud, booming into the metal sink with a deafening crash. It
seemed that the choice was mine. I could be their passive victim
if I wished.

'Fuck OFF!'

As my shout raged I took the big screw by his tunic and flung him crashing against the urinal wall, then ran to the far side of the recess where a mop was standing. I snatched it up quickly, ran back to the still tottering screw, and brought it down savagely once, twice, three times on his head, splintering the handle. This took only seconds. The other screw came at me and I threw the remains of the mop into his face. One of them pressed the riot bell and its pandemonium began screaming. As I hurtled on to the landing another screw, Murphy, came charging out of the office a few cells down from the recess, looking for the trouble. My steel dinner tray was still lying outside my cell and I sent it crashing and skimming along the floor, hoping to trip him up. It thumped against his toes and hurt them badly, as he told the Visiting Committee later. He was off work for two weeks.

With the first screws pounding hard on my heels I raced along the Ones and flew up the stairs to the Twos, the ground floor level in Walton. A P.O. tried to bar my way at the top and I booted him with ruthless accuracy in the balls. He collapsed like a pile of plastic bricks hit by a cannonball. All the lads upstairs were cheering now, clapping and stamping and banging steel trays, shouting tumultuous support. The din was terrific, and screws were running from all directions and spilling into the wing from the gate at the end. I ran along the wire-sided passageway which runs down the wing centre with half the screws breathing down my neck and the rest rushing at me from the front, brandishing rabid sticks. When the crash came I dived on the first and hit him with all my strength and anger. Punches and kicks jarred into me from all sides and a forearm closed my windpipe. A minute later, still struggling, I passed out.

When I awoke I was on the floor of my cell. My shirt was off, my overalls and underpants were at my ankles, and they had thrown vast quantities of water over me. After a long time they came in, took my blankets without a word, and went out again. They did not come back. The sound of the Beasts and the other Block lads getting their food came faintly through my two doors, but they did not bring any to me. Through my little window I saw the lights of the prison go out. Mine was left on.

For a time there were shouted conversations through the windows. Later there was only the odd call from an insomniac here and there until the whole prison went gradually quiet.

Total silence followed. Cold, wet, bored and angry, I slid the rubber mattress out of its case and laid myself upon it on the floor. It seemed that they were determined to try to humiliate me. Okay, let them try. I would show them what manner of man they were pushing. After a time I began picking little lumps from the mattress, and throwing them over my shoulder. Pick, pick. Pick, pick, pick. Pick. In a couple of hours it was in pieces around me. I sat cross-legged and pushed them together in a heap, then started again from the beginning, tearing each little piece in half and throwing the bits behind me. The night passed, and a grey light filtered into the dirty yellow cast by my electric bulb. When the first eye appeared at my spyhole in the morning I was sitting in a great heap of the stuff. The door opened.

'Yer never brought me blankets,' I said softly. 'Now fuck off.'

He closed the door without a word. Ten minutes later he was back, with another screw.

'Breakfast, Gaskin.'

'I don't want any.' They put the tray on the floor and slid it over. 'Don't fuckin' put it in 'ere.' I picked it up to put it outside again but they had shut the door, so I hurled it against the wall and left it where it fell.

During the afternoon I dozed off on the cold floor, uncomfortable in body but more content in mind now that I had begun to use a new weapon. That night they moved me to a different cell. This time they didn't give me anything, not even a mattress, so I just lay on the floor till morning.

'Breakfast, Gaskin.'

'Fuck off.' I shoved the tray with my foot and the food slopped on to the landing. 'I told yer, I don't want any.'

Later in the morning the Governor came down. I didn't stand up, just lay there looking at him.

'What's wrong with you?' he demanded.

No answer.

'You'll have to buck your ideas up, Gaskin, or you'll never get out of here.' He looked at me coldly. 'D'you understand? Never.'

Still no answer.

'You'll lose remission,' he said.

Only the Borstal could lose me time. Anyway, I still hadn't been up for the burglaries I'd done while on the run, so what was the point in worrying? For two more days I didn't eat. I dozed for most of the time, kept very still when awake, and lay for hours thoughtfully stroking the rough bricks in front of me. The Borstal I had yet to finish and the unknown sentence I had still to get caused me anguish when I thought about them. If I had stuck it out at Finnimore Wood I probably would have been due for release by now. What the hell. It was too late to do anything about that. Probably it had always been too late for me, with the breaks I had had. One thing was certain, my spirit was still strong. I would resist every effort they made to break it.

At the end of the first day they silently put a mattress in my cell, on the morning of the second they put blankets in and left them there all day, though you're not allowed them on the Block. On the third day, when I started to eat, I found that they gave me better food than before and more of it. Violence worked, then.

The magistrate's half-moon glasses shone as he lifted his eyes from the papers in front of him, and stared at me unfeelingly. I stared fearlessly into his faraway eyes as he spoke.

'My words last time had no effect, then, Gaskin?' Silence. 'You will be kept on restricted location for twenty-eight days on each charge, up to the maximum of fixty-six days. We recommend a loss of thirty days' remission for each charge of assault. On the charges of malicious damage ... '

In all, he recommended a loss of ten months' remission. At this rate the Governor would be right. I'd never get out.

Though I was still on the Block, life was easier. Lads left roll-ups and matches in the recess for me, and though the screws must have known about it they turned a blind eye. One screw was good to me.

'Pssst!'

When I looked up a single cigarette and match would spill through the spyhole and fall to the floor. By the time I reached them the outer door would be closed. Neither of us ever mentioned it. He lives in Walton, and when I see him outside I always let on.

An Irish screw used to turn my cell over for home-made weapons, but otherwise I was left in peace. At such times I'd read or merely stare at the walls, thinking. What did they think I was, locking me away like this all the time? As far as I was concerned my whole life had been spent in prison, I was seventeen and had done the equivalent of two life sentences. When outrage overcame me I'd stand in the middle of my cell flexing my muscles, taking deep breaths, spoiling for a fight.

Kick, slam. Kick, slam. Kick, slam. 'Gimme some books! Gimme some books! Gimme some books!'

The steel door took my blows till the outer one opened.

'What, Gaskin? Books? Okay, don't get your knickers in a knot.'

They brought me some then, including some new ones from Fritz. At other times they were less amenable. Whenever they showed any intransigence I smashed up, immediately, completely. The Governor dealt with these incidents and we came to know one another well.

' . . . and a recommended loss of seven days' remission. Take him away.'

Two screws walked me back to the Block and opened my cell.

'Er, can I go for a book, boss?'

'Where to, Gaskin?'

'The servery lad's cell at the end.'

'No,' the other said, 'you can't.'

That morning I had taken the clothes-rail from my locker and hidden it in my bed. Now I pulled it out and charged at them, yelling. They rushed out of my cell and slammed the door. A mouth appeared at the spyhole.

'Silly little bleeder. You'll get hurt if you carry on like this.'

'Bastard!'

I spat at the disappearing mouth and the closing outer door, then stood banging the steel and screaming through the spyhole for a long time, perhaps four hours. Every time one of them went past I'd let fly afresh.

'Come IN, come IN, come in 'ERE, come in 'ERE!' Bang!Bang!Bang! 'I'll smash yer to BITS!'

In the end they brought the doctor, a woman.

'What's all this about, Gaskin?' There were three screws with her, and they stood around the cell with their arms folded, watching. 'Here, drink this.' She put a little plastic cup in my hand. Largactyl. 'It'll calm you down.'

When they had gone I turned in and was soon in a deep, drugged sleep. Next day they gave me everything I asked for. It was all or nothing for me now. Since there was no way I could get out of the prison and enjoy liberty I concentrated everything upon the defence of my inner freedom. If they tried to take away even one tiny privilege they could have the lot, I would smash up, beat up, let my anger uncivilize me and attack them, fearlessly.

It was a morning in the middle of May, when I had been in Walton for about eight weeks. A key clattered into the lock. The tumblers clicked into their places and the door swung open.

'Gaskin?' I nodded. He ticked a sheet of paper. 'Liverpool Crown today, come on.'

They took me down early, before the normal prisoners who were going out or to court that day, and except for some screws Reception was empty. A little screw, one of the type who always meant trouble for me, led me past the sweatboxes where prisoners are left to await their escort and stopped at a beast box at the far end of Reception. This is a square steel box with a bench fixed inside, where they put the Beasts out of harm's way. He unlocked it.

'In there, Gaskin.'

'No.' My voice was quiet and sure. 'I'm not goin' in there. That's for Beasts.'

He poked me in the chest. 'Go on. Get in.'

'No.'

Another, harder poke. 'Move it, Gaskin. Into that box.'

He poked me again and that nudged me into action. BANG! My fist slammed hammer hard into his nose, spreading it over half his face. He lay at my feet, splattered. A second screw raced over from the far side and I dived on to him as he came, put an unbreakable headlock on to him and flung him across a table with me on top. We crashed over it and fell through a chair to the floor. They ran in then from everywhere to the tune of the shrieking bells. Though I was pulled, dragged, punched, kicked and baton-smacked I held on to this unknown, hated screw, slamming blow after blow into him. It was just like a street fight to me. When they overpowered me, two held my arms while a third drove punches into my stomach. The pain floored me, my guts writhed and I tried to force a vomit to make them stop but deep down, really deep down, I didn't give a toss. Not for them, their court, their red-robed judge, their stinking prison or anything else. When they had finished they flung me into the beast box and I lay there gasping. In five minutes I had recovered enough to mount a drum-roll of thumps and kicks on the door.

'I wanna doctor! I wanna doctor! I wanna doctor!'

Fifteen minutes later the key turned in the lock. One of the doctors was standing outside.

'What's all this?' he snapped in his best cellside manner.

'Look, doctor. Look at these bruises.'

I took my shirt off and showed him the new red marks which now overlaid the old black, blue and yellowing ones. Walton's doctors seemed to be short-sighted when it came to bruises, and this one was no exception.

'Where?' He brought his eyes forward till they were centimetres from the most livid bruise. 'I can't see anything. There's nothing wrong with you.'

I longed to slam my fist into his face too.

At the court I was lucky.

'You're already doing a Borstal sentence, and in spite of your escape from custody and the offences you committed while at liberty I want to give that sentence a chance to work. For this reason I'm sending you for a new term in Borstal, the sentence to run concurrently with the one you are already serving. Take him down.'

This was the best outcome I could have hoped for. When they took me back to Walton they put me straight into the Block. The prospect of doing another Borstal, this time definitely in a secure prison like Hindley, was a daunting one, yet it had to be done. At the same time I was still in a war situation with the prison authority, and felt as determined as ever not to concede one millimetre of my pride. Freedom seemed so far in the future that I quickly forgot about it, and concentrated instead on events as they happened.

Next afternoon, another Visiting Committee. The eyes behind the half-moon glasses watched me coldly, like a biologist's examining a new specimen.

'Twenty-eight days' restricted location, twenty-eight days' loss of privileges, and a recommended loss of sixty days' remission. We don't want to see you in front of us again, Gaskin. Understand?'

The corners of my mouth turned down, and I shrugged. The screws who took me to the Block tried to revert to the original regime.

'Right, blankets out, Gaskin. And the mattress.'

'Take 'em yerselves if yer want 'em.'

They did, and gave a thorough search. 'Where did you get this tobacco?'

When I said nothing they flung it on to the landing and went out, slamming the door locked. Time passed. Eventually the doors opened again and a screw stood there with my steel meal tray.

'Here's your tea, Gaskin.'

'Yeh?' My body blocked the doorway. 'Try shovin' it up yer arse'ole, pal.'

The screw who opened me up next morning put my blankets and mattress in first, without a word. Only then did he bring my breakfast. I took it.

A few days later they decided to move me to Strangeways. This time when they put me into the beast box on Reception I did not resist. I had been staring at the metal walls for half an hour when I heard activity outside.

'Beast!' BANG! 'Beast!' BANG! 'Beast!' BANG!

'An-im-al!' THUMP!THUMP!THUMP!

'Monster!' BANG!BANG!BANG! 'Monster!' BANG!BANG!BANG!

The kicks and thumps of the guys outside crashed in my ears, deafening in the confined space of the box.

'I'm not a beast,' I growled, 'I'm on the Block.'

There was a pause.

'It must be that blond feller,' said a voice. Papers rustled, a matchbox rattled, and some roll-ups and loose matches were pushed under the door.

' 'Ere y'are, kid.'

'Ta, lads.'

At Strangeways they took me straight through the wing and into the Block.

'Mattress and blankets outside, lad.'

Fair enough, for the present at any rate. They banged the door shut and I sat on the floor, staring at walls. Half an hour later they were back.

'You're to see the Governor, Gaskin.'

The ugliest man I've ever seen sat with his hands flat on the desk in front of him. One ear was half eaten away and he seemed to have scales rather than skin. I heard later he'd been badly burned in the course of some heroic action during the war. He put his finger on a word in my file and looked up.

'Gaskin.' His lips were slack, his teeth yellow. 'I see you've been on the Block for a long time in Liverpool. This is a different prison, not connected in any way with Walton, so I've decided to take you out and let you make a fresh start. I'm putting you on Rule 43b.'

That was a joke. Rule 43b is where they put you 'in the interests of the good order and discipline of the prison'. It's how they take you out of the prison population when you haven't committed an offence, and it's the same as the Block except that it's easier. You have your mattress and blankets in the cell all day and you're allowed to smoke.

'All right, Governor.'

The Rule 43b cells were in the same row as the Block, and once I was in mine I had a good think about my predicament. Perhaps it was time for me to get back on the wing, where I could try to settle down and get a release date. I was still determined not to sacrifice an iota of self-esteem but perhaps the prison authorities, stupid though they were, had learned that by now. After a while I banged on the door until an eye appeared at the spyhole.

'I'm now on official 'unger strike,' I told it. 'I'm not eatin' nothin' till I'm put back on normal location. Right?'

To make sure my protest was recognized I put in a written application for normal location to the Governor that day, and one on every consecutive day of my protest. This is one of your rights in prison. He ignored them all, and in spite of the applications ignored my hunger strike too for the first three days. By the seventh day my head was light, dizziness struck me when I tried to stand, and for most of the time I slept lightly, having many peculiar dreams. I had almost forgotten I was on hunger strike, and the idea of food did not bother me. In mid-afternoon they opened me up unexpectedly.

'The doctor's here to see you, Gaskin,' the screw said.

My head lolled towards him. 'Yeh? What for, like?'

'It's a rule. You've been on hunger strike four days.'

'Huh. Yer never won no maths prizes at school, did yer?'

The doctor spoke in that stern, superior, medical way. 'Carry on like this and you'll do yourself permanent physical damage,' he said at the end, 'you realize that, do you?'

'Yeh, doctor, but I've got to stick up for me rights. I'm not givin' in this time, even if I 'ave to die.'

I turned away with an effort, and stared at the wall.

Later the Governor came to my cell with his full retinue of Chief, two P.O.s, and a medic in a white jacket. As I've said, he was the most repellent-looking person I've ever had to meet. With his unhealthy skin and mangy ear he looked like a terminal case of skin cancer. When the medical screw had helped me to my feet the Governor put his infernal face next to mine.

'You'll go out of here in a wooden box if you carry on like this,' he said, his breath stinking like a sick dog's.

I moved away from the stench. 'Fair enough, Governor.'

They stood looking at me.

'You'd better start eating, lad,' the Governor said.

'I'll do that, Governor ... ' they brightened up when I said this, 'when I'm put back on normal location.'

This deflated them and they went out, muttering. An hour later a different P.O. opened me up.

'Eat your dinner, Gaskin. You're going on the wing.'

Strangely, I didn't enjoy the food. I even left some. As soon as I finished they put me on H-wing in the first cell on H2, next door to the office. On Monday they took me to the Canteen for my pay, which, since I hadn't been sentenced to loss of earnings but merely prevented from spending them, had been mounting up while I was on the Block. I found I had six quid to spend and bought sweets, shampoo, soap, chocolate bars and tobacco. It was good to be able to mix with the other lads again. Later that week the wing P.O. sent for me.

'You're going to Wormwood Scrubs on Tuesday, Gaskin.'

That was all right. The more moving I did the better it broke up my time. When Tuesday came I was sent up to London with a busload of others, most of whom seemed to be homosexual.

'Can I sit with you, Blondie?'

'No. Piss off.'

We stopped at Winson Green prison in Birmingham for dinner, then sped down the M1 to London. It was strange to look at the world again and to watch people doing ordinary things, coming out of shops or waiting for buses. It seemed to come so naturally to them, yet it wasn't even possible for me. In the Scrubs they put me on the Ones in B-wing, where it would be easy to watch me. After three days another batch of Communist books and magazines arrived from Fritz. Three days later, to my surprise, they put me on a bus to Huntercombe.

'Hey,' the kid next to me said as we rolled along, 'look at that.'

'What?'

'That. It's a whatsit, innit? A thingie.'

'A regatta.'

'Yeh, that's it. A regatta.'

'So fuckin' what, like?'

It was now July 1977, and Wimbledon was in full swing on the radio in Reception when we arrived. For some reason I didn't bring Fritz's books through with me, but left them in my property. They put us on C-wing, then took us for our interviews with the Governor. My days of standing rigidly at attention were over. I watched him ironically with my head to one side, my lips pursed.

'Ah, Gaskin. So you decided to come back to us, did you?' He tamped his pipe triumphantly. 'Thought you might. Well, you've ruined your chances of bettering yourself in Borstal, so you're stuck here till we decide you're fit for release.' He softened, looked at me in a reasonably human way, and glanced at my file. 'You've been given a concurrent sentence, I see.'

At this point I did straighten up. 'Yeh. Look, Governor, I've done four months since they captured me for that offence. That time should count off me sentence, reelly.'

'Hmm.' He nodded like one of those toy dogs with its head on a spring that people keep in their cars. 'What we'll do is give you an E.D.R. six months three days from the date you got your concurrent sentence. That's the minimum we can give you, so watch your step and stay out of trouble. All right?'

That was fair. It meant I had under five months left.

'Right, Governor.'

'And Gaskin ... ' he said as I turned to go.

'Uh?'

'Try and settle down, will you?'

Three days passed before I remembered my books, and made an application to have them out of my property. Nothing happened. Another day went by, and next morning I went up to the P.O. outside the wing office.

'Er, I've 'ad no reply to me application about me books. Do I get 'em, or what?'

He put his hands behind his back and lifted himself pompously on to his toes a few times.

'No,' he said. 'Your application's been turned down.'

'Right.'

Anger at this attack on my rights gushed through me, making me feel as I had before my tantrums at New Heys. I pulled my cell door to and stood looking at the things there. They were not my things. I took a deep, deep breath to spread the adrenalin through me, picked up a chair, roared savagely, and laid into them. In less than a minute everything in there was smashed to bits, including the large windows which were an unusual and supposedly humane feature of the Huntercombe cells. Then I came out, banging the door behind me. Four or five screws pounded along the landing.

'What? What was it? What was that?'

'Er, it's okay,' I said. 'Cool it. It was on'y me smashin' me cell up, nothin' out o' the ordinary, like.'

They whizzed me straight into the Block, which was on the Ones.

'I want me BOOKS! I want me BOOKS! I want me BOOKS!' I hammered and sang till the whole wing knew. After an hour the door opened.

'Here you are, Gaskin.'

The screw threw in a few thrillers and Westerns and closed the door before I could throw them at him.

Next morning they took me back to Wormwood Scrubs in a taxi.

'Gaskin again? Put him on the Fours.'

There was another lad in my cell, and I wasn't even on punishment. As I accustomed myself to the routine it began to seem possible that I might do my time without further trouble. A week later they called me up for Allocation.

'You've been re-allocated, Gaskin.' Silence. 'Aren't you going to ask where? Just to give me a bit of job satisfaction for doing all this work?' He motioned to the contents of my file, which were strewn over his desk.

'Where?' I asked.

'Feltham.'

'Feltham? *Feltham?* But that's for nutters!'

The allocation screw nodded, smiling. 'That's right, Gaskin.'

Back in my cell I threw myself despairingly on to the bed. Feltham. I remembered the square building squatting behind its high fence, a threatening place of straitjackets and padded cells. Why couldn't they just leave me here? One thing was certain. I would resist.

The guy in the cell next to mine was a crazy, half-Spanish kid called Sasportas. He was scheduled for return to Feltham, having been kicked out of there once after a one-man riot. He had climbed on to a roof and rained slates on the screws for a few hours, watched by the Press and T.V.

'Sas,' I suggested the same day, 'they're on about sendin' *me* to Feltham now. What d'yer say about a demonstration?'

His eyes blazed at the prospect of action. 'All right, Scouse. I'm into it. What shall we do?'

'Take me cell-mate 'ostage, like, an' threaten to do 'im in.'

Sas laughed. The idea was right up his crazy street. 'Okay, Scouse, yer on. It sounds like a good 'un to me.'

My cellmate was all right so we told him the plan. He even agreed to co-operate. We smuggled water and bread into the cell to keep us alive for as long as it might take, and stole brush-handle clubs from the cleaner's cell at the end of the landing. Then we got our dinners and sat down to wait, having decided to take our hostage at afternoon slop-out. In the meantime something went wrong. After dinner a key rasped in the lock. The door opened.

'Right, Meredith,' the screw said. 'Visit.'

'Today?' The lad was surprised. He looked at me meaningfully as he went out. 'I'll see yer *later*, Scouse.'

When we were opened for slop-out Sas charged along to my cell. After a minute's talk we decided to carry on with the demo, and rushed into my cell and slammed the door, then jammed the metal beds end-to-end along it. They fitted exactly, vice-tight, making the door effectively unopenable. We piled lockers, chairs and other junk on the end by the door, and waited.

Sas had his eye to the spyhole.

'Hey!' he hissed. 'One's comin'.'

'Yeh? 'As he seen us?'

'Think so. 'Ang on. No. No, he's gone past.'

We sat there for an hour feeling impatient and rather silly. The more we talked the more convinced did I become that Sas really *was* mad. Not that I mustn't have often seemed so in those days. Eventually, when we had given up looking and were sitting on the beds leafing through some *Penthouse* magazines, we heard activity outside. They had finally seen us. A mouth appeared at the spyhole, its lips jerking like a clam with convulsions.

'What do you think you're up to, you pair of little pricks? Open this door.'

'We're not prepared to negotiate with you,' Sas said. 'Fetch us a senior screw.'

'I'll negotiate your bollocks up your arse and down through your bloody nose if you don't open that fucking door,' said the screw.

After him another one came, then a P.O.

'We want yer to lissen to our demands,' I told him.

'Demands? What are you on about, Gaskin? What demands?'

'That you don't send us to Feltham,' I replied. 'It's for nutters.'

He looked at me through the spyhole, sagely. I realized they would be even more convinced of my lunacy now. It was too late to do anything about it, though. There was no alternative but to carry on.

Sas was at the spyhole when the Governor came.

'You get out of my way,' I heard him say, 'I want Gaskin. At least he's not completely off his rocker.'

'Fuck off! Fuck off! Fuck off!' Sas screamed, trying to spit through the little aperture.

' 'Ang on a minute, Sas.' I put my hand on his shoulder, and felt it tense like a hawser under strain. 'If he wants to talk I'd better 'ave a word.'

He moved out of the way and I peered through the circular hole. The Governor was standing outside, arms folded, lips clamped tight together.

'This is stupid, Gaskin. You must see that. Come out peaceably while you still can, before everything gets worse.'

'I'm not goin' to Feltham,' I said.

'Yes you are, and this little escapade makes it even more certain. So get used to the idea, and start listening to reason.' He made some promises. 'If you come out now I'll stay here and make sure you're treated decently. I'll even tell the V.C. you showed common sense, and that'll make them easier on you.'

'Look,' I said, my image of the place crouched still and threatening in my memory, 'I'm not goin' there. That's all I want to talk about.'

He gave up then and walked away.

The cell doors on either side of a prison landing never face one another directly, there is a solid stretch of wall opposite each one. This is done with a purpose. It is for the jack. They have this big jack that reaches from one side of the wing to the other, and with it they can push down anything you can put up. Now, Sas and I took turns watching them get it ready. Four screws started to turn the giant handle, and in a little while the door gave its first creak.

'Right,' Sas said immediately, 'we'll burn the fuckin' place up.'

He set to work smashing up lockers and chairs, and tearing paper. As he bent to the task I watched him closely. He *was* mad. His cheeks hung slack and slab-like, but vibrated with a fierce inner passion. The extent of his lunacy suddenly came home to me.

'Don't be daft, Sas. Who are we goin' to burn, like?'

He ignored me and struck a match. Flames rose. The rubber mattress belched black smoke, and I inadvertently breathed some of it in.

'Stop it, Sas,' I choked. Dense smoke rose in a solid plume, and stung my eyes. 'Yer crazy doin' that.'

Behind us the door buckled slightly, a sharp pistol-crack of sound.

'Burn!' he croaked, his voice hoarse and obsessive. 'Burn the fuckers! Burn 'em alive!'

My brush-handle cracked on to his head as sharp as the buckling door. No one was going to burn *me*. When he looked like fighting I hit him again, harder, then set about tackling the blaze. As I kicked the last smoulders dead the door shot in with a bang and the confined space filled with screws. Sas and I, faced with the common enemy, turned to fight. Our sticks had clattered for only a few seconds when we were overpowered by a barrage of batons, punches and vicious, steel-capped kicks. There were about twenty of them and they split up into two groups to boot us along the landing and down the stairs to the Block, Sas in front. I heard him roaring and yelling his way down, one step at a time, drenched in a downpour of punches while I was still being kicked along the Fours.

They took us to separate cells and gave us both a hammering. As in Walton, two screws held my arms while a third hit me. The two holders pinioned my elbows against a wall, and the hitter had a medical screw to direct him.

Baff! His fist shot into me like a piston, doubling me up.

'Oof!'

'Not there,' the medic said, 'higher up.' The striker poked me with a forefinger. 'No, to the left,' the medic said. Another poke. 'Yes, there.'

His fist shot again.

'Oof!'

Sas got it worse than I did. When I saw him later his face was really bashed, with two enormously swollen black eyes, lips puffed to banana proportions, and even his cheekbones afloat. My own fat lip and slight nosebleed made me feel mildly ashamed.

They took us to new cells, mine on a landing under the authority of a fat P.O. who was obsessed with order and cleanliness. You could see your face in all his cell floors. I sat with my head in my hands staring at my anguished reflection, and when he waddled in I jumped up, determined to resist any attack.

'Right, Gaskin,' he said, 'now you keep this cell *clean*, understand? Have you got any polish?'

'Eh?' After the events of the day it was hard to believe this was happening.

'Don't worry if you haven't,' he said. 'I'll drop some in to you tomorrow.'

He went off duty at eight o'clock, and I sat with a dull ember of rage glowing inside me. Rage at my powerlessness, at the way I was always at the mercy of events. As I went over the happenings of the day the ember flared, the fire grew. By the time I stood in the middle of my cell, flexing my muscles and feeling my strength, it was a conflagration which left no room for fear. At five past eight I smashed up.

I was an expert at it by now and everything that could be smashed, was. I left the big modern windows, the ones that were supposed to make you feel human, till last. Only when the door flew open and the stick-waving screws bore down on me did I use what was left of the locker to splatter the glass. Thrown into the fallen shards, I kicked for all I was worth as they dragged me to the far side of the landing and hurtled me into another cell. This time I took a bang to the head and my vision was glaring, the lit surfaces jerky as I wiped blood from my face and looked around. The cell was completely empty, bare of everything breakable.

Except windows. Having no implement I smashed them with my elbows, immediately, yelling and screaming.

'BASTERDS, BASTERDS, BASTERDS!'

They ran in again and dragged me fighting across the wing to the padded cell, where two of them knelt on me while a third put me into a straitjacket. I screamed incessantly while it was going on. One of them fetched a hose and poured cold water over me but I carried on screaming till they went out. My eyes were closed and I saw nothing, felt nothing but the black void. After five minutes the medical screw who had directed my beating-up came in. His face was horrible as his nails bit into my nose with eye-watering hardness. My mouth opened and he poured the bitter largactyl down my throat.

'It'd be cyanide if I had my way, Gaskin.'

Though I fought to keep my eyes open, a comatose darkness soon overwhelmed me.

They took the straitjacket off in the morning, and put me in the bare cell whose windows I had smashed. I lay on the floor staring miserably at the chipped walls. After an hour the door was unlocked. The cell-proud P.O. stood fatly in the doorway.

'Get up, Gaskin.'

My body and my mind were completely numb. I knew what was about to happen, and got shakily to my feet. He walked over to me and stood close. His rheumy eyes were pink at the rims. Like a frog's.

'My cells!'

When his fist crashed its lightning explosion doubled me up, but I folded with less than a grunt. I lay in a river of pain, and when it had washed me I struggled to my feet again, managing by a huge effort of will to keep my hands at my sides. If there is a point at which pain loses its terror, I had reached it. His fist crashed again, and this time I squirmed for longer. When the pain receded I stood once more before him, proud and defiant, and looked into his eyes. They were glazed with age, their rims sore with the years he had spent staring at this wing and the lads passing through it. As I watched them something eased, as though a plug had been pulled and his desire to hurt me had drained away. He turned on his heel and went out.

There seemed to be nothing I could do to change things, so I wandered through the days in a kind of dream. I felt very tired and slept as much as I could, glad when I woke up that another bit of my life was over. Sas and I were exercised at the same time, on opposite sides of a huge circle, but were not allowed to talk. Often one of us walked faster to try and catch the other, but as soon as we drew close they separated us again. Sometimes, without realizing it, we both accelerated at the same time and ended up going as though in a walking race, as far apart as ever. An unspoken plan to jump on to a workshop roof and attack the slates evolved between us, but we made sure nothing ever came of it. For Sas, anyway, our demonstration had worked. He never went back to Feltham. He was too loony even for them, and finished his time at the Scrubs.

The fat P.O. was now a changed man towards me, and came to unlock me every night before he went off.

'Want to clean out the office for me, Gaskin?'

'Er, yeh. All right.'

He would hand me a dustpan and brush and stand out on the wing, smoking his last fag of the day. It was a funny thing, and not what you'd expect from such a tidy man, but every night there were a lot of long dog-ends on the floor that had somehow missed the ashtray, and even two or three live matches scattered amongst them.

After a week they moved me out of the Block and put me on normal location. Next day I was taken, with seven others, to Feltham.

9 | *Model Prisoner, Free Man*

The first thing they did in Reception was to give me the books Huntercombe had not allowed me.

'Centre House for you, Gaskin,' the Reception screw said, slapping me matily on the back. 'You'll like it there, it's right next door to the Block.'

We were driven from Reception to our Houses in a barred van, and as I looked at the grim buildings with their bars and barbed wire I have to admit I was frightened. Other lads were dropped at North, South, East and West Houses, each of which held about sixty boys. In theory the House populations were mixed, but in fact each House catered for a different kind of deviant. East House guys were usually violent, North House contained most of the junkies and intellectual nuts, South House had most of the queers, West House most of the spaced-out characters with whom nothing could ever be done. All the guys who might go off their heads and kill at any moment were on Centre, because it was close to the Block.

'One for us, sir?' the Centre gate screw asked as the van stopped outside.

'Yes, sir.'

He unlocked his gate, stepped out, locked it behind him, came over and took my handcuff in his fist. 'Don't try anything, kid.'

Inside, it was more or less like the wing of an adult prison. The cell doors were wooden, but still had spyholes. As in most places you had to work on wing cleaners for the first couple of weeks, scrubbing floors. They had Grades there, A to E. E was the lowest, and you were on the Block if you had it. They also had a Trust Rating lettered in the same way. When I arrived I was DD, from which I had to work my way up to AA for release.

From the first, the other lads didn't bother me. Most of them had a low I.Q. as far as I could judge.

'Er, hiya Gazzer. Remember me?'

'Eh? No, should I?'

'Richardson. We was in The Meadows together a few years back.'

'Oh, yeh.' I turned my back on him. He had been an idiot then, and would be one still. I had no wish to be associated with him.

Many were raving nuts who could kick off at any time, and one or two were hard cases. On my first night I was watching the box when two lads came over.

'Come from the Pool do yer, lar?'

'Yeh.'

'Thought so, yer common as muck.' He grinned. 'Us too.'

'What's it like in 'ere, then?' I asked.

'Bearable,' he said, offering me his tobacco tin, 'if yer reasonably sane. Yer don't want to be one o' these divvies, do yer, gettin' thrown in the Block all the time an' actin' as a target for tranquillizer darts?'

Before I could answer his mate said, 'Look out. 'Ere's Rafferty.'

A big bearded guy with eyes like Rasputin walked dazedly past. The first Scouser took back the tin I was holding out.

'That's Rafferty,' he explained. ''E's an idiot too, but 'e'd crack yer skull open as soon as look at yer.'

'We won't be with yer for long,' his mate said. 'We've on'y got two weeks to do.'

At Feltham every kid had a Case Officer, a screw who looked

out for him personally. Mine was Mr Bligh, and I met him on my second day. He had been case screw to my two Liverpool friends, and they had asked him to take me on.

'All right, Gaskin.' He gave me a playful jab in the chest, which surprised me. He was a well-built young bloke and the jab hurt. Then he shook hands, which surprised me even more. 'So I've got another Liverpudlian, have I?' He screwed his face up pugilistically. 'Are yer frum de Dingle, lah?' His appalling imitation of our accent made me smile. 'I should be getting danger money,' he said, and we both laughed.

When we had been chatting for a while I forgot he was a screw, and began to like him.

'Gaskin,' he said, 'I can see you're not like some of the nutters we get in here, "divvies" as you Scousers call them.' He smiled, then nodded gravely. 'You've had a rough ride through Borstal up to now. How do you feel about going easy on yourself for a change?'

'Yeh, Mr Bligh. If people can just stay off me back, like.'

He looked into me. 'They will here, Gaskin. You're in a Borstal, though. You can't expect anyone to behave like a children's nanny, can you?'

'I don't want 'em to, Mr Bligh.'

'Right. Well, I'll tell you what I propose, Gaskin. A bargain, right? You keep your nose clean and we'll retain your Huntercombe release date. That's in spite of your recent troubles. We can't be fairer than that, can we? Watch out, though. Step out of line, even once, and it'll cost you.'

'Okay, Mr Bligh. Yer've got yerself a deal.'

My release date was 11th November. I had less than four months left to do. It only remained for me to accustom myself to another routine, something I did with sumptuous ease since my whole life had trained me for it. Already I felt a genuine affection for Mr Bligh. He was the first screw who had ever spoken to me like a human being, or taken the trouble to find out how I felt about things. Now that I had made my compact with him I threw myself totally into fulfilling my part.

There was Parade twice a day at Feltham, a kind of smartness inspection, and my uniforms were soon flawless, perfectly laundered, tailored and pressed. In exchange for a fag the lad in the next cell polished my boots till the Governor could see his face in them. I started to set myself up with the trappings of institutionalization, and 'baroned' tobacco and money – lending it out at high interest rates – to help me afford the things which would make life tolerable. The Liverpool lads went out, giving me their bookcases and other possessions to enhance my status.

'Your cell's certainly up to scratch,' Mr Bligh said, looking round.

'Ta, Mr Bligh. I've been doin' me best, like, about what we said.'

When I came off wing cleaners they put me into the Laundry, which was better. There were only eight kids in there, all smaller and softer than me, and three or four of them were divvies. Our working clothes at Feltham were a dark blue jacket and trousers which everyone bleached to the palest possible blue, almost white, and tried to keep clean and smartly ironed. You were paid in cash and Canteen was three times a week, so it was easy to make money by washing and pressing other lads' kit. Not that I did it myself. I'd just toss it to one of the divvies.

' 'Ere, kid. Wash these.'

Since everyone in Feltham was nuts, it didn't take as great an effort for me to be well-behaved as it had in other places. In most institutions if I behaved in my normal, relaxed way I'd find myself in trouble. Here, when I acted normally they thought I was good, and compared to the divvies I was. Thus it was possible for me to get away with a lot, and in that way Feltham reminded me of a junior approved school or somewhere like that. In every other way, though, it was far harder. Nothing ever happened quietly in Centre House. A lot of guys screamed and threw tantrums when they were upset, and when someone went off their head they went right off it, with no half measures. The screws knew what to expect, and were wary. In all the time I was there none of them ever hit me.

Work was boring, and we got up to all kinds of mischief to pass the time. Crazy things happened.

'I'll be back in half an hour, lads,' the screw would say, then go off for a natter with his mate the Kitchen screw. 'If the phone rings tell 'em I've gone out a minute before.'

He would lock us in and leave us to our own devices. There was a divvy called Collins who had a grievance about his release date, and on one such morning we started winding him up about it.

'I done *six* days in the police cells,' he said, pounding his thin fist on the windowledge, then holding it tremblingly to his face. 'Even if they *do* only give you two-thirds, they should have given me four.'

He pounded the ledge again, then wrung his arm from elbow to fingertip. 'Two. *Two!* The Governor won't listen. Just won't listen!'

It turned out he still had six months to do. A normal person wouldn't even have thought about it till nearer his release.

'Why don't you have a demonstration?' one guy said. 'It's the only thing that works, isn't it lads?'

'Yeh. Yer've got to show 'em they can't fuck yer around.'

'It should be the twelfth,' Collins bleated, almost in tears, 'not the fourteenth. The fourteenth! That's *two* extra days!'

That afternoon when the screw let us out to unload dirty washing from the van, this fruitcake broke away from the party and ran wildly across the yard.

'Collins!' the screw shouted. 'Come back here. Where d'you think you're bloody well going? Collins!'

In seconds he was shinning up a tall drainpipe, through sharp tangles of barbed wire, to the roof. The screw stood at the bottom looking up. When a spot of blood from Collins's cut hands splashed on to his overall he stepped back.

'I'll throw myself off! I want my rights! My release date's all to cock!'

Laughing, we watched from the Laundry window while they talked him down. In the end a ladder was put up to the roof and he descended it, to be marched away to the Block. Poor nut. He was in tears about his release date at the finish, when he realized his protest had put it further away.

The reasonably sane kids hated the nutters. If that seems cruel, try living with them for a few months. None of us was naturally cruel, but we gave those divvies hell. When we were alone in the Laundry we held competitions to see which of them could stay in the dryer the longest.

''Ey, Thompson. Yer a bottleless bastard, yer know.'

'I'm not.'

'Yer are. Isn't he, lads?'

'Yep,' one of the sane guys would reply. 'He's got a yeller streak the width of an airport runway right down his back.'

In the end we would talk him into climbing into the machine, a front loader with a glass door.

'Don't shut the door! Promise you won't shut the door!'

All of them said that. Usually we did shut it, though. Then we'd switch it on, pull up chairs and sit there laughing while the poor nut went round and round, his face twisted with fear, silently screaming. If he stayed in a long time we'd give him a cheer and a clap when he came out, and they were often enormously pleased by this. It was the only time anyone was nice to them, and it made them really happy. We wanted to try them in the washing machine too, but could find no way of doing it without drowning them. The Laundry screw didn't like divvies any more than we did, and merely ticked us off when he caught us tormenting them.

'The P.O. wants you, Gaskin.'

Feltham had been my home for four weeks now, and I had made myself get used to it. The place was as oppressive and monotonous as any other prison, but with freedom like a rising sun on my horizon I put the harrowing experiences of recent months behind me, and threw myself totally into the life there. Now, I gave my boots a quick rub, straightened my tie in my cell mirror, and went down to the P.O.'s office.

'Yer wanted me, sir?'

'Ah, Gaskin. Yes. Sit down for a minute.'

'Ta, sir.'

'Now, I want to ask you something. You're not by any chance baroning, are you?'

'Er, baronin' sir? No, sir. Honest.'

'Well,' he tapped his teeth seriously with his ballpoint, 'one or two of my officers have got the impression you are. It's a serious business, Gaskin. If I found out you *were* baroning, especially after this little talk, your feet wouldn't touch. Are you with me?'

'Yeh, sir.'

'Right, you can go.'

After that I was more cautious, and gave debtors longer to pay. Later, when I became more important in the social system of Centre House, the same P.O. often asked for my help. At such times I felt proud that he had trusted me, and preened myself mentally on what a responsible fellow I was.

'Gaskin, sit down. Now keep this one under your hat, eh? My officers tell me that Smith is picking on Chapman, making his life unbearable. Chapman's been suicidal in the past, as you probably know. I've been watching you of late, Gaskin, and Mr Bligh agrees that you're shaping up well. If you were to have a word in Smith's ear it would do something for me, as well as for poor old Chapman. It'd be better coming from you than a member of staff. Do you catch my drift?'

'Okay, sir. I'll grab Smithy's lug'ole for yer, like.'

'Thanks, Gaskin.'

The screws told off anyone they caught bullying, but as soon as their backs were turned it happened again. When I told a bully he stayed told.

For some reason changing jobs was really difficult at Feltham, but in my four months there I had as many jobs as other lads had in the full fourteen months' stretch. There were a number of parties, Concrete Moulders, Kitchen, Laundry, Gardens, Boiler House, and General Joes who filled in wherever there was need. When my Grade and Trust Rating reached BB I managed to get on to the Boiler House party, which was less boring than the Laundry.

One screw on Centre House had a hearing problem, and this was an unending source of fun. He lip-read more than he heard, and if you were careful about the shape of your mouth you could say anything to him.

'Can I shove me cock in yer gob, shit?'

'Eh? What did you say, Gaskin?'

'Er, can I get the SHOVEL for this JOB, sir?'

'Yes, Gaskin. Carry on.'

'Okay, sir. Will yer swallow me spunk as well?'

'Eh?'

'I'll get ONE for the BUNKER as well.'

There were three of us on the Boiler House with only three boilers to maintain, so our day was leisurely. We took our time filling the barrows, then sauntered around with them, stopping frequently for cups of tea and fags. We worked Saturday mornings, which meant missing the General Inspection which the whole Borstal had to undergo. Out all day with my barrow it was easy for me to pass my overalls and shirts through the Laundry window, and get them back washed and crisply ironed for the lesser inspections which punctuated our daily routine. Between these diversions I leaned on my shovel, dreaming of freedom.

You would probably think a Borstal could never be a home, and call my life as a model prisoner at Feltham one of institutionalization. A home was something I had never had, and once I ceased smashing up and settled down to do my time I *was* at home there. My pride in my cell was as fierce as the fat Scrubs P.O.'s for his office. Often in prison you see the old lags embroidering cushion covers or laboriously cutting doilies out of paper towels for their locker tops, and I began to take that kind of attitude. You were only allowed one picture board but I had three, all covered with pictures of Liverpool Football Club. In time my bookcases became crammed with books, most of which I never looked at, but which I kept for the way they enhanced my cell. The Governor made a little protest about it on every General Inspection, which was one reason why I preferred working.

'Too many books again, Gaskin. Are you running a bloody library in here? How is it you've got so many when no one else in the House has even a bookcase?'

'Er, I got these from the cupboard downstairs, sir. The divvies keep rippin' 'em up. Look, sir.' I held out a torn paperback which I'd lovingly restored. 'I've reelly fixed it, sir. I 'ad to put tape inside, sir, like that, an' I've backed it with polythene.'

'Hmm.' He examined it. 'Very good. All right, Gaskin, but you'll have to give some of them back. We can't have the cells full of books, it's a fire risk.'

'Yeh, sir. Okay, sir.'

He told me this every week. The following week there always seemed to be more, and we went through it all over again. After every Inspection he complimented me on my cell.

Draped across the table there was a cloth with pictures of Spanish dancers on it, which I had found in the Laundry and affectionately washed and ironed. Plastic aeroplanes I'd made up from kits hung from the ceiling and veteran cars, similarly made, were parked on shelves and locker top. All that was missing was a wooden plaque with Home Sweet Home written on it in pokerwork. No one was allowed to walk on my highly polished floor, and squares of old blanket were left by the door for visitors to skate around on. There was always a bottle of orange cordial and a packet of biscuits on top of my locker, and my tobacco was stacked inside. Nobody ever touched it. If it had ever gone I would simply have walked into someone else's cell and taken theirs. If it had happened twice I would have taken everyone's, and all the lads on the wing knew it.

Life was as easy as it can be in a Borstal.

'Steak an' kidney pie, eh? Give us two slices o' that.'

'Okay, Scouse.'

Glancing to see if the Kitchen screw was looking, the lad would pile them on. With my BB rating came outings to the baths on Saturday mornings, another useful Inspection-dodger. Four went from each House, and every time I applied I was successful. Every House had its own football team, and Centre selected me to play in the Saturday afternoon matches. The losing team was awarded an old pisspot at the end of the game, and the victorious team took it over to them. When we took it to East, the violent House, or when they brought it to us, threats were shouted on both sides and the air was charged with aggression. It was great stuff to me then.

Mr Bligh was more like a friend than a screw. He helped me get hold of political books and magazines, even the P.R.O.P. publication.

'Here you are, Gaskin,' he said when it arrived. 'All you have to do is sign this undertaking that you won't show it to anyone else.'

Of course I showed it to people who could understand it, but there weren't many of them in Feltham.

When Brenda came up to visit me, Mr Bligh walked over to talk to us.

'Graham's a natural leader,' he said, offering us cigarettes. 'He's doing all right here, and he'll be something one day if he puts his mind to it.'

I smiled at Brenda when he had gone. 'Nice bloke, eh Bren?'

Time passed more quickly now. With only a few weeks left I was sacked from the Boiler House, so wing cleaners was my job when they gave me my Home Leave date. A fortnight before it arrived an incident happened which, for a time, looked like having serious consequences. It was bang-up time and I came on to the landing late. A little screw I hated was twirling his keys outside my door.

'Come on, Gaskin. Move yer fuckin' arse.'

I was already moving fast. To run would have been humiliating, so I carried on at the same pace.

'MOVE, Gaskin.'

I slowed down. When he reached out and grabbed my arm it stiffened me.

'Into yer kennel,' he said.

It was one of those times when I just couldn't take it.

'Fuck *off*.' A contemptuous two-palmed push sent him reeling. He did a backward roll along the landing and his little legs waggled furiously in the air. 'I'll go in when I'm ready,' I said.

Waiting to go on Governor's, I was scared stiff lest he took away my BB rating, which would mean waiting another month at least for my Home Leave and release. He gave me a dressing down, then softened.

'Mr Bligh's put in an excellent report about you, Gaskin, so I'm not going to alter your Grade this time. If there's a repeat performance you'll leave here a CC. Clear?'

Home Leave extended from Thursday morning until the last train back on Tuesday night. When the day arrived I was numb, and going out seemed to have lost its meaning. My head was done in by all that prison. You always imagine you'll feel ecstatic, but when the day comes it is never like that. Sometimes you're merely dead from the neck up, as happened to me that day, at others you can be acutely depressed. Sitting next to Mr Bligh in the Borstal minibus my mind was a blank. On the station platform he handed me my rail warrant.

'Well, have a good time, Gaskin. I won't bother with the usual lecture about making sure you come back. Whatever else you are, you're not stupid.'

The train took me to London, and as the numbness wore off my feelings made themselves known. One moment I was ecstatic, the next terrified.

'Hiya, Bren.'

'Put a lock on the fridge,' she called out, smiling almost shyly, 'our Graham's arrived.'

Brenda was into the quiet life with her steady boyfriend, but on the second afternoon I met a girl called Angie in the pub and went with her to her flat, which was in the next street. Her many visitors smoked dope incessantly, and it was good to try the stuff again. They introduced me to heavier drugs like speed. People knocked at the door at all hours, and it took me a while to discover that Angie was selling something. It turned out to be methadone, an analgesic. Some of her customers were junkies who substituted it for heroin, and one or two were troublesome.

One night when she answered the door I heard her arguing with one of them.

'Look, that's me price an' if you don't like it, *lump* it.'

They reached the point where the man was shouting, and I stood up. Angie called at that moment.

'Graham, can you come 'ere a minute?'

The junkie blanched when he saw the size of me. He hadn't expected a rough and unruly convict.

'Er, it's okay,' he said quickly. 'There's no trouble.'

'Yer dead right there isn't.'

I grabbed his neck, dragged him into the passage, and started to pound his head against the wall. This was normal behaviour to me now, having spent so much time inside.

'That's enough,' Angie said immediately. 'Leave 'im be now, Graham.'

She sold him the stuff then at the price she wanted, and gave him a final instruction.

'Don't come back.'

In the daytimes Brenda gave me money to go to the bookies, at night she took me to the pub.

'Relax, Graham.' She gave me a serious look. 'You've got to adjust to bein' outside, or you'll just keep goin' back in.'

That was what worried me. I spent the whole time trying to unwind.

In Feltham again, I had only four weeks left. They put me on Con Moulders, the concrete shop. The screw in charge was an oldish guy who had been an unarmed combat instructor in the Army. Like us, he hated nutters.

'Have a ciggy, lads,' he said on the first morning.

'Er, thanks, sir.'

'I don't give 'em to nutters, though.'

He nodded towards Richardson, the Meadows guy, who was also on Con Moulders, and was standing outside on his own. There was another Centre House lad with us, and a hard case from East completed the party. There was nothing whatever to do. The machines were all broken, so we couldn't make concrete. The screw sat in his office all day reading Westerns, and we whiled away the time sitting on a four-wheeled truck outside.

For the first few days the East House kid and I had a hard time of it while we sized one another up. He watched my reactions to everything he said, so I made sure they were aggressive.

'Christ.' He'd indicate a passing screw. ''E's a fuckin' pain, that one.'

'Yeh, yer right.' I'd look at the lad confidingly. 'I'd love to cave 'is skull in, wouldn't you?'

Both of us would laugh. In time the East House kid realized that I would never turn on him, though I'd fight murderously if attacked. When we had each other's measure we became friends. He was due out a week before me and we made arrangements to meet outside, which we never kept.

All day we sat on the four-wheeled truck, bored to stupefaction, talking and larking about. Richardson, our resident divvy, came in for most of the stick.

'Give us yer socks, Richardson.'

He would take them off and obligingly roll them up so we could have a game of football. When we grew bored with it we invariably kicked them over a high roof. The screw watched from his office window, laughing. He often tormented Richardson himself. Proud of his prowess as a boxer, he gave punching lessons in his office to the East House kid and me.

'Come here, Richardson.'

Smiling lamely, half-flinching, the lad sidled into his office where the screw took up a boxing stance in front of him.

'Right, you want to hit with the maximum power, see? Bring your arm right back, swing your body like this, and push hard from the shoulder.' Thwack! He slammed a deadening blow into Richardson's shoulder. 'Got it? You have a go, Gaskin.'

While Richardson gritted his teeth, I did.

Thwack!

'No, not like that. Move your whole body from the waist, and swing your shoulder. Like *this*.'

Thwack! Richardson reeled across the room and went crashing into the desk, then stood grinning foolishly, and rubbed his aching shoulder.

'Christ, Richardson, you can't half take it,' the East House kid said when his turn came. When Richardson turned away he grinned at us.

Sometimes the screw took the cushion from his chair and made Richardson hold it across his middle. BLAM! The screw laughed as Richardson spun across the office and juddered into the far wall.

'Good job I let you have that cushion, eh?'

'Yeh, sir. Thanks.'

All of us would laugh. For our first two weeks on Con Moulders we had no work at all so Richardson got this for a couple of hours a day, and was covered in bruises. Sometimes he weaved about like a boxer while it was happening, acting as though he were part of the game because the alternative, being merely a live punchbag, was too humiliating even for a divvy like him.

This period is fixed in my mind as a time when time stopped. My imminent freedom lured and terrified me by turns. How would I live? Would I be able, this time, to blend in somewhere, find a home perhaps, survive? Perhaps I would meet a girl. Whatever was going to happen I wished it would hurry up and *happen*. The boredom was total. All we did was play sockball, torment Richardson, race around on the truck until we hit something or a screw told us to stop. It got so bad that I started taking a book with me, but even that was no good. The others were too distracting.

'Right, lads,' the screw said one morning, 'we'll be General Joes today.' He had grown tired of his cowboy books at last. 'We start by cleaning the Officers' Club.'

After that we did a bit of work every day, sweeping up or moving rubbish, and time passed more quickly.

The final day arrived. Smiling, outwardly self-confident, clapped on the back by pals wherever I went, I shed the trappings of my institutionalization. My model aeroplanes went to one friend, my books, bookcases, tablecloths and specially tailored clothes to others, and I gave generous dropsies of tobacco and money to people I liked. That night I lay tossing and turning for hours, unable to sleep as always. Next day was Mr Bligh's day off, but he was in Reception at eight o'clock to say goodbye, which was good of him.

'Well, Gaskin. It's come at last, eh?'

'Yeh, looks like it, Mr Bligh.' A fresh bag of butterflies released itself into my stomach. 'Thanks for everythin', sir.'

'You know how to thank me, son. Stay out of places like this.'

My chest was tight with anxiety as I walked out to the van. I sat on the station platform, fear and hope at war inside me.

When the train came in a middle-aged lady alighted. She smiled at my hang-dog expression.

'Cheer up.'

As soon as I looked into her eyes, I did.

'Wait till you're my age,' she said, 'then you'll know.'

As the train started to move my feelings broke.

'Ha-HEY!'

Heads turned, some of them smiling doubtfully. I smiled back, free at last. Really free, not merely on the run, surrounded by institutions waiting to gobble me up. At that moment I felt the first twinge of pain from my tooth.

It was a steady ache by the time I arrived at Brenda's. She took a look.

'It's an abscess on your gum, Graham. Pity it's a Friday, you'll 'ave to suffer the whole weekend now.'

On the Monday morning she gave me two letters of intro-duction to friends in North Wales. 'They'll look after you, Graham. I'm sure you'll settle into somethin'. You'll 'ave to, eh?' She pressed something into my hand. 'Take these, they might 'elp with the tooth.'

'Are they painkillers?'

'No, valium.'

They were no earthly use, but it was typical of her to give me what she could.

The first friend, Sandra Keating, lived in Colwyn Bay. She had once been to St Vincent's with Brenda to visit me, so wasn't a total stranger. When I arrived in the town I booked into a hotel for two days and left my gear there. Then I found her flat.

'Yes?'

'Er, I'm Graham Gaskin, Brenda's brother.'

'Oh, come in, love.' She was a blonde girl, and nice-looking. 'This is Joanne.'

A small, fattish girl smiled and poured me a cup of tea.

'I've got a letter for yer. Off our kid, like.'

The two girls made me welcome, took me to the pub, and brought me back dead drunk.

'Come on, you drunken sod,' Sandra said. 'Get in my bed for tonight.'

I went to sleep holding her tight in my arms, but couldn't do anything else. It was great to sleep with someone after all that time alone.

Next morning Pete appeared in the flat. He was okay, and promptly gobbled up Brenda's valium.

'Come on,' he said when he heard my trouble, 'we'll find you a dentist.'

When we went back I formed the impression that Joanne was his girlfriend. As the day wore on I realized the feelings were all on her side. She was always sitting next to him and he was always telling her to move away. Probably he threw the odd fuck into her when he felt generous. She was attractive enough, with a big arse and tight jeans.

That afternoon we went to the pub again.

'This is the life, eh Graham?' Sandra Keating said.

'Er, yeh. Yeh, sure.' The alcohol had had a sledgehammer effect upon me the night before, so today I took it easier.

'AVE your glasses please,' the barmen shouted at the end. 'COME along now.'

'I'll fetch me stuff from that 'otel,' I said.

Joanne glanced at me, then looked away. 'I'll keep you company if you like,' she said.

'Yeh. Okay. Come if yer want.'

The hotel hadn't been paid for nothing, after all. Joanne and I spent seven hours in the bed, and for the first time in my life everything went right. The act was performed, perfectly. Then we did it again, and again. Burglaries, beatings up, straitjackets and strict regimes flowed out of me, or seemed to. It was only a lovely illusion, they are still there. She wanted us to stay the night, but I craved company so we went to see Sandra and Pete.

Brenda's second letter was to her friend Hamish who lived along the coast in the little town of Llanfairfechan, and next morning I decided to pay him a call. By that time Joanne was clinging to me as she had to Pete the previous day, with as fraying an effect upon my nerves.

'I'll come with you,' she said.

Bluntness seemed the only way. 'What for? Yer not with me, Joanne, just because we 'ad a roll in the 'ay.'

Pete laughed soundlessly behind her. 'You can't stay here either,' he chipped in, 'driving *me* up the wall.'

'Hamish is my friend too,' she said. 'I'll go and see him if I want to.'

There was no stopping her. We rode side by side and silent as the bus weaved its way below heathery hills to Llanfairfechan, a little town on a narrow shelf of flat land beside the sea.

Still saying nothing we called at the flat, which was over a chipshop in Bankfield Village Road, the main and almost the only street that cuts across the town.

Knock!Knock! Knock!Knock!Knock!Knock! From within, the sound of many voices. A record player blared in one room, a tinny radio piped in another. Rap!Rap!Rap!Rap!Rap! A dog began to bark, and the voices were raised higher as the speakers strove to make themselves heard. I turned my back to the door and pounded away with my heel. BOOM!BOOM!BOOM!BOOM!BOOM! For an instant there was silence. Then more dogs began to yap and howl, and footsteps clattered down the stairs.

'Hello, David.'

The only answer Joanne got was a pair of jeaned legs flying upstairs to rejoin the fray.

In the kitchen I sat, painfully shy and out of place, at a long table full of people. The place was knee-deep in dogs, and to combat my isolation I stroked one.

'D'you want a cup o' tea, Joanne?'

The speaker, David, poised the teapot in mid-air and gave me the look reserved for strangers.

'Ta, David.' She indicated me with a jerk of her head. 'This is Graham, Brenda Gaskin's brother.'

A slow-moving giant at the far end of the table stood up. '*Brenda's* brother?' Surprise and pleasure animated him. He leaned over and my hand was swallowed in his enormous fist. 'Nice to meet you, Graham. I'm Hamish.'

'Do *you* want a cup o' tea?' David Boon asked.

'Oh, do I get one now that yer know who I am?'

Everyone laughed, and the atmosphere grew more relaxed.

The flat was like a madhouse, crowded for eighteen hours a day. As well as Hamish and David Boon there was an Irish guy there, Frannie Logan, and a lad called Jim Jones whose three little kids and big collie shared his room. Two terriers lived in the kitchen. The flat was small, but there was a room upstairs that was empty save for a mosaic of dog-turds on the floor. Hamish read Brenda's letter, and it was accepted amongst the lads that I could stay.

'I thought you said *I* could have that room?' Joanne complained when it was mentioned.

'Did I?' Hamish stroked his chin. 'Oh. We'll just see 'ow it goes then, eh?'

After a few more words the subject was dropped. It lay, unresolved, a further barrier between Joanne and myself.

Alcohol has always made me do things which shame me when I'm sober, and I had become unused to it in Borstal, which aggravated this. When I reeled back from the pub on my second afternoon, blind drunk, Joanne was sitting in the kitchen. Her very presence enraged me, but she still carried the memory of our evening of love in her broad-arsed form, and I placed my hand on her breast. Its feminine wobble and unroused nipple penetrated layers of drunkenness to touch a part of me that was, in spite of how it seems, tender. My voice was thick with alcohol.

'Get on the deck.'

'What?'

I lurched forward, blindly amorous. 'On the carpet, Joanne.' My weight almost toppled her over. 'I wanna screw yer.'

She slipped out from under my arm, and sent me sprawling. 'Get away.' Her eyes had a virtuous beauty that held no vestige of her usual passivity. 'You'll never touch me again after this. What do you think I am? Your whore? *Yours?*' She trilled derision.

Smack! At the first slap Hamish charged in and lifted me bodily away from her. Boozy despair at my callousness overwhelmed me, and I had to keep from crying.

'Sorry, 'Amish.' I blundered towards the stairs. 'Sorry, Joanne. Sorry I'm 'orrible. Sorry.'

Upstairs, I lay comatose among the dog-turds. Joanne had left by the time I revived. I swept the room, mopped it out with strong disinfectant, and moved in.

It didn't take me long to settle into their lifestyle.

'Er, are yer into smokin' a joint, like?'

Hamish put his arm up his own back and advanced upon me backwards. 'Twist that.'

That was our life. That and boozing, visiting friends, entertaining the incessant callers. The thoughts I had had in Feltham about blending into the world of normal people occurred to me less frequently. After all, I belonged to something now, with Hamish and the rest. When doubts assailed me I doused them with booze, or hid them in a cloud of hashish smoke.

Hamish, David Boon and Frannie Logan were night people,

and made sleep impossible save during the day. If you dozed off after dark they shoved a joint into your mouth. One night I dropped off with my head on the side of the armchair, and awoke terrified as something soft and warm fastened itself suffocatingly over my nose. When my eyelids shot up I found myself staring into the bright, crazy eyes of Frannie Logan. His mouth was over my nose like a warm clam.

WHOOOSSHHH! As he blew I gave an involuntary gasp, and the cannabis smoke inflated my lungs to bursting point. The rest of them sat around the edges of the room, giggling.

Frannie was great. When things slowed down he ran in like a madman.

'Hoho, heyheyHEY! What's the matter, Graham, can't yer sleep?'

Then he'd set about us all, tickle one under the armpits, pour water over another, and start a wrestling match into which everyone was drawn. The couch went over every single night I was there. All night and every night we were awake, talking nothing but nonsense.

'Graham, what's up? Can't you find a cup? Here.' Hamish chucked me a packet of Polyfilla. 'Get some water from the kitchen, you'll knock one together in no time. Use the stereo for a potter's wheel.'

A couple of times when we were drunk I had arguments with David Boon. He was much older than me, twenty-one, but was younger than the rest and seemed it. We were lurching drunk.

'Come on, treasure,' he said, 'sit on me knee an' I'll tell you a story.'

Blam! When he stood up he was holding a cut eye.

'Come on, lads,' he said later the same night, 'let's do a raid on the fridge.' He worked days in the chipshop below and was able to keep the keys. As I stood hesitantly at the top of the stairs his voice floated up to me. 'I bet Graham could murder half a dozen pies.'

These sorties into the chippie were a regular thing. We came out smearing ourselves with food, had pie fights on the stairs, orgies of grease in the kitchen. Food obsessed us. There was a chocolate machine outside the little shop over the road, and we spent hours rustling up the necessary coins.

' 'Ave you got a ten pence, Graham?'

'Me? What're yer askin' me for? It's me that's been keepin' yer in chocolate all week. Anyway, I'm skint.'

When we had the coins there were arguments about who should go.

'It's your turn, Graham. You haven't been for days.'

'I 'AVE.'

'When?'

'Last night. You were bein' sick in the sink when I come back, remember?'

'Did you? Did he? Did he go for chocolate then?'

Often, in the middle of the night, Frannie and I would take the dogs down to the beach for a run. It was pitch black down there except for creamy waves splashing the sea wall. You could hear the shingle rolling as the tide pulled it this way and that.

'Give us a fag, Graham.'

'Yeh. 'Ere, Fran.'

The match flared, lit our faces, hissed as it fell into the black water. Frannie spent hours sitting on the sea wall looking out at the Irish Sea. It was as though he was thinking about his childhood and his home on the other side. He probably wasn't, but there was something good in it anyway.

At six in the morning, stoned out of our minds, the lot of us went over to the little shop across the road for sweets and bottles of pop.

'All right, boys. Lavley morning.'

'Lavleeeeeeee!' we'd chorus.

Whenever the shopkeeper spoke I went into paroxysms of giggling. He had spent his entire life in these few streets crouched next to the sea, and thought we were from a different world. We were. At about nine o'clock we'd filter off to bed, and the house would be quiet all day save for our snores rumbling. Jim Jones brought his kids home from school at four.

'Yaaa-AAAAH! Oooo-eeEE! Where's my DOGGY?'

Later I organized my day so I went to bed in the afternoon, before they came home. When I rose they were in bed again, fast asleep.

Jim had his own business, 'Have Van Will Travel', and drove around all day in his Commer truck disposing of trash and moving furniture.

'This is me wife, Graham,' he said one day. She was a dirty, horrid little thing, part human, mostly junkie. A big black mongrel bounded over to me.

'Yeh? Is this yer dog, love?' It was squirming in and out of my legs, daft as a brush.

'Yes,' she said, then paused. 'D'you want him?'

The idea of having my own dog to follow me through the mountains was too good to resist. 'Er, yeh. Okay. Ta.'

'Look after him, though.'

After that Dan went everywhere with me, on my country drives with Jim Jones and up to the remote mountain cottage where we scored our dope.

'You can work with me today, Graham,' he often said. 'Only a fiver, though.'

It wasn't much, but it gave me something to do. I was still only seventeen, and got just over eleven pounds a week on the dole, so it helped. At other times I'd stay at home all day with Bob Big Deal. This pleasant fellow smoked dope with us constantly, but never contributed anything all the time I was there.

My eighteenth birthday came and went, and 1977 crept towards its close. Things worsened between David Boon and myself. The flat was in his name as well as Hamish's, so just before Christmas Dan and I moved out. Fear nagged at me as I assembled my few possessions on the last morning. I sensed, dimly, that I was due for another drift downwards. Tom Drew, one of our visitors, lived in a hotel room in Colwyn Bay that had two beds.

'Come down there if you want, Graham. I'll try to smuggle you in.'

The first night it went well, but on the second we came back drunk.

CRASSHH!

'Watch it,' Tom hissed, 'you'll have the landlord out.'

'Uh? Yeh, okay.' Now, wasn't there a telephone table around here somewhere? Dan trotted ahead of me, tail flailing. Oh no.

CRASSHHDIINNG!

The landlord's door flew open.

'What's this? Eh? What's going' on, Mr Drew? You know you can't 'ave visitors after eleven o'clock.'

No more desolate place can exist than a holiday town at night, in mid-winter, when you've neither roof for your head nor fire for your body. Dan and I tramped the streets until eight o'clock next morning. Then, unable to stand the cold any longer, we called on Sandra Keating. She was all right that day, but on the second morning she came and sat on the couch where I was sleeping.

'Er, look Graham. I haven't much room, and with Pete staying too. You know.'

With my clothes slung in a bundle over my shoulder I went back to Llanfairfechan, but not to the chipshop. David was still there, and that would mean trouble. An empty house on the other side of the road had been renovated and replastered, so I broke a window at the back and moved in. Bob Big Deal gave me a mattress and a portable stove, so I was reasonably well set up. On Christmas Eve I went shopping.

'A pound o' sausages, love. Er, 'alf a pound o' bacon, a packet o' coffee, a loaf ... A thingie o' marge an' four tins o' dogfood.'

My Christmas fare thus taken care of, I left Dan in the house and went off to a party. When I came back in the early hours of Christmas morning, pissed, a scene of utter devastation greeted me. Dan had scoffed everything. The cellophane which had wrapped my bacon and sausages was strewn, in tiny pieces, over every centimetre of the floor. Even the coffee had been opened and flung around, there were little heaps and trails of it everywhere. The tub of marge had been licked clean. Everything not in a tin had been wolfed, and the only stuff in tins was the dogfood.

On Christmas Night I kicked the chipshop's rear door in. Back at the house, I mournfully opened a tin of dogfood and tipped its contents on to the floor, then sat down to a meal of cold pies and colder Coca-Cola. That I was on the threshold of a life of crime was obvious, but no matter how I racked my brains I could think of no way out.

''Appy Christmas, mate.'

Dan's tail wagged, thump thump, contritely.

Larceny drew me, not that I had a choice. The North Wales coast is a bleak and windy place in winter and I was homeless, and more of an outsider than ever. On New Year's Eve I burgled the canteen of a hospital, breaking into the building through the Gym. Splatt! When the glass had tinkled away I reached through and opened the window. On its far side I went down some stairs, kicked my way through two doors into a corridor, and attacked the canteen door. After thuds from my boot and repeated shoulder charges it gave in, and I found myself in a staff shop full of festive gear. With twenty lighters and the same number of watches in my pockets, six thousand fags and a thousand cigars in a carrier bag, and a tin of Cadbury's Roses under my arm for myself, I climbed out into the grounds again.

WOOF! WOOF!WOOF!WOOF! WOOF!

'Shurrup, Dan. Shush, lad, for Jesus' sake.'

That night I put a ladder against the window of the chipshop flat, and climbed in to sleep by the lecky fire. Next afternoon I met Bob Big Deal in Station Road.

'Hiya, Graham. What's 'appening?'

'Er, I'm tryin' to sell this lot.' I briefly opened the bag. 'Any ideas?'

He took me to different places and we sold some cigars and fags. Still carrying the remainder, I went with him to another party. We emerged in the small hours, behind some very drunken lads who went the opposite way. We had gone only a few paces when we heard glass breaking.

CHIANGLE-PIANNNG!

One of the silly gets had caved a window in along the street. We walked on. A minute later a police car appeared from nowhere and swished to a halt beside us.

'Hang on a second, son.' Slam! One cop was out of the car and standing next to me, and his mate was following. 'What have you got in that bag?'

Hurling the loot at his face I ran as fast as my legs would carry me, with both cops hard on my heels. I left the road behind me and plunged through an overgrown garden and across a field. A horse stopped grazing to watch me pass. One cop was still breathing down my neck as I went full tilt down a muddy bank and SPLASSHHH! into an icy river. It was a mountain stream, fast-flowing and swollen with winter rains, and the cold water hacked my breath away. It came halfway up my thighs and wading was difficult, but I was glad it was deep and cold. It made the cop stop chasing me.

Bob Big Deal was questioned about me, and later released. Next day as I was lying on my mattress in the empty house in Bankfield Village Road two cop cars squealed to a halt outside. They kicked the door of the chipshop flat open, and poured into it looking for me.

'Hush, boy.' Dan's muzzle was in my hands. 'Shhhh.'

They brought Hamish out and put him in one of the cars. He had had some dope and was busted through me, which made me feel awful. Next morning I moved to the next town along the coast, Penmaenmawr.

I knew a lad there, Buzz, and stayed with him a few days. At night I travelled the coast looking for places to rob. It was at this time that I met Colin and Jan in a pub, and they first took me to their house in Abergele. It was a squat licensed to them by the council, known always as what it had formerly been, The Button Factory. It was an eerie place of cavernous rooms, peopled by ghostly chunks of dead machinery in canvas shrouds. Colin was a Birmingham bloke of about thirty, with long hair and a beard, and Jan was small and plumpish. They were unlikely friends, but good people who never once closed their door to me.

Now I was a night hunter padding silently through the streets, preying on the weak window, the unguarded door. One night, out of my head on booze and dope, I did a smash and grab, badly, scooping up watches and Ronson lighters with fingers cut by the breaking glass. The following day I hitched with Dan to Liverpool, sold the lot, and stayed some days. On my way back I stayed overnight with Col and Jan, then made my way in broad daylight to Buzz's place in Penmaenmawr. On a later expedition I found a derelict garage near Colwyn Bay which I used as a stash for my loot, and sometimes a bedroom. One night, near the station in Abergele with another lad, I spotted a jeweller's whose plate glass looked unbreakable. There were coaches parked nearby and we slept in one, fitfully, till four in the morning. The black sky had jewels of its own as I dropped a chunk of iron into a carrier bag, the idea being to hit a hole in the glass without the projectile following through.

BLATT! Damn, the handles tore away and the iron shot through the display, knocking most of the gear beyond my reach as I had feared. I grabbed a tray of gold rings, and stuck most of them down as we ran away since the other lad had done nothing but dither. Dan had an extra tin of dogfood that night, in Liverpool.

Buzz's idea of a good time was to blow some dope and go for a walk in the hills. On one of these outings he spotted a holiday cottage on a remote hillside, furnished but empty.

'It's completely isolated, Graham. The nearest neighbour's a farm on a hill two miles away. You'll be safe as houses up there.'

With a bag of groceries in my arms and Dan at my heels I walked up, broke a back window, and moved in. When I switched the electricity on everything worked. There was a radiogram, and I took it upstairs to the room I had chosen, and draped a bedspread over the window to rule out any possibility of the faraway hillfarm seeing my light. Then I boarded the broken pane in the back door with a neat square of plywood.

'Okay, Dan?' He whined joyfully, his tail thumping as I opened his tin. 'Like it 'ere, boy?'

Once again, a home of sorts. In the daytime I slept, at night I crept into Penmaenmawr to break into shops or collect the money Brenda sent to Buzz's. The thought of going back to prison terrified me, but there was no way out of my predicament that I could see so I merely carried on with it, doing the best I could. Prowling the coast and preying on easy meat, I survived a while longer as an outlaw. One night in the lane leading to my Colwyn Bay garage the lights of a cop car were turned suddenly, transfixingly on. A freeze of light glared the hedges. In less than a second I was through a fence and running, running. Dan ran off at a tangent, barking joyously at first. It was the last time I ever saw him. I heard his happiness change to despair as he crashed through the undergrowth looking for me. A loudhailer crackled.

'GASKIN.' Static whined, then cleared. 'GASKIN, GIVE YOURSELF UP. YOU CAN'T GET AWAY. GIVE YOURSELF UP, GASKIN.'

They knew it was me, all right. I'd have some explaining to do when they caught me.

Two days later I burgled a Do-It-Yourself shop in Penmaenmawr and made a good haul, filling three plastic bags with tools which I hid in a derelict house. They almost cost me my freedom. Somehow the police stumbled on to them and kept a watch on the place, waiting for me to pick them up. Buzz went into the shop next day to buy some putty. The shopkeeper was talking into the telephone, and motioned him to wait.

'You've found 'em, 'ave you Constable Evans? That was quick. No, I don't mind waitin' to get 'em back, not if it 'elps you catch the bugger.'

When Buzz found me I was on my way to collect them.

It was Friday. All day long I had lain in my holiday cottage, dogless now as well as miserable, trying to think of a way out of the trap I was in. No solution had come to me. If I went back to Liverpool it would be the same thing all over again, and if I tried London I'd only find myself in Brenda's way. Dusk was in the air as I walked down the hill, the lights of Penmaenmawr taking an added twinkle below me as the gloom deepened. Even thieves like to see crows winging roostwards, and the mountain-side was a fine thing to be free on. I rounded a bend, and SCREECH! A plain car swerved to block the narrow lane in front of me and three heavy C.I.D. men rushed sweatily out. Escape was impossible. I ran, desperately, but one cut me off and the others collared me.

'Right, Gaskin. We've a ruddy great list o' your doings, boy.'

10 | *Running*

At Conwy police station they questioned me for hours but could not get through to me enough to scare me, and in the end they only charged me with two offences. At one o'clock on Saturday morning two flat-hatted cops clicked me into handcuffs and drove me under the castle walls out of Conwy, and over the bridge to Llandudno. The modern police station there had more cells, and later that morning a special court would sit to remand me. Along a stark corridor we went, past the Charge Room and the sliding door that led up to the court. A steel gate closed off a little passage with six neat cells on one side of it.

At ten o'clock the court remanded me in police custody till the Monday.

'Er, I want a solicitor.'

Though I did not know it then, this was the wisest move I ever made. For the rest of that day I lay on my bunk, unable to concentrate on the rubbishy thrillers they had thrown me. The six bare sides of the cell made a merciless cube that cramped me, a cruel prism that pressed claustrophobia into me. I lay with my arms at my sides, longing to scream or to fling myself at the door, but telling myself the hopelessness of it, willing myself to lie still. Later I dozed for a time.

In the evening Buzz brought my good clothes down. The cop made me leave them outside the door in their plastic bag, in case I put my head in it. They lay with my belt and laced shoes, always taken in case you decide on capital punishment for yourself. Occasionally I drummed out rhythms on the pipes with my tin mug to which the only other prisoner, an oldish guy in the cell next to the gate, replied. On Sunday afternoon they took us outside for twenty minutes, and we sat in a little yard staring at a postage stamp of sky four storeys up. It was such a small bit of the world to be allowed that I scorned it, and looked instead at my fellow prisoner, an obvious old lag. He sat with his hands on his knees, looking up contentedly.

"Ere y'are, mate.' Buzz had brought fags. "Ave one o' these.'

Monday morning brought a fatalistic acceptance of my lot. Okay, so I was back inside. So what? It wasn't new. Footsteps approached, and without listening I heard the familiar sequence of sounds. The steel gate at the end of the passage was unlocked, opened, closed, and locked again. The footsteps came nearer. A key rasped and my cell door swung open.

'Your solicitor's here, Gaskin.'

The cop stood aside to let in a man in blue pinstripe.

'How d'you do? I'm Mr Bellis. Now, the first thing . . .' the cop leant against the wall outside, boredly studying his shoes, '. . . no chance of bail, Mr Gaskin,' said the lawyer, snappily professional. 'No point in our even applying. A straight remand to Risley, and nothing we can do about it.'

He smiled brightly, and walked out of my life forever.

'Er, can I change me clothes before I go?'

The cop yawned. 'All right, Gaskin, but be quick. You're on in a minute.'

He left my door open and took Bellis out through the steel gate. When his key had turned in the lock their footsteps clacked out of earshot. Luck, or perhaps a wish for privacy, made me change behind the cell door. As I was lacing my second shoe a fresh cop came in through the gate, locked it behind him, and opened up the other prisoner.

'Right, Griffiths. Court.'

'Umph.' A resigned grunt from the poor man. A pause. 'The young feller's already gone up, has he?'

'Yep.' The cop rattled his keys. 'Think so.'

He came along to check, and popped his head into my cell. He was young. His clear skin and shiny hair were a metre away as his face bobbed in and out, staring straight ahead. He did not look behind the door, but clattered back to his charge and a few seconds later unlocked the gate. The sliding door that leads to the court opened, then rattled shut. I was alone in eerie silence.

Dimly aware that something momentous was looming, I had as yet no idea what it might be. It was only the need for a fag that sent me along to the absent prisoner's cell. Three Park Drive lay in a packet by his bed, surrounded by painfully short dog-ends. Since he was so poor I left them. On the way back to my cell a half-impression struck me, and fear rippled my guts. Had I heard the cop re-locking the iron gate? From the corner of my eye it looked slightly ajar. The enormity of this swamped me. I stepped back into my cell and stood trembling. It wasn't possible. Yet when I plucked up the courage to go and look, it was. The gate was standing as cold and black and metallic as ever, but unlocked and slightly open.

During all this time cops were banging in and out of the Charge Room, whose door was almost directly opposite. When things were quiet I stepped out of the gate, gingerly. There were two sinks there and I turned a tap on to see if the noise would bring them. It made a tremendous din, but no one came. For another moment I dithered, then the encompassing walls made me decisive. I threw on my jacket and stepped forward, stopping a breathless metre from the Charge Room door. It was wide open. Inside, spoons rattled on saucers, cops guffawed, struck matches, shouted. I took a deep breath and flitted past. No apprehending bellow followed me. At the end of the corridor, a door. Would it lead outside? I ran along on tiptoe, opened it, and stepped into a small square yard enclosed on all its sides by the building. Fumbling the door closed behind me, I looked around wildly for a drainpipe on which to climb out. Then I noticed a gap in the wall at the far end and ran through it. I was in the station grounds.

Walking quickly without looking back, I reached the police

car park and started to cross it, weaving in and out among silent pandas. After twenty paces a cop holding a walkie-talkie stepped around a corner of the building, looking up at a high window. When he came into view my pace slowed. I walked up to him with as much nonchalance as I could muster, and we drew level.

'India Two to Control,' he said. 'Testing, testing.'

I carried on at the same speed through the gate and into the street, then pelted along the busy pavements. Heads turned and people stared but I fled regardless, dodging housewives with shopping bags, jumping into the gutter often for a clear run. When I had put some distance between myself and the police station I slowed down to a fast walk, for an even faster think.

They would be combing the town for me any minute, that much was certain. Where would they think I was heading? Penmaenmawr? Or the other way, Colwyn Bay and Liverpool? More important, which way *should* I go? My first need was to hide till I could formulate a plan.

Running again, I zigzagged through streets of guest houses till I reached the public gardens below the Great Orme. Here was a way. By crossing over the mountain I could leave the town behind me. I slogged up the steep gardens, climbed a stone wall at the top, and dropped on to the heathery mountainside. Steadily onwards and upwards I went, maintaining speed though my legs were leadening to two dull aches. I leapt ditches, dragged myself through thorny hedges and scaled slippery walls till at last, gasping, I topped the summit. After lying face down in spiky heather, panting, I got to my feet and plunged down the other side, exhilarated. After a few moments I pulled up with a shock.

There was no way down. A sheer cliff face of grey rock yawned in front of me, the wintry Atlantic pulverizing house-sized rocks at its base hundreds of feet below. Seagulls wheeled high above, expressing my frustration in their cries. I would have to go back.

After the short, exhausting climb back to the peak I made a cautious descent to a point above the gardens. In summer the heather would have hidden me, but not now, in January. I had to make do with some leafless bushes, from which I could watch the gardens and the street below. Jim Jones's mother lived there, and I watched on the off chance that he might appear in his pick-up. Time passed. Then, to my horror, a policeman came into the gardens with an Alsatian dog straining on a short chain in front of him. They climbed the slope and went over the wall at the top, following the route I had taken earlier. By now I was terrified. It would take them a long time to follow me here, but when they were out of sight I dashed to a new hiding place at the top of the gardens. A workman came into view. He had been hidden by a rise in the ground before, and I now saw that he was turning over the soil below a long row of saplings. He took his coat off as I watched and threw it over a bush, stuffing his Army & Navy jungle hat into the pocket. As he worked he moved away from it, and as he moved away so I crept closer. Debutantes' eyes never stared at an Yves St Laurent gown as did mine at that donkey jacket. When he was far enough away I flitted across a rosegarden, pinched it, and scuttled behind a shelter to try it on. I wound my long hair into a ball, shoved the hat over it, and turned my coat collar up so no one should see my blondness. Then I walked off the Orme and down the street to the beach.

Soon I reached a golf course, and crossed it. My destination was The Button Factory in Abergele, since Colin and Jan were friends I could trust. With the golf course behind me I avoided the road, and plodded instead over high hills till a point came when I had to go down and cross it. When the narrow strip of tarmac was empty I streaked over, disappearing into hills again on the far side. Before Rhos, the little resort between Llandudno and Colwyn Bay, the road runs along a narrow ledge of rock beside the sea, and it is impossible to cross the mountains. I nervously followed the main road into the town, then disappeared into quieter streets. After crossing the Rhos golf course I made my way back to the beach. The tide was far, far out and I walked beside the water till Colwyn Bay was behind me. I was now in an area I knew well from recent thieving expeditions, and had my route planned out. I had to cross the grounds of the North Wales Police Headquarters, but that was unimportant. They only see what they expect to see, and the last person they expected to find in the grounds of their H.Q. at that moment was me. I took a round-about route to avoid my secret garage, which they might be watching. After a long walk, mostly along the beach, Abergele hove into view. The Button Factory was on the main road, and I took my time approaching it.

Bang! BangBangBang! Bang!

It was getting dark. Electric light fell upon me when Jan opened the door. When she recognized me she looked exactly as though someone had grabbed her throat, shutting off her breath.

'Graham!' She grasped my lapels in shaking hands and pulled me inside, slamming the door. 'Oh, Graham.'

She charged along the passage ahead of me, her plump arse wobbling a semaphore of shock. 'Col! Col! Colin! It's Graham, Colin. He's *here*!'

Colin emerged from the living room, rubbing his eyes clownishly. He grinned. 'We've just been hearin' about you on the radio, mate.'

In a chair by the fire, with my elbows on my knees and my head in my hands, I gave in at last to a prolonged fit of shaking. When I came out of it I was exhilarated. The cell walls had miraculously fallen away and I was free again. I took a deep breath, and shook the stale smell of prison from my hair.

As if my problems weren't bad enough I was now famous, at any rate in North Wales. The report of my escape was the main item on the evening news on T.V., and gave their idea of which direction I would take out of Llandudno. It was frighteningly accurate. Motorists on the coast road were asked to look out for me, it was believed I would head for Liverpool. A mug-shot of me took up the entire screen when the report ended. Colin leaned over and switched off.

'So,' I said, "ow do I get away, then?'

There was a thoughtful silence.

'Promise you won't laugh,' Jan said.

'Eh?'

'The best idea would be for you to go as a woman, Graham.'

Colin and I hooted with laughter, but she persisted. 'With your blond hair and fair skin they'd never suss you.'

'Ah, come on, Jan. Be serious, girl. Yer'll never talk me into that.'

It took her over an hour to dress me and make up my face. She began by supervising my shave, the closest I'd ever had and also the most extensive. It included my legs. She packed a bra with rolled-up socks, put me into a long dress and applied face powder, lipstick and eye make-up. Someone had left a pair of court shoes in a bag of stuff on one of the moribund button machines, and though they were much too small I found that walking was just possible when I squeezed my feet into them. It was also acutely painful. In the end even I had to admit that I did look like a woman. A slut, perhaps, but definitely a female.

'Try and sit a bit more gracefully,' Jan said when the transformation was complete.

I ceased picking my ear, and put the leg that lay sprawled over the arm of the chair back with the other.

'Okay,' I said. 'I'm anybody's.'

Colin laughed. 'Right, Graham. Let's go an' try it out, then.'

'Do we 'ave to?' My heart sank at the prospect. 'Yeh, okay. We do. Get a bag, Col, we'll rob some milk from the dairy.'

They parked a loaded milk float in the street overnight, and we often relieved them of much-needed pintas. When we left the house Colin put his arm through mine and we started off along the main road, me clacking along at his side and swinging my arse when we passed any people. Apart from the crippling shoes, it was easy.

Chink, clink. We filled the bag and walked home. As we were approaching The Button Factory a man in a passing car stared hard at me, and jammed his brakes on urgently. He overshot the front door by about twenty metres, then turned in his seat to watch me.

Bang!Bang!Bang!Bang! To my horror, his reversing lights came on as I hammered. 'Come on, Janet, come *on*!' I whispered, scared stiff. 'I'm sussed!'

As the car shot backwards, its engine a high-pitched whine, our door opened. The driver, drawing level, stared whitely as I passed through. In a paranoiac sweat I ran wildly through The Button Factory, searching desperately for a back way out or a place to hide, expecting the inevitable knocking to begin at any moment. It did not. When my nervousness had subsided we sat down to discuss the mystery. After a time Jan voiced the thought that had crossed all of our minds.

'He must have fancied you, Graham.'

Our laughter may linger there still, silent amid the rusting machines.

Next morning they lent me a couple of quid, and stood grinning on their doorstep as I tip-tapped away to the bus stop clutching a bag with my clothes inside it. A Coastliner goes express to Chester, but I feared police scrutiny and climbed on to a local bus instead.

'Single to Rhyl, please,' I piped in a ludicrous falsetto.

Bzzzzzzp. The machine spat a ticket into the conductor's hand. 'Thirty-five pence, love.'

When he had gone I kicked off my high heels. My feet throbbed relief. Crossing my stockinged legs as I primly ignored the leers of my fellow passengers, I felt inwardly quite confident. The sight of an obvious detective watching the buses at Rhyl changed my mood, but I clacked brazenly past him in my agonizing shoes and climbed aboard the Chester bus. Upstairs I chose a seat where I could watch him, sat down, eased the shoes off and lit a fag. The detective's presence in the corner of my eye filled me with nauseous apprehension, and I couldn't help looking at him. He glanced up and our eyes met. It dawned on me that for the last minute I had been taking deep, anxious, masculine drags on the fag, which was held like a gun in my fist. He watched me jam it clumsily between two fingertips. The bus's engine thumped into life and he looked away, uninterested.

Halfway to Chester nervousness overcame me. The passengers seemed to be giving me funny looks, so I left the bus at the next stop. Experience had taught me to wait for lifts, but today was different. As soon as I had put one not unshapely leg in front of the other and extended my thumb, a car stopped. The driver was oldish, and male.

'Make yourself comfy, love. Put the radio on if you want.'

He drove through the towns in furious bursts, tearing around corners and screeching to a halt centimetres from packed zebra crossings, then crawled with tortoise slowness through the countryside, furtively eyeing my sock-filled bodice and footballer's legs. It may have been this that gave him the bursts of speed. He didn't try anything on.

At Chester station, an unforeseen problem. Which toilet should I use to change my clothes? Entering the Gents as a girl might mean trouble, as might leaving the Ladies as a man. In the end I watched till I was sure the Gents was empty, then dashed in undetected and found a cubicle. Five minutes later I strolled out again, comfortably masculine.

Ten minutes after that I was on the road again, thumb held hopefully out. As I stood in the drizzle with the cars flying callously past, my euphoria at having escaped became a little blighted. After all, what progress had I made? I was back in the trap that had held me before my arrest, only now it was worse. I was a fugitive as well.

When I got to Liverpool I took a bus to Rice Lane.

'Two sugars, Gazz?' Valerie asked.

'Five please, Val.'

'*Five?* D'yer know what that stuff does to yer body?' In the end she compromised on three.

There was a lull in the conversation. Leo leaned forward. ''Ave yer thought o' tryin' The Crypt, Gazzer?'

'The Crypt? What's that?'

He looked vaguely embarrassed. 'Well, it's for dossers, like, reelly. It'd keep yer off the streets till yer get fixed up, though.'

'Yeh? Where is it, Lee?'

'In town. In the cellar under the Mersey Funnel.'

'What, that new cathedral?'

'Yeh.'

The bus dropped me in Lime Street, and in a few minutes I had walked up the hill to the Catholic cathedral and found the place, a refuge for homeless derelicts. I stood in the street outside. If there had been anywhere else to go I would have gone there, even if it had been hundreds of miles away and I could only have stayed for a day. Later I often did this to get away from The Crypt, spending hours on the road getting to Brenda's or The Button Factory where I would have a meal, stay a night, and come straight back. Now, I plucked up my courage and went inside.

There were about twenty beds around the walls, all full of fleas as I later discovered, and some tables where a lot of drunks and hobos were supping tea. Most looked verminous, and some had bags stuffed full with newspapers which they kept close to themselves, like valuables. I stood in the doorway until a guy came over.

'Hello there,' he said, 'I'm John Rossington, the project leader. Got no place to stay?'

'Er, no.'

'Well, you can stay here. We've a rule that says only for three consecutive nights, though.' He was quite young, and looked all right. 'For a lot of these men,' he indicated the dosser-filled tables, '. . . that means moving to the Salvation Army hostel at

Arden House for a night, then coming back here for the next three. What's your name?'

'Graham.'

'All right then, Graham. Take a bath if you want one. Most of these never bother.'

I lay in the hot water wondering what to do next. Though I was glad to have escaped what would have been certain prison, there was still no way out of my real problem. It seemed there was no place for me save in society's bins. If it wasn't prison or a mental hospital, it was a dosshouse. Still, I *was* free, the water *was* hot, I *was* clean. Not many positive things it's true, but some. I spent every subsequent night at The Crypt in the bath.

Over the next couple of days I met winos who remembered me from the Rosie Munro era, and began to visit the pubs which catered for this human flotsam and jetsam. Some of the guys in The Crypt were young, like Scotch Ian.

'Hold oot yer hand, Scoose.'

He pulled out a plastic bottle and rattled some capsules on to my palm.

'What are they?'

He gave me a faraway grin. 'Valium.'

'Valium? Tranquillizers? What are they like?'

'What are they like?' He grimaced, nodded his head, laughed noiselessly. 'They make it bearable, that's what they're like. Get a few down ye wi' the drink an' ye go aff yer heed.'

Now that I'd slipped into my place as a derelict it wasn't that hard to survive. There was no way I could change anything, so I drank cider and took valium to cushion the knocks of everyday life. My days were spent mooching around town. There was a place in Manchester Street called the Single Homeless, a sort of soup kitchen where a social worker gave you a meal chit and you got something to eat, never enough to fill you. Wendy, a pretty, copper-haired girl of about twenty-six, seemed different from most social workers and we soon developed a good relationship, laughing and joking whenever we met. As far as the hardships allowed I had a good think. It was obvious that if I carried on with crime I'd soon be back inside, so I started visiting the Jobcentre daily. On my third visit they gave me a card. Mr Costas Angeli, proprietor of the Cooker Market in Hardman Street near the city centre, was in need of a young labourer.

Standing in a warehouse in which half-dismantled cookers were piled to the roof, I expected some kind of formal interview. A dark, wavy-haired man, well-built and smartly dressed, stepped out of an office at the back. In spite of his Greek appearance his accent was pure Liverpool.

'Jobcentre send yer?'

'Yeh.'

'Good lad. Step inside.'

He took me into the workshop. 'What's yer name? Graham? Okay, Graham. This is Norm an' this is Mike.' Two screwdrivers stopped turning while their wielders nodded. 'Call me Coss.' He pottered about, telling me the job. 'When d'yer wanna start, son? Tomorrow?'

'Er . . .'

'Tell yer what, kid. Start Monday. Nine o'clock sharp, right?'

'Okay, Coss.'

After my three nights in The Crypt I went to the Salvation Army at Arden House. They gave me a chit saying they would accept me and I took it to social security, telling them I'd found a job.

'Where did you sign on last, Mr Gaskin?'

If my file was sent from North Wales they would find out I was wanted, and tell the police my address.

'Er, I never 'ave, mate.'

After that things changed a little for the better, and I was rewarded with the knowledge that my own efforts had brought about the change. Coss confirmed that I was starting work and they paid my first week at Arden House. On Saturday they sent me a Giro to buy working clothes.

At five minutes to nine on the Monday morning I arrived at the Cooker Market, nervous at starting in my first job. There was no one there. I stood for ten minutes, then sat on the step. At twenty-five to ten a red B.M.W. slid to a halt opposite me, and Coss climbed out.

'Bang on time, eh lad? Very good.' He laughed, and nodded at the gorgeous blonde lady in the driver's seat. 'That's the wife. Yer'll be seein' a lot of 'er, she runs the shop in Grove Street where we sell this junk.'

The job was great. Coss was a lovely bloke, an out-and-out villain. Norm stayed in the warehouse fixing the cookers while Mike and I took them to Grove Street in the van, then delivered cookers from there to customers all over the city. After a week Mike left and his place was taken by Derek. He was black, with a bald head like an enlarged Easter egg.

'Jesus,' he said when Coss introduced us. ''E's a fine example o' the Master Race, eh?'

We were friends from the first.

By now valium had become a regular feature of my life, insulating me from my fears. The lads at The Crypt taught me how to obtain it. You turned up at a random doctor's, gave him a bogus name and a spiel about things upsetting you, and came away with a prescription for a hundred capsules. It was that simple. So it was with my mind benumbed and my gestures exaggeratedly slow that I rode all day with Derek, delivering and fitting cookers. We made some money in tips, but most of it came from fiddles. People were incredibly stupid. When they came into the Grove Street shop and bought a gas cooker, Mrs Coss asked them if they wanted it fitted, which they always did. It cost £6, and was done with a rubber hose.

Derek would turn to them blandly. 'D'yer want a copper fit or a 'ose, love?'

'Er, I dunno. They said at the shop that yer'd fit it, like.'

He'd look at me exasperatedly. 'They never explain, do they Graham?' Turning back to the woman, 'Was it six quid they charged yer?'

'Yeh.'

'That's for a copper fit, love. It's two quid more for a 'ose, but it means yer'll be able to move the cooker around. To clean be'ind it, like.'

They nearly always agreed, so we got £2 for ourselves on every job. When the odd person did baulk at paying it was awkward. We didn't actually do copper fits, only hoses. Derek would grin plausibly.

'Tell yer what, Graham. We'll give 'er one on the 'ouse, shall we? Don't say nothin' to the boss though, love.'

This usually assured us of a tip. Sometimes when people bought their cooker Mrs Coss forgot to arrange the fitting.

'D'yer want it fitted, love?'

'Eh? Too bloody true, I've got to cook me feller's tea on that in 'alf an hour.'

'It's seven quid, love. We'll do it for a fiver if yer don't mention it at the shop.'

The cookers were guaranteed, and maintenance work gave us a chance to make money on parts. Derek was a natural actor, and could have been a star Othello if the breaks had been different. He'd dismantle the cooker, wrestle a part loose and stand looking at it, spanner poised, lips pursed morosely like a doctor preparing to tell you bad news.

'I'm afraid this one needs a split-ring commutator, love.' He'd look her in the eye. 'They're fourteen quid new, but we can put in a reconditioned for a fiver.'

One afternoon we serviced a cooker in a nineteenth-floor flat in a block called Greenheys on Cantril Farm, a desolate housing waste near Huyton. On this particular day I had popped more valium than usual and was stumbling around in a dream, galaxies away from the dim reality in which Derek and everyone else moved. We emerged blinking from the lift and stepped streetwards.

''Ow many 'ave yer 'ad today, Graham?'

'Uh? Wha'?'

'Never mind.' He glanced at his watch. 'Knockin' off time. Where shall I drop yer?'

'Drop me. Yeh, yeh. Mmm. Okay.'

'Where, Graham? *Where* shall I drop yer?'

A lucid moment wiped valium away. 'Er, anywhere near the Sally Army, please Derek.'

We drove along in his van, Derek whistling a current Soul hit through his teeth and me nodding at his side. In spite of the drug I noticed the vanload of police by the A.B.C. cinema before we reached it. The driver had his elbow outside and was looking in his mirror. As we came up behind he said something to the others and when we had passed they pulled out and overtook us, the red sign on their roof flashing, Stop! Stop! Stop! Derek hissed with annoyance, and pulled over.

'Yer get used to this when yer as black as me, Graham.'

Three uniformed cops and a plain clothes man walked over. The C.I.D. man stuck his head through the window.

'Give me the keys first. Now out of the car, both of you.'

We stood on the pavement. It was rush hour and a main road, and little groups of people formed outside the shops to watch us. Two cops started to search the car, opening the boot and taking the carpets up to look underneath.

'Let's see yer documents, then,' the C.I.D. man said to Derek.

Fear filtered slowly through to me, made remote by valium. The third cop, left with nothing to do, started asking me questions.

'What's yer name, son?'

My mind thought, This is a mistake, but my mouth said: 'Why? I'm not drivin' the bloody car, am I?'

He snatched a handful of my shirt and jutted his face into mine. 'Get this straight, kid. Give me any more lip an' yer get yours busted, right? Then yer'll answer me questions down at the station. Now what's yer name?'

'Paul Griffiths,' I said.

'Where d'yer live, Paul?'

'Er, Canny Farm.'

'Where in Cantril Farm?'

I chased the name of the flats we'd just left through valium mazes. 'The Hey,' I said.

'There's no such place in Cantril Farm.'

'Er, no. Greenhey,' I stuttered, remembering. The clear part of my mind cursed valium.

His eyes glittered menacingly, aeons away. 'Yer don't know where yer live?'

'No. I mean, yeh. We on'y moved in last week.'

'Ever been in trouble with the police?'

'No.'

He looked at me closely, making me realize my fear and my fleeing eyes. 'Why've yer got this attitude, then?'

'What attitude?' An upsurge of anger swamped the valium. 'I 'aven't got no fuckin' attitude. I've 'ad a 'ard day at work, mate, an' I want to finish. Why don't yer let me?'

The C.I.D. bloke finished with Derek then. 'Right, lads. Yer can go.'

Watched doubtfully by the constable, we drove away.

One day I turned from a shop window to find Wendy tapping my shoulder.

'How are you, Graham? We've missed you at Single Homeless. Where've you been?'

'I've got a job, Wendy. So I can afford me own food now.'

She laughed. 'Good. What about a place? Have you got somewhere?'

'No.' I shook my head. 'On'y The Crypt an' the Sally Army.'

'Hmm.' She looked thoughtful. 'Tell me where you work, Graham, and if I can do something to help I'll get in touch.'

One dinner hour a week later she picked me up in her car and took me to Halfway House, a hostel on Princes Avenue. It was owned by a charity that favours prison reform, and looked better than the Salvation Army. The staff were young, and though one of them slept in every night none actually lived there. The idea of moving into the place was attractive, and caused me to make an error of judgment. I decided to tell a social worker the truth. We were driving back, Wendy intent on the traffic. I glanced at the delicate features beneath her copper hair, and plunged in.

'Can I be straight with yer, Wendy?'

'Yes, Graham.' She smiled sideways. 'I'm glad you want to be.'

'I'm on the run.' It was out, then. She concentrated on her driving. 'The police are after me in North Wales.'

'Oh, Graham,' she said sadly, 'you can't stay at Halfway House, then.'

My migrations between The Crypt and Arden House continued. You were supposed to be in The Crypt by eight but John Rossington, the project leader who had welcomed me that first night, was quickly becoming a friend and let me stay in the pub till ten. Afterwards, drowsy with beer and valium, I'd lie in the hot water trying to close my ears to the depressing coughs and sudden, bitter quarrels of the derelicts next door. Some weekends I thumbed it down to stay with Brenda. Hitching was hard in winter, but it made a change from lying in the bath in The Crypt, and there was a hot meal and a bed to look forward to at the end of it. A couple of months passed in this way.

On the night of the 1978 Derby match, Liverpool versus Everton, I strolled down to Goodison Park for something to do. The streets near the ground were humming with excitement and scuffles were going on everywhere, most of them caused as far as I could tell by the presence of the police. Trouble was the last thing I wanted, but it was fun to watch. Whenever the action came too close I sidled away, taking care not to become involved. Escaping from one punch-up, though, I inadvertently blundered into another, and before I knew what was happening fists were flying all around and someone had kicked me. A lad next to me biffed a cop, and a different cop got me in a headlock and pushed me against a police horse. As the animal's stiff hair rubbed my face like a nailbrush the copper gave me a dig in the face.

'Gerroff, will yer?'

I took hold of his tunic, heaved him off, and ran. There was a lull in the fighting just then and the nearby police fanned out to catch me. It was like a game of British Bulldog at Northfields as I weaved through them, dodging this way and that. In the end they nabbed me, took me into the little substation under the football ground, and stuck me in a cell. I could have wept. The misery of the past weeks looked like freedom now that cell walls were around me. My despair filled the confined space thickly, bouncing off the walls and coming back to me more concentrated than before. After half an hour they drove me to Walton Lane police station.

The desk sergeant was forty years old and built like a brick shithouse. He put the heels of his hands on the edge of the table and pushed his considerable weight upwards till his feet left the floor. 'Name?'

'Paul Griffiths.'

He dropped down, flushed with exertion. 'Where d'you live, Paul?'

'47, Andrew Street.'

My Dad's old house, now occupied by another family. It was such a trivial offence that I hoped they wouldn't check. After some more questions the sergeant put me into a side room and went away. Ten minutes later he returned. When I tried to stand he pushed me back into the chair.

'Your name's not Paul Griffiths and you don't live in Andrew Street,' he said patiently. 'Now who are you and where do you live?'

For a split second my mind was a total blank. It dragged itself through the weeks and months of stifled hours that awaited me in prison, and cleared. The struggle must continue.

'Look, sergeant.' I glanced at his face, ashamed, then looked at my feet. 'I'm sorry for bein' such a divvy. I'll tell yer the truth now.'

He sat on the desk at my side, clenching and unclenching his fist in some weightlifter's exercise. 'Your name'll do for a start.'

'Graham Gaskell.'

'Date of birth?'

'Second o' the twelfth, fifty-eight.'

He wrote it down and gave it to a constable to check. Every criminal knows they need your correct name and date of birth to lift your record from C.R.O., and the date I had just given him was wrong. The last digit should have been a nine.

'Ever been in trouble with the law, Graham?'

'No, sergeant.' I shook my head. 'Never.'

'Been lucky so far, eh? Where d'you live, then?'

'Er, nowhere reelly,' I said.

His suspicion returned. 'You must live somewhere. Where are your parents?'

'They're both dead.'

He jumped down from the desk and stood in front of me flexing his shoulder muscles. 'Come on, Graham, what are you scared of? Have you got something at home you don't want us to find?'

'No, honest, it's like I told yer. I'm 'omeless. I 'ad a bedsit in Lark Lane but I got chucked out for not payin' me rent. That was before I started me job, like.'

'Job? Who d'you work for, then?'

I told him, then picked up a telephone directory and leafed through it till I found Coss's home number.

'Look, give 'im a ring. 'E'll vouch for me.'

'Stand over there, then.' When I was at the far side of the room he dialled the number. As soon as he looked away I edged closer.

'Hello, is that Mr Angeli?'

'Yes,' I heard, very faintly. Shifting along by moving my weight sideways, toe to heel, heel to toe, I moved slowly nearer.

'City police here. I'm ringing to ask if you have a Mr Gaskell working for you?'

'Er ...' I measured Coss's hesitation in frantic heartbeats. Come on, Coss. Please come on. '... is that Graham?' he crackled, still very far away.

'That's right,' the sergeant said.

'Yes, he works for me.' Coss paused. 'He's a nice lad.'

'Do you know where he lives, Mr Angeli?'

I edged closer.

'No.' Coss's voice was clearer now. 'He's between flats at the moment.'

Coss, you old rogue. Tremendously relieved, I was charged under the name of Graham Gaskell with a breach of the peace.

The desk sergeant lifted the heavy typewriter between his outstretched palms, up and down, up and down. 'You can't have bail, I'm afraid. No fixed abode, see. Don't worry, though. It'll only be a fine in the morning.'

They took me to the Bridewell in central Liverpool and clanged me into a dungeon for the night. Though I was still desperately afraid of discovery, at least I now had hope. My fingers were crossed that no cop from the old days would recognize me, and none did.

'The court will rise.'

Everyone stood up, and the magistrates trooped in. The Clerk of the Court riffled his papers until they sat down.

'First case, your honours, a breach of the peace.' He turned to me. 'Are you Graham Gaskell?'

'Yeh.'

'And are you at present . . .' he glanced at a paper, 'of no fixed abode?'

'Er, yeh sir. Till I find a flat, like.'

'Gaskell, you're charged that at Goodison Park football ground on 13th March 1978 you behaved in a manner likely to cause a breach of the peace. Do you plead Guilty or Not Guilty?'

'Guilty, sir.'

The offence was trivial. The chief magistrate gave me a lecture and a £29 fine.

'Do you need time to pay?'

'Yeh. I've on'y got a quid on me.'

They muttered. 'The fine must be paid in four weeks. You may leave the court.'

I made my way to work, smiling. That was one fine that would never be paid.

For the next few weeks I carried on much as before, but taking valium in ever larger amounts. Life on the run meant intense pressure and the drug, supposedly my escape, added to my difficulties. I began to have the odd day off work, and this got worse until it was only on odd days that I went in. Eventually my job floated off into the past, like a dinghy cut free of the barge that tows it along. One night I popped a huge number of valium and it was so freezing in The Crypt that I crept into the stifling boiler room to sleep. Heat and the valium kept me unconscious till eleven in the morning, and when I stumbled into The Crypt it was empty. Worse, I was locked in. The exit door had a mortise lock that looked unbreakable.

'*Je*sus.' My voice splashed the concrete walls and oozed down them like slime. 'What do I do now?'

Nosing about in the office, I found £13 cash and two allowance books in a desk drawer. One book was a woman's, for £28 every Monday, the other was for only £13 but was a man's, and would be easier to cash. They must have been left with John Rossington for safe keeping. Social security would issue new books as soon as the theft was discovered, so I had no qualms about robbing the wretched derelicts to whom they obviously belonged. The government had never done anything but oppress me, and I jumped at the chance of robbing it.

With a chisel and a crowbar from the boiler room, I attacked the door. Once on the far side I made it look like a break-in, put the tools back, and scarpered. John Rossington later told me what time he discovered the theft and it was uncomfortably close, within minutes.

In town I booked into the Y.M.C.A. for the night, then found a doctor and got a scrip for a hundred valium. I collected them from the chemist but didn't take them that night.

Next afternoon I was strolling down Bold Street when someone shouted my name.

'Graham! Graham! Hang on a minute, will ye?'

Scotch Ian, the valium popper, crossed the road. He was wearing a bobble hat and jeans with the arse hanging out.

'Lissen, Graham,' he said as he approached, 'I've a few quid. D'ye fancy takin' a train oot somewheer diff'rent for the day? We'll go tae a doctor first an' get some . . .'

Before he had finished I pulled the bottle of Roche 10 from my pocket. He nodded, giving me his silent laugh.

'Ye're a tiger, Graham, so y'are.'

We popped some there and then, and having decided upon Crosby as a destination, walked through gusty streets to the station. The allowance books were dodgy things to carry, so I hid them under a stone in the station car park when we arrived. Then we went drinking in the thick-carpeted pubs of the town.

'Will ye have a wee one, Graham?'

'Yeh, get us a Pernod. 'Ere.' I handed him a capsule. 'We'll chase 'em down with a weer one still, eh?'

As the night progressed we drank harder and heavier, gulping down further tranquillizers whenever the thought struck us. The reality of our surroundings gradually became disjointed, retreating to unconscious regions of our minds. The solid citizens of Crosby, grouped in jovial bunches around us, became more and more remote, fleeing or engulfing when we looked at them, and their voices washed over us in confused eddies of sound. By closing time the pub was like an ill-remembered dream.

'A bottle o' cider to take out, please mate.'

We popped further valium to protect ourselves against the cold as we staggered along the street. It took us ages to get to the station, and by the time we reached it the last train had gone, so we turned and walked back through the quiet streets.

The surrounding streetlamps lit our faces weirdly as we stood looking at the empty house.

'Even if there's nae money in there,' Ian said, 'it'd be a place tae kip, an' I could do wi' that, I'll tell ye.'

We went round the back, put the cider bottle down in the alley and climbed the wall, wobbling precariously at the top and more or less falling into the garden.

'Ian, hush.' I pointed. A light had gone on in a house behind us. We watched a woman seat herself near the window and open a book.

'A' clear,' he said. 'Come on, I'll have the two of us in there in a wee jiffy.'

He climbed on to the kitchen windowsill and began pulling ineptly at a ventilation flap.

'Out o' me way,' I said after a minute. 'Lemme do it.'

Perched on the sides of my feet, I put my fingertips in the narrow gap and tugged. CRASSHH! Blood streamed as the sound of shattering glass ruptured the night air. The lighted window across the way shot up, and the woman started squawking. Clumsy with booze and valium, we clambered back over the wall.

'Ooch!'

Ian fell with a painful thud on the far side, but though winded did not forget to scoop up the cider bottle as we charged past. My cut hand splashed dark poppies of blood on to the pavement as we ran. Ten minutes later, with much nervous fidgeting and not a little noise, we stole a battered Mini from outside a house and roared off towards the M6 and London.

'Pop a couple o' vallies,' Ian yelled over the noise of the engine as I stared at my cut hand, 'it'll deaden the pain.'

As I looked at the deep gash I realized there *was* no pain. I swallowed a capsule anyway and bound the wound with an oily rag. At Knutsford we pulled into the services, clambered out of the passenger door because the other wouldn't open, and looked at the car park with bleary eyes.

Plodding wearily upstairs to the cafeteria, it chanced that I looked down through the window. A gleaming Range Rover had appeared below and two policemen were standing next to it holding Ian by his arms. Their three faces looked up at me, an eerily lit tableau frozen by neon signs. Fear clenched my heart as my run began.

I flew up the stairs and along the passage that spans the motorway, then cascaded down through the entrance area on the other side. Heads turned from Space Invader machines to watch me pass. At top speed I raced across the wide car park and into the dark fields beyond, entering their shadow as a cop emerged from the services entrance. He took his hat off and looked around perplexedly, scratching his head. Keeping in shadow I jogged along in pitch darkness parallel to the motorway, hoping to reach an entry point to it. Twice the Range Rover sped past, burning up the country roads in search of me. Each time I threw myself down and lay in deep shadow till the danger had passed.

Three miles later, very tired, I climbed an embankment and saw a motorway sliproad below. The combination of adrenalin, exertion, alcohol and valium overcame me then and I collapsed and rolled down to the dark road, where I lay stupefied in the ditch. When I came to blood was leaking from my cut hand again. I got to my feet and stood shakily at the roadside. After half an hour an ancient lorry chugged around the corner and stopped, catching me in the glare of its lights. Its engine thundered and black smoke belched from its exhaust. The door swung open.

'Where are yer headin', kid?'

'Liverpool, mate.'

'Bootle docks do yer?'

As soon as I was seated, sleep came. When the lorrydriver nudged me awake the streets were still dark, but full of people hurrying to work. In a valium trance I lurched on to a bus, gave a false name and address when I found my money had gone, and went back to sleep.

''Ey, love. 'Ey! Come on, sleepin' beauty.' I opened my eyes. An old woman was leaning over from the seat in front, prodding me and smiling. 'Is this yer stop, love? Walton?'

I staggered from the bus and wandered into the Casualty Department of Walton Hospital to get my hand stitched. It was still in its dirty rag and the receptionist looked at me strangely.

'What's your name, love?'

'Gaskell. Graham Gaskell.'

'Take a seat over there.'

Sleep returned as soon as I sat down. I dimly heard them calling my name several times before it registered, when I followed a nurse into a cubicle, sat down, and promptly fell asleep again.

'Mr Gaskell.' Someone shook me. 'Mr Gaskell, Mr Gaskell.' I jerked myself awake. A young doctor with glasses and an earnest expression was examining my cut. 'How did you do this, Mr Gaskell?'

'Er, I dunno.' Sleep pulled me back. I slid into it.

'Mr Gaskell.' Shake, shake. 'Mr Gaskell.'

'Yeh?' My eyelids lifted slowly. 'Wass the problum?'

'How did you get your cut? Was it on glass?'

'Yeh, glass.' Back to sleep.

'Mr Gaskell.' Shake, shake, shake. 'Mr Gaskell.'

'What, man?'

'Why do you keep falling asleep, Mr Gaskell?'

'I dunno.'

After much pressure, and then only so he would let me go back to sleep, I dug into my pocket and listlessly pulled out the plastic valium bottle. It dropped from my fingers and clattered across the floor, completely empty. He continued to shake. I continued to doze.

'Why did you take them, Mr Gaskell?'

'Eh? I don't know. Didn't know what they were.'

'How many were in it?'

'Hmm? A 'undred. I never took 'em all meself. There was two of us.'

He jerked me awake while he stitched my hand.

'Come and lie here, Mr Gaskell.' They helped me on to a trolley. 'Drink this.'

When I had drunk the stuff I went back to sleep. A nurse shook me. 'Drink this, Mr Gaskell.'

'Wha'? I don't want 'ny more.'

'It's water, love. Drink it.'

As soon as I lay down to sleep again, nausea erupted. The nurse was ready with a bowl and I puked and puked into it, a horrible mess in which half-digested valium shells were prominent. It was twenty-four hours before I woke again.

Halfway through my cup of tea a psychiatrist arrived at my bedside.

'Why did you take all those tranquillizers, Mr Gaskell? Were you thinking of leaving us?'

'Er, no. I went on the booze with me mate an' some lad sold us 'em. 'E said they were great. I didn't know what they were, doctor, honest.'

'Will you try it again?'

'Oh no, doctor. No way. I'm not so stupid.'

At noon they discharged me. For a time I sat in a bus shelter around the corner, thinking. I had escaped capture once again, but this time I felt no exhilaration whatever. How many more times would I get away with it before they caught me? I watched people passing. All of them seemed to have a destination and a purpose, while I had none. It was freezing, and I was penniless as usual. What I needed most at that moment was warmth and companionship, a place where I could relax.

I hitched to Abergele to visit Colin and Jan, arriving at The Button Factory after dark. A tall girl with henna'd hair opened the door.

'Er, hiya. Is Colin there? I'm a friend of 'is, like. Graham.'

'Oh, you're Graham, are you? Great.' She preceded me into the living room. 'I'm Gina. I've really wanted to meet you, you're famous round here.'

Gina would be famous herself later, when she stabbed her lover and was sent to prison for manslaughter.

In Wales, where nothing much happens, it was a big thing that I'd escaped from Llandudno police cells and been on T.V., and I revelled in the glory for the rest of the evening as we drank numberless cups of tea. At midnight Colin and Jan went to bed. Gina and I talked a while longer, and later a comfortable silence fell. Looking at her, I felt good. She was an easy person with whom to be at rest.

'Er, Gina.'

'Hmm?'

'Can I sleep with yer?'

She glanced at me, then looked into the fire. 'All right. Stay on your side of the bed, though.'

We went in. Ten minutes later we were making love.

A few happy days passed, then I had to think about money. Staying at The Button Factory was impossible, and wherever else I went I would need cash. One early morning at the beginning of April I set off along the A55 to hitch to Liverpool. There was a touch of spring in the air and luck was with me, the first car that stopped took me all the way. It is several miles from Liverpool city centre to Crosby and I had no choice but to walk it. The allowance books were still under the stone where I had left them in the station car park. I shoved them into the waistband of my jeans and jumped the train into town, seeking the guard out rather than waiting for him to catch me.

'Look, mate, it sounds ridiculous this. I was leanin' out o' the window cleanin' me nails with the ticket, an' it blew out o' me 'and, like. Can I give yer me name an' address?'

They always believe a story as incredible as that one.

I hitched through the Mersey Tunnel and back to Abergele, arriving there late at night. In the morning I filled in the Change of Address parts in the books and Gina cashed the woman's in one post office, I did the man's in the little sub-post office near The Button Factory. We scored some dope and I gave Jan something to pay for what I had eaten, which didn't leave much over.

It is never wise to stay too long in any one place when you are on the run, and though I didn't feel like it I knew it was time to move. Today was Friday and I decided to catch a bus to London the following morning. Brenda's boyfriend was away at weekends and during these fugitive months I often went down there, stayed until Monday morning, then hitched back to Liverpool. It was a long way to go for a bed and something to eat, but to me it was worth it. It got me away from police who knew me, and even a few hours in a decent home away from The Crypt made it worth the journey. This week I had an added reason for going. The books could be cashed again on Monday, and it would be far safer to do it in London. That night Gina and I had a little talk.

'What are you going to do, Graham?'

'Go down to London an' stay the weekend with me sister.'

'Yes, but what are you going to *do*?' She squeezed my arm. 'You can't go on like this, Graham. You'll get caught before long, and come out again to the same thing. It could go on for ever.'

'Huh.' I shook her hand off and bent my head glumly forward. 'D'yer think I don't know that? D'yer think I like bein' like this? I've tried to get out of it loads o' times, but somethin' always fucks up. There just doesn't seem to *be* a way out.'

The room was silent save for the crackling of the fire.

Next morning I took the bus to London, but Brenda wasn't there. I rang throughout the day, and when there was still no reply went to King's Cross and spent eight hours in an all-night café. On Sunday morning I called at Brenda's again.

'I'm sorry, Graham.' She shook her head. 'It'd be all right with me, but 'e 'asn't gone this week,' she glanced at the door behind which her boyfriend was sleeping, 'an' 'e just won't 'ave it.'

'I expect I'll survive,' I said, turning to go.

''Ang on a minute, Graham.' She went into the kitchen and came out with a copy of *Time Out*. 'They 'ave adverts in 'ere for places to kip. Crash pads, like.'

It would still be best to cash the books in London, so I went to a café and looked through it till I found an advertisement for S.H.A.R.E., an organization that helped the single homeless. The address was in Westbourne Park, and after losing myself repeatedly on the Tube I eventually found it. The office was very disorganized, with three guys lounging about amid the clutter.

'We can't help you,' one said, 'we don't do crash pads.'

'Shit, man, I'm stuck for somewhere to sleep. On'y for to-night, like. If I get me 'ead down on the street the pigs'll 'ave me.'

Their leader, a bald guy of about thirty, relented. 'Go round to our house, then.' He scrawled the address on an envelope. 'There'll be someone in.'

The house was nearby, and the big bloke who answered my knock showed me into a scruffy living room where people were sitting around talking. I built a joint and had a smoke with them. After an hour the guys from the office came back carrying some party cans of beer, the bald one with a young girl in tow. She was nice, but painfully thin and plain-looking. We started to drink and the big guy who had opened the door to me, an ex-junkie, took continual nips at some kind of cough mixture. After a time he brought out a bottle of tuinal, a tranquillizer like valium, and started handing the pills around.

'Hey, turn the radio up.'

Soon everyone was dancing to the music, smoking joints, popping tuinal, and drinking. This went on until people grew tired and gradually, one by one, crashed out on the floor. Every hour through the night I awoke, and each time there were fewer people in the room. When they had all gone I switched the radio off, dragged the curtain down from the window, and curled up beneath it on the floor.

The sound of someone moving around woke me. It was morning. The thin girl who had been with the group's leader was mooching about in her nightie, tidying up. She bent to pick something up, and I saw that she was wearing no knickers. Then she did it again, and again. Was it deliberate? No matter. The sight of a raw sex first thing in the morning was pleasant enough.

When I got a chance I pulled the ex-junkie to one side.

'Are yer goin' out now?'

He grinned lopsidedly. 'Yeah, I'm going to get some cough mixture. Why?'

'D'yer want to make yerself a few quid?'

'Yeah, okay. How?'

In the post office I filled in two Change of Address forms. He cashed the woman's book as though collecting the money for her, and I did the man's.

''Ere y'are, lar.' I gave him back some of the notes. 'Seven quid. Not bad for two minutes' work, eh?'

Before I caught a bus to the motorway I dropped the man's book down a grid. The woman's meant £28 for me the following Monday.

A lorry dropped me at Knutsford services, and I had something to eat. Later, waiting on the sliproad for a lift, with money in my pocket and Gina waiting for me in Abergele, the world looked all right. It wasn't. A police car slid round the side of the services building and stopped. Its two occupants stared for a minute, and then it crawled over. They got out.

'Where're yer off to, son?'

'Liverpool, mate.'

'I'm not yer mate. Usually travel this way, do yer?'

'Well, yeh. When I'm skint, like.'

The other said, 'Let's see what you've got, then,' and plunged a hand into my pocket.

''Ey, yer can't do that.'

'No?' The first cop prodded me derisively, then tried a pocket too. His hand came out holding the allowance book. 'Interestin'.' He glanced at the cover. 'Yer name's not Mary McCandless, is it?'

Laughing, they put me in their car and drove me to a little substation next to the services.

'What's yer name?'

'Graham Gaskell.'

'Date o' birth?'

'Second o' the twelfth, fifty-eight.'

One of them scuttled away to telex.

'Where did you get this book, Gaskell?'

'From a feller in London. I give 'im a fiver for it, like.'

'What was his name?'

'Dunno. 'E was a Scouser, though. I wish I 'adn't bought it now.'

'Ever been in trouble with the law?'

'Yeh, once. I got done for a breach o' the peace in Liverpool.'

Two city police arrived later and took me by car to St Anne's Street police station in central Liverpool. All the way I acted like a real divvy, as thick as two short ones, staring into space as though in shock at my folly.

'First I go to a football match an' get meself done for disturbin' the peace,' I whined, 'then as if that's not enough I 'ave to buy this bloody book an' get meself in *more* trouble.'

When we arrived at St Anne's Street I continued with the act, adding mannerisms borrowed from Richardson and other Feltham morons. 'Yeh, well, er, I didn't understand, like. Not really. I bought the book off this bloke 'cos 'e needed the money, so 'e said.' I rubbed my palms down my face from forehead to chin. 'Oh, I'm a bloody *fool*.'

They swallowed it and were soon immensely irritated with me, the more so because I seemed too pathetic to hit. Then one of the C.I.D. men went to see the woman who owned the book.

She had a new one by now, and merely said she had given it to John Rossington to mind for her.

'Right, Gaskell,' the cop said when he returned, 'don't give me any more crap about buying that book in London. You told the old girl your name was John Rossington, right? You're not as thick as you've been making out, are you? What did you do, buy her a few drinks?'

They hadn't connected the book with the burglary at The Crypt, so confession seemed in order.

'Yeh, that's more or less what 'appened. I didn't want to get the ole girl in trouble so I kept me gob shut about 'er.'

He was happy at getting such an easy conviction. 'Tell you what, Gaskell. We don't want to drag the old lady through court, do we?'

'Er, no.'

'Well, how about this? You plead guilty tomorrow and get it dealt with there and then, and we'll forget the book's been cashed and only do you for receiving. That's fair enough, isn't it?'

'Yeh, that's cool, man. Thanks.'

They took my photograph and fingerprints under the name Gaskell, stamped F.O. on my file to show I was a First Offender (!), and sent me to the Bridewell till morning. In my cell I lay on the hard bunk with the prison smell in my nose, my mind a battlefield. Would I get away with it again? It didn't seem possible. After eight sleepless hours the cell cop opened me up and a solicitor breezed in.

'Good morning, Mr Gaskell. I'm from the firm of . . .'

'What d'yer want?' I demanded. 'I never asked for no lawyer.'

He smiled disdainfully. 'I've been assigned to defend you, Mr Gaskell. Now I've looked at the papers in your case and had a little chat with the prosecution, and my advice is this: ask for an adjournment for social enquiry reports. It's in your interest that . . .'

A typical lawyer, he had scented cash and wanted to spin things out.

'No,' I stated. 'We'll get it done this mornin'. The police want it that way an' so do I. Just play it like I tell yer.'

'You're very sure for a first offender,' he said, visibly annoyed.

'I'm sure o' this much.' I looked him in the eye. 'It's goin' to be a guilty plea followed by a simple fine. Right? That's what I agreed with the busies, an' I don't want 'em breathin' down me neck for breakin' me word.'

When this was clear I gave him a fictitious autobiography, telling him I was studying Engineering at Hendon Tech. He went out and a few minutes later the cop unlocked me for court.

They read out the first charge, theft of the book.

'Do you plead Guilty or Not Guilty?'

'Not Guilty, sir.'

'On the second charge, receiving the book knowing it to have been stolen, do you plead Guilty or Not Guilty?'

'Guilty, sir.'

The prosecutor stood up. 'In that case, Your Honour, we'll drop the charge of theft.'

My lawyer got to his feet and churned out the spiel I had fed him. 'My client . . . only one minor offence prior to this . . . man of good character . . . deeply sorry . . . ashamed at standing before you today.'

After a brief natter with his sidekicks, the chief magistrate addressed me. 'Mr Gaskell.'

'Yeh? Er, sir?'

'We haven't forgotten what it is to be a struggling student,' a nostalgic smile drifted across his lips, 'and we know it is easy to give in to a sudden temptation.' He furrowed his brows sternly. 'But though we understand your behaviour, we cannot excuse it. You have broken the law.' He paused to let this sink in, then relaxed and leaned back. 'You look an intelligent man, Gaskell, and because of this, and the naïveté you showed in buying this book from a trickster, we're going to put this incident down to an impetuous moment. You are fined £10. You may step down.'

The Clerk of the Court gave me four weeks to pay. The unpaid breach of the peace fine was not mentioned, and five minutes later I was back on the streets, free.

The mugs! I laughed aloud. Three times they had caught me, and three times I had slipped out of their hands. Passers-by half-smiled at me, wondering what was the joke.

Val and Leo found me on their doorstep again.

'Another piece o' toast, Gazz?'

I held out my plate. 'Please, Val.'

'Well, where's it goin' to be this time?' asked Leo.

As usually happened when the pressure was on I went to The Button Factory. Gina was still there and my only regret was that I could not stay, settle down like a normal person, and have a long rest. After a few days I returned to Liverpool, and for the next fortnight I stayed again at The Crypt, hounded, stealing what I could, standing in soup kitchen queues. It seemed that it would go on for ever. One weekend at the end of April, four months after my escape from Llandudno police cells, I hitched to Abergele again to see Gina.

The four of us were sitting down to a meal that evening when there was a knock at the door. Colin let two guys in, Tom, a Manchester lad I knew slightly, and his mate.

'Hiya, Graham. 'Ow goes it?'

'Not bad, Tom. Build a joint if yer want one, there's some dope on the mantelpiece.'

They stayed an hour, then left.

'Gina, I'm just goin' up to yer room for 'alf an hour.'

She smiled mysteriously. 'Does that mean . . .?'

'No.' I grinned. 'Well, yeh. Not yet, though. I'll write to me sister first.'

'All right,' she said, smiling still. 'We've plenty of time.'

11 | *Out of the Depths*

'Dear Brenda,' I wrote, and tapped my teeth, awaiting inspiration. Clump, bump. I listened. Bump, bang. Something made me peep out. Torches were flashing in the darkness, heavy boots were feeling their way on the stairs. Police! I looked around wildly, but there was nowhere to hide. Their voices were near the top of the stairs so I stood behind Gina's door and put the light out. As I did so a burst of static streamed from one of their walkie-talkies, and Colin heard it and charged out of his room across the landing.

''Ey, what are *you* lot doin' here? You can't go breakin' into people's houses any more than I can. Show me your bloody warrant.'

'We have reason to believe you're harbouring a fugitive,' said a voice.

'There's no fugitive here, mate. No warrant either, I'll bet. Come on, let's see it.'

While one talked to Colin the rest fanned out along the

corridor, opening doors, checking rooms. There were eight or nine cops there now and more kept arriving. Thunderous footsteps plodded up to Gina's door, and it opened. A little cop marched into the room, glanced around, and saw me.

'He's here, Sarge.'

Others came running, and their hands snatched greedily at me. With one holding either wrist they led me downstairs, past the policewoman sitting with Gina, and into the street where a convoy of vehicles waited. Radios crackled, torches flashed, a dog savaged its door when it saw me. What could have been more normal? For the time being I felt nothing, and was merely an observer. They snapped handcuffs on to both my wrists, put me in a car in the middle of the line, and showed off all the way to Colwyn Bay police station. Three happy coppers kept me company in my cell, and five minutes later an inspector walked in, smiling.

'So this is the famous escaper, eh? Tell us how you did it, lad.'

The station had a festive air now that I was caught, and many policemen and women came down to have a peek at me. In the middle of the night they took me to Llandudno, where I was received more sourly. Next morning the court remanded me to Risley.

It was back to the life I had always known.

'EXERCISE!' Bash, clang. 'Slop out!' Clatter, crash. 'Into yer boxes.'

Back to my cage. Free or imprisoned, it seemed that I must always live like an animal. Probably I should have been making plans for when I got out, but all I did was worry about how long I'd get.

My case came up early in May. Gina, Colin, Jan, Frannie Logan and others were in the court to watch me. I stood dry-mouthed while the magistrate made fussy notes on his jotter. Eventually he looked up.

'Graham Gaskin,' he said, 'you have wrought such a trail of havoc along this coast that we considered sending you to a higher court today, where a heavier sentence could be meted out to you.' He paused to see if his words were having the desired effect. When my blanched expression told him they were, he continued. 'At your age you must be sentenced either to eighteen months and over, or to six months and under, and eighteen months would be longer than you deserve.' He underlined a word on the pad in front of him. 'You will go to prison for six months. Take him down.'

My friends' faces were a sympathetic blur as the cell cop led me downstairs.

There were about fifteen Y.P.s waiting to go through Reception when the Welsh cops dropped me at Walton, and most had been in before. Their conversation was entirely about prisons.

'Wasn't you in Strangeways a while back? Yeh? Thought so. Me too, oh, er, end o' seventy-six. 'Member that Kitchen P.O., the ex-boxer?'

'Yair. Twat, wasn't 'e?'

For myself I sat quietly, taking no part in it. The Reception P.O. singled me out. My record was in front of him with the details of my numerous assaults on staff prominent in red type over several pages. He knew what he was getting, and acted accordingly.

'Hello, Gaskin,' he said affably.

'Er, hiya.'

'Well, what's it to be this time?' He paused. 'The Block or normal location?'

'Oh, I think I'll try normal location,' I said.

'Right.' He nodded, beaming. 'Good lad.'

As the day progressed I realized I was going to have an easy time in Walton. My behaviour during my Borstal sentence had put me down forever as a violent man, not to be given pressure, and the screws acted accordingly. On my first morning on B-wing the P.O. sent for me.

'Gaskin?'

'Yeh.'

'We're making you stairs cleaner. Ask the officer on the Ones for what you need.'

It is the cushiest job on the wing. The stairs took only a short time to clean and my cell was open all day, so I could go down to the Ones and talk to the servery lads, or wander about at will. The majority of the Y.P.s were in the M.R.A. Shop stripping cables, which is slave labour and really dirty work. My life was one of leisure in comparison.

They put me on the Fives where the landing officer was Rafferty, a good screw who did his job without giving anyone pressure. My cellmate was a three-year man, Parker, who had lived in Wales and knew some of my friends. His cell was smart and he had a radio, but after two days he got on my nerves. He was studying A levels, as any idiot can do if he gets a long sentence, and he thought this made him an intellectual.

'No one objects to discipline,' he told me one day, 'but the screws use it as a panacea for all kinds o' repression.'

'Pan o' what, did yer say?'

'Er, panacea,' he said lamely. 'A kind of excuse, like.'

I looked the word up and, sure enough, it meant something entirely different. After a week I moved, with Rafferty's help, into a single cell. This was better. I could slam my door and spend all evening reading, or working on my latest poem.

Many lads in Walton weren't strangers to me but guys I knew from earlier institutions, some when I was as young as seven or eight. The tragedy is that they are still there, walking from wing to workshop to exercise yard, and they all have stories like mine to tell. On Sunday nights we went to the Gym for five-a-side football. All the teams had the names of League Clubs, and this was taken seriously by everyone. Mine was Tranmere Rovers, and there were three other hard men on it. A lad called Snatter, whom I knew from Parkfield and Menlove Avenue, was in goal. Watford was top of the League and in this team too there was a kid I knew, Tommy McMullen, a tiny, dead hard little bloke who had been in St Vincent's.

'All right, Gazzer?' He jigged about on the landing whenever we met, dribbling and heading an imaginary ball. 'It'll be ten nil again when I flash these magic feet on Sunday.'

Time passed slowly, but doing it was easy. Life wasn't hard and I didn't lose a day's remission, so my term was almost exactly four months. With three days left I hurt my toe in the Gym and had to go in the prison hospital. One of the jail's social workers came to see me and I told him I was going to London, to stay with Brenda. I hadn't asked her about this, but we had been corresponding and I was sure it would be all right. Now that I was eighteen and officially out of care he gave me the address of the Probation and Aftercare office I would have to visit, telling me I would be able to ask there for any help I might need. Social services had never done this before. Even when I was on licence from Borstal they alone had supervised me.

On my last night I was brought back to the wing and given my pay, so I bought as much tobacco as I could and handed it round to my mates. Next morning, 1st September 1978, they gave me a few quid and a rail warrant to London. I felt no elation whatever, only an ill-defined fear.

She stood unyieldingly in the doorway. 'You can't stay 'ere, Graham.' She jerked her head at the closed living room door. ''E won't 'ave it.'

'Ah, come on, Bren. Not even for tonight?'

'I'm sorry, Graham.' Her lips closed to a thin line and she shut the door in my face. It is the only time she has ever done the dirty on me.

Half a day's tramping later I found the Probation Office, the only thing I could think of.

'No, Mr Gaskin, we definitely *can't* give you a rail warrant to Liverpool. You'll have to use your money.'

'Yeh? That's great, that is. 'Ow do I live when I get there?'

'That's not our concern.'

The Walton social worker had advised me to ask for any help I needed, but he hadn't said I'd get it. I caught a Tube to Edgware and trudged to the M1, which was miles away and took hours. At the entrance to it some guys were trying to fix their car and I stood next to them, thumb out. After ten minutes a Pakistani family stopped and took me to the first services. I was stuck there for the rest of the night. For the first half I sat inside the entrance asking lorry-drivers, but at three in the morning a security man told me to wait outside. It was cold for September.

'Er, can yer take us north, mate?'

'Sorry, son. I'm going the other way.'

'Yeh?' I'd ask their backs. ''Ow are yer goin' to do that on a motorway?'

At six o'clock a tanker driver took me to Knutsford, where I was eventually picked up by three Tottenham supporters, on their way in a battered Cortina to watch their team play at Anfield. I sat in the back seat. As soon as we were moving my neighbour leaned forward and yelled.

'Fackin' 'ell, are we goin' to PULVERIZE them Scarsers today!' He smacked his fist into his palm, THWACK! and looked me over, grinning.

In fifteen seconds the car was doing over ninety.

'Wait till they see a REAL team in action,' the driver shouted. 'Shall we get pissed up there tonight, lads? Sicken all them fackin' Scarsers?'

'Might 'ave to flatten a few if we do,' his neighbour said.

Mine thwacked his palm again. I wondered for a time if they intended beating me up. To add to my nervousness the driver was fast, but not skilful. They carried on raving till we reached the outskirts of Liverpool, but as we went into the city they became meeker, and their tough boasts grew less frequent until they fizzled out altogether. By the time we hit town all three were silent. The driver continued to burn it up from lane to lane. In Scotland Road something funny happened.

We were stuck, revving impatiently, at some traffic lights. They changed to green and our driver shot us forward, cutting viciously in front of an Avenger that was trying to pull out to our right. The more gentlemanly car behind us flashed the Avenger on and it kept right on our tail, its driver glaring with rage. His wife, sitting on the back seat with two little kids, said something to pacify him but at the next red light he jumped out and charged along to us. Our driver fumbled with his door but wasn't quick enough. The angry motorist nearly ripped it from its hinges.

'What the fuck're yer PLAYIN' at?' he roared. 'Yer nearly took the front off me CAR then, an' I've got me WIFE inside an' me KIDS!'

'Don't come that,' the passenger seat guy said, 'we 'ad right of . . .'

Crack, smack! The irate Liverpudlian reached in, gave passenger and driver a lightning dig each, then strode back to his aptly-named car. The lights were green again and we moved off. Nobody said a word. When I looked at the fist-banger beside me he seemed somehow smaller, and I wondered how he had ever frightened me. At the corner by the football ground they dropped me.

'Ta very much, lads.'

'That's all right, Scarse,' one of them said, wearily. 'Seeyer.'

Their enthusiasm had fired my interest in the match, and I went in to watch it. Liverpool won seven nil.

That night I booked into the Y.M.C.A. All my money had gone by the next evening, so at eight o'clock I was standing outside The Crypt. For a long time I looked at the doorway, loath to go in. If there had been anywhere I could have gone I would have turned away.

'Graham!' John Rossington put the big teapot down and walked over, pleased. 'How *are* you? Where've you *been?*'

'In prison, John.'

'Oh.' Silence. He looked at me strangely, and it wasn't until later that I realized his expression had been one of pain. 'Welcome home, then.'

So it was back to bursting fleas on the bedpost, to foul air shot with the moans of the hopeless. Next morning one of the young guys gave me some valium and I popped them, more out of disgust than anything else. This was to be my world, so I would make it bearable at least. After three days' sitting on waste ground with guys from The Crypt, swigging cider to help the valium divorce me from my eighteen years, it was as though I had never been away. In the Single Homeless I ran into Wendy again.

She slid a mug of tea across the counter, shaking her head sadly. 'So you've been in prison now, Graham?'

Amber lights flew in her hair, made brighter and less real by valium.

'I've been in prison all me life, love.'

As I was leaving she gave me an ancient overcoat. That evening I was trudging past Coss Angeli's establishment, the Cooker Market in Hardman Street, when an emaciated kitten ran out from behind a bin, tail in the air, mewing plaintively.

''Ello, puss.' I dropped to my heels and gave it a thorough stroking, then walked on. It followed. I stopped and plapped the sole of my boot on the ground to scare it off. 'Go on. Go on, puss, I can't do nothin' for yer.' It sat down in mid-pavement.

Around the corner I stopped, looking at black buildings made still dimmer by the drug. The sky was charcoal grey. Where should I walk? All directions led nowhere so I sat on a doorstep and went into a valium doze. When a cold, wet, tiny thing touched the back of my hand I opened my eyes. The cat rubbed itself against my leg, purring.

'Okay, puss.' She fitted neatly into the pocket of the coat Wendy had given me. ''Ave it yer own way, then.'

One night when I was lying on my bed in The Crypt bombed out on valium as usual, Wendy walked into the place. She looked fresh and pretty in those grim surroundings.

'Come on, Graham,' she said. 'You deserve better than this. We're going to Halfway House.'

The place was run by Nigel, a fattish guy with a dome of skin curtained on three sides by hair, and two part-time helpers. Barry was a Rastafarian with dreadlocks and the compulsory floppy hat, and Cathy an enormously fat girl who laughed a lot. They gave me a copy of the rules to read then went home, leaving Barry to sleep in. As I fell asleep my head was full of dreams. Perhaps I would get a job again, save up, buy a car . . .

Next morning I teamed up with Jed, the lad who shared my room. He was a little guy, quiet and smiling, and had grown up in care too. His girlfriend lived at Halfway House as well, and he seemed very placid to me then.

'D'yer fancy a blow, Graham?'

'Yeh. Sure do, Jed.'

He stuck some papers together and crumbled hashish into a cigarette. We were halfway through smoking it when the door opened and in walked Barry, the Rasta member of staff. To my surprise he didn't blow a fuse when he saw the joint, but threw himself into a chair and stuck his feet on the coffee table.

'How's it going, lads?'

Jed handed him the joint and he drew on it like a veteran smoker. Later, as we left the house, Barry slipped a small brown paper packet into my hand.

'Welcome to Halfway, Graham.'

When I opened it outside it was top quality marijuana.

Jed's girlfriend went away somewhere that day, so the two of us were thrown together. It was only with him that I felt relaxed. Though Halfway was better than The Crypt, I felt a terrible foreboding from the moment I woke up there. My dreams of stability now seemed incredible. By the time Saturday came Jed and I were good mates. It was Nigel's day off and we were both relieved when he drove away, his fat head stuck out of the window as he bawled last minute instructions. We went to a nearby coffee bar.

'Cathy sleeps in tonight,' Jed said.

'What, the fat one? So what, like?'

He stirred his coffee thoughtfully. 'Yer wanna see 'er when she 'as a couple o' bevvies, Graham. Dyin' for a bit, she is. Creams in 'er dry goods, honest.'

'Yeh? Yer don't fancy 'er, do yer?'

'No.' He shook his head frankly. 'Me bird's back tomorrow, too. Still,' he stirred his coffee some more, 'it *is* tomorrow she comes back, an' Cathy *would* be into it.'

By afternoon we had decided it would help if we had some drugs, so we went to a few doctors. Most turned us away as usual, one or two even noting our false names to tell the police, but in the end we got some downers that were heavier than valium. We popped a couple on the way back to Halfway, where we found Cathy asleep in front of the television.

'D'yer fancy comin' out for a drink, Cath? It's Saturday night, like.'

'Erm, all right. Just give me a minute.'

In the pub, she got drunk quickly. Jed dropped some capsules into her palm. ' 'Ere y'are, girl.'

'Oh thanks. What are they?'

'Some kind o' trancs. Try gettin' 'em down yer neck.'

We asked the barmaid to turn the juke box up and the evening took off, became unhinged, and floated away into dreamland. At ten o'clock Cathy surprised us by pulling out a bottle of Benylin Expectorant, a cough mixture much favoured by junkies, and pouring it into our lager. By closing time all three of us were wiped out. Cathy collapsed outside the pub and it took all our strength to get her on to her feet again.

'Comfy now, Cath?' She watched with glazed eyes as we settled her enormous bulk on to the bed in the staffroom. 'Don't go away, girl, we'll be back soon. We're goin' to get some dope.'

We stepped into the streets. Cars slipped by in slow motion, like imaginary things, and the houses belonged in Toytown. We floated along to the Ibo Club in Parliament Street, popping more downers as we went.

'You wan' buy smoke stuff?' He wore a long dirty robe and his face was crisscrossed with tribal markings. 'Ganja?'

After one drink we walked through dreamy streets to Halfway, popping yet more downers on the way. Cathy was stretched out asleep exactly as we had left her, and my cat was curled up with its paws in her hair.

The rest is a kind of blur. Somehow I rolled a joint and Cathy, now completely out of her head, smoked it with me. A long, low moaning drifted in from the passage outside, where Jed lay crumpled against the skirtingboard.

'Oooooooooooh. Ooooo-oooo-oooo-ooooooooooooh.'

Cathy and I were stretched out on the bed while I stripped her, both of us dropping off frequently into barbiturate stupors. After half an hour her bra came off, and her breasts rolled out like barrels. In slow motion I unzipped my flies and lolled a limp tassel into her hand, then BLAM! The door flew open. It gradually penetrated my brain that Nigel, our leader, was standing in the doorway with lamplight gleaming on his dome.

'Good GOD, Cathy! What are you DOING? For Heaven's SAKE, I just don't believe this!'

Rolling from the bed to the floor I zipped myself slowly, and floated outside to stoop over Jed. He was kneeling with his head against the wall, still moaning.

'Ooooooooooooooooooooh.'

'Jed. Jed, lar. Come on.'

He followed me into the kitchen like a zombie and we gathered up all the food we could find, loaves, a lettuce, a tub of marge and some onions, and staggered upstairs to our room. Below us we could hear Nigel, a pleading note entering his voice.

'Cath, come on. What's wrong with you, Cath?'

We ripped bread and numbly smeared marge on to it with our fingers, spreading grease across our faces and strewing crumbs on the floor like confetti. Afterwards, with laborious slowness, I made a joint which stunk of burnt fat when I lit it. Later I woke sprawled out with my shoulders against the wall, Jed's head on my chest.

'Oooooo-ooooooh. Ooooooooooooooooooh.'

'It's all right, Jed.' I stroked his hair. 'It's all right.'

Time passed dimly, until I realized I was being led downstairs by men in uniform. 'Me leg!' I shouted. 'Watch me leg! Ouch, me leg's done in!' Terrified that a stabbing pain would shoot through my foot if I put it on to the floor, I was hopping. There was nothing wrong with my leg and in a way I knew this, yet I wasn't shamming. It was a weird effect of the drug.

As they were putting me into their gleaming ambulance I noticed that I had no shoes or socks on. My feet were faraway blotches of light and this caused me to weep, quietly, before blackness enveloped me. I woke in a hospital corridor lying on a stretcher trolley. Next to me, on another, lay Jed.

'No! No! Aaaaaaaaaagh!' His scream drowned in a gurgle, then he started shouting, 'Kill me! Kill me! Kill me!'

Doctors, nurses and porters were milling around him, some holding him down while others tried to get a tube into his throat.

'I'm not 'avin' this,' I shouted, terrified. 'I'm not 'AVIN' it! I know me fuckin' rights.'

Such shouts were a reflex to me. Crashing to the floor, I picked myself up and ran towards the entrance. A nurse made as if to follow me but someone shouted, 'Leave him. This one's serious,' and they bent over Jed again.

My feet blobbed white on the black pavements all the way to Halfway House. Barry was there. He bundled Nigel into the staffroom and led me, half weeping, up to my room, where he undressed me and put me to bed.

'Here.' He put a little joint in my hand. 'I'll stay with you till you've smoked that, then you must go to sleep.'

Nigel was very self-righteous next morning. 'We're giving you a day's notice,' he said. 'We want you out of here tomorrow.'

The following morning Wendy arrived and took me to a boarding house in Bootle. There were four old dossers in my room, and the place stank worse than Rosie Munro's. Even my cat didn't like it. Wendy returned next day with my Giro from Halfway House.

'You'll have to send £2.50 for your night's lodging,' she said, and went with me to the post office to make sure that I did. Afterwards we stood on the pavement outside.

'What'll you do now, Graham?'

I shrugged. 'Dunno. I'm goin' to London to see me sister. I'll 'ave a think while I'm down there.'

With my cat peeping out of my coat pocket I thumbed it slowly to the motorway. For once I had had no valium, so as I stood at the roadside I had no choice but to think about my situation. It was now October, and five weeks had passed since I came out of prison. It seemed like five years. In five years' time, probably, there would still be no escape for me, only the occasional transfer from the prison of the streets to the real prison at Walton. After two freezing hours a lorry stopped.

'M6, mate?'

It was dark as I climbed in. The wheels devoured the road and an endless white line whizzed away beneath the lorry.

There would be nothing for me in London, I knew. This pointless journey was the act of a convict pounding his cell wall, a bird crashing into the side of its cage.

Brenda opened the door, her face stiff and mask-like.

''E's away tonight, so you can stay. But on'y tonight, Graham.'

In the morning she was kinder, and pressed a note into my hand as I was leaving. ''Ere you are, Graham. I'm sorry things 'ave been so 'ard for you.' She shook her head. 'I've got me *own* life to live, you know.'

Back in Liverpool I went to the Day Centre, another dossers' venue. The first person I saw was Jed.

''Ow are yer, Jed lar? Got out of 'ospital all right, eh? Where are yer stayin'?'

'Yer won't believe this,' he said, 'but me an' me tart are stayin' with Fat Cath. She got the boot from 'Alfway an' offered to put us up.'

'Yeh? Incredible.'

The flat was in Belvedere Road, not far from Halfway. It was nicely decorated and furnished.

'You can stay for a little while, Graham,' Cathy said, 'but you can't bring that cat in here. It's forbidden by the lease.'

'All right, Cath.'

I took the cat out and left her under a bush by the front door.

''Ow about poppin' some valium?' I asked when I went back in. We sat playing Cathy's four records and after a while Naomi, Jed's girlfriend, went for some cider. We were soon drunk and stoned. An hour later Cathy sent me for more booze and as I was coming back I saw my cat, shivering under the bush where I had left her. I dropped her into my pocket and went inside.

Jed and I used to feed valium and booze to Cathy till she didn't know what she was doing, then strip her and have intercourse with her. It sounds horrible and it was. We comforted ourselves with the thought that she must have known it was going on, as indeed she must. My life at that time was one of utter despair. That is not an excuse. It is merely a fact.

One evening when we were all out of our heads as usual, Jed wandered into the kitchen and did not come back.

'Je-e-ed,' Naomi mumbled, slurred with valium. 'Are you all right, Jed?' Silence. When she had called many times she hauled herself to her feet and lurched away to look for him.

CRASSHBANGLEDANNG! Pots and pans cascaded from the draining board as she blundered into them. 'Oh no! Graham, Cathy, come quick. Jed's DYIN'!'

We fell across the room and stumbled into the kitchen. Jed was lying on the floor, watching with glazed eyes as blood spurted every few seconds from his wrist. A broken glass lay beside him and one shard of it was clutched in his unmutilated hand. I held the vein closed and staggered out of the flat with him, but fell on the stairs. Someone must have phoned the police because they arrived a minute later and took him away.

Naomi was crying. 'D'yer think he'll die, Graham? Do yer?'

'Don't worry, love. 'E'll be back in the mornin'.'

Sure enough at four a.m. there he was, waking me, showing me the stitches, smiling quietly. I found that my face, hair and shirtfront were soaked with his blood.

'We're sorry, Cathy.' The cat mewed goodbye from my pocket. 'We really are.'

We were. She stared at the floor.

That night I trudged wearily up to The Crypt. John Rossington shook his head sadly and threw me a clean towel.

It may not seem possible, but my descent into despair had not yet reached its limit. Things had been hard in the past but a pinpoint of hope had always burned, infinitesimal, but bright and unwavering as a star. When I had lain in darkness as Lawrence's feet beat the stairs to bring me the bite of the cane, it had twinkled, faint but undousable. The stroking hands of Malcolm Bishop had failed to smother it. When I had woken from a largactyl stupor with a screw in the cell doorway waiting to thump me, it had burned, minute but infernal. Now it had gone out. The prisons, dosshouses and lunatic asylums that were my future lay in a sharp focus even valium could not blur. Yet escape, *my* escape, was near. It was to be brought about by my own ingenuity and my will to resist, but first I had to drown in hopelessness, to drag myself along the sea-bed of my soul and come through it alive.

One valium Friday in October 1978 found me walking through a dream to Dale Street, and the offices of the social services department. They put me into Wendy's office and I sat there, cat in pocket, head in hands.

'Graham,' she sounded weary as she came in, 'there's nothing we can do for you. You've abused every . . .'

'There's one thing yer can do,' I said.

'?'

'Talk to me.'

She rested her eyes on my face, sighed and sat down. 'What have you been taking?' she asked. 'You're on something, aren't you?'

The question didn't merit an answer. My fingers snatched air on the table in front of me. 'I'm goin' to tell yer somethin' now, Wendy, an' I want yer to lissen. I can't carry on like this no more. I'd rather die.' I tried, tried to force the power of what I was saying through my eyes and into hers. 'That Crypt's doin' me 'ead in. Now answer me one question. 'Ow d'yer think I got to be like this?'

'I don't know, Graham.'

'Yer do, Wendy. Yer do.' Blindly from the bottom of my mind a clear thought emerged, rose like air through water, and popped into my mouth. 'Get me file. 'Ave a read through it an' see the life yer've given me, you lot. Go on, Wendy, get it now, me file, an' we'll look through it together.'

'I can't do that, Graham,' she said quietly.

'Can't do it?' My anger was a searchlight through the valium. 'Can't do it? Who are youse lot to keep a secret file on me?' My chair clattered over as I swayed to my feet. 'I wanna see me file, Wendy. I want me fuckin' FILE.'

At that moment two male social workers walked into the room, for all the world like the heavy mob on the Block in Wormwood Scrubs. Another confinement in police cells would have faced me if I'd carried on, so I blundered streetwards. Eighteen years earlier my Grandma had snatched me from the arms of my mother before her suicide. Now I scooped my cat from my pocket and laid it, mewing, on a table in the reception area as I lurched through.

'I don't CARE any more,' I shouted as I went out. 'Remember that.'

Muttering, 'I don't care, I don't care,' I tottered along busy Dale Street. People stared at me. 'I don't give a SHIT,' I told the lamp-posts and the shop windows. They fled past, not caring either.

At the end of Dale Street there is a flyover, one of the primary routes into town, down which the cars fly like rocks down a quarry chute. It was empty when I reached it, which is unusual.

I stepped numbly off the kerb, made my way to the middle, turned towards the traffic and walked up its gentle slope. A moment later a tidal wave of cars and lorries hurled itself around the corner at the top, metallic, belching blue smoke, roaring in my ears as it rushed towards me. I closed my eyes and walked on, my head battered by the scream of klaxons and the shriek of skidding tyres.

CRASSHHBASHHBOOOM! One car smashed into another and the second clanged into the guard rail at the side of the road. A third slammed me sideways and the air was a great wrenching and ripping and rending of metal. I flew across concrete with the acrid stench of burning rubber saturating me.

Footsteps clattered over. 'Here, lad. Can yer get up? Grab his arms, pal.' Hands grasped me. 'That's it. Come on.' I felt myself moving.

Voices murmured.

'What's up with 'im?'

'Heart attack? Can't be. He's only a kid.'

I opened my eyes to terrifying faces and a sky the colour of concrete, and closed them again immediately. Blackness took me. I came to in a hospital bed.

Wendy arrived later and took me to a hostel in Anfield, a place for mental patients making their way into the world. For the rest of that day I stared into space, shaking my head when approached. Over the weekend I ate, slept, had baths, watched television, and suffered fits of the shakes. On Monday morning the lady in charge handed me a bus ticket.

'You're to go to social services in Dale Street, love.'

One of the chiefs was there and he led me into Wendy's office, where she was sitting at her desk. There was a chair facing her, and on the desk in front of it were three files. The thick one was mine, and the two slimmer ones Brenda's and Robert's.

'You can look at them for an hour,' the chief said, pursing his lips disagreeably, 'since you insist.'

He left. Wendy smiled, shaking hair like burnished copper. 'I've something else for you, Graham.'

She went out of the room. When she came back she flung me a bundle of fur that caught claws on my lapels, miaowing.

'Ta, Wendy. Thanks for lookin' after 'er.'

There was complete silence in the room. I leafed through the pages, pondering. What I read made me only mildly angry. The lives the social workers were writing about, my early years and those of my sister and brother, corresponded only hazily to our reality. After fifteen minutes the phone rang, and Wendy picked it up.

'Yes?' She listened. 'What, now? Can't it wait?' She glanced at me thoughtfully. 'Well, I *could*, I suppose. Yes. In a couple of minutes, then.'

She put it down.

'Graham,' she said.

'Hmm?'

'If I go upstairs for a minute, do I have your word that you won't take any pieces out of the files? It'd get me into awful trouble, you know.'

'Yeh. Okay, Wendy.'

'You promise?'

'Yeh.'

She went out.

Far, far in the depths of my mind I thought of taking it, but it wouldn't have happened if, five minutes after she went, I hadn't reached some parts which made me profoundly angry. The first was a memo that had passed between two social workers, its subject the fostering of myself to a single man, Malcolm Bishop. It was a supreme rationalization and ended with the words, hastily scrawled, 'Shouldn't we bend the rules this time and send Graham along?' Remembering early mornings when I had woken to Malcolm's insistent hands, to his mouth moving leech-like along my body, I became enraged. On the very next page there was a self-congratulatory sheet, also in connection with Malcolm, whose opening words angered me further. 'Our work in this case will go down in the annals of social work history as one of sustained and genuine *care* . . .' That did it. Just one of the places they had sent me to would have been enough to destroy a person. I had been unlucky enough to go to them all, and here were social services patting themselves on the back for the good job they had done.

Only my promise to Wendy worried me. She was all right. Nevertheless, she was part of the machine. Technically, anyway, I wouldn't be breaking my word. I wasn't taking any *parts* out. With rattling hands I scooped my cat from the floor, dropped her into my pocket, and picked up the file. I dithered for a moment, then shoved it under my coat and strode through the reception area into Dale Street.

Certain that a hue and cry would come flying out any moment after me I stepped in time to the thumps of my heart, and with many backward glances, till I turned the corner into Old Hall Street. The offices of the *Liverpool Echo* were in front of me and I went through the doors and up to a security man who was standing in the foyer.

'Er, mate. Erm, lissen, like . . .' I took a deep breath and said with sudden clarity, 'Can I see a reporter?'

'Take a seat over there,' he said.

After a few minutes a reporter came down. 'What can we do for you?'

'I've got a social services file 'ere. D'yer wanna talk about it?'

He pulled some chairs over, gave me a fag and a cup of coffee, checked that the file was genuine, and shot away. In a minute he was back with the news editor, a tall, smart, self-assured man called Vincent Kelly. He took me downstairs to his office.

'Right, Mr Gaskin. Can I call you Graham? Okay, Graham, let's have a look at this, shall we?'

For a couple of hours he looked through it, asking me questions about my life as he did so. Afterwards he took me to the canteen for something to eat. I kept the file clutched tightly under my arm. Now that I had it no one was going to take it away.

'Is it all right if I photocopy some pieces of this?' he asked when we were back in his office.

'Yeh, okay. Bring 'em back, though.'

'We've done all we can for today,' he said later, when it was dark outside. 'Will you come back at noon tomorrow and bring the file with you?'

'Yeh, okay.'

'Here.' He dug into his pocket and gave me some notes. 'That'll get you a bed for the night. It's from me, though, not the *Echo*.' He smiled. 'Don't go thinking you're being paid for your story, because you're not.'

'Ta, Vince.'

I left the *Echo* offices with the precious dossier under my arm, a different person from the young derelict who had tramped those streets in recent weeks. The spark of hope which had sustained me through the hard years was back, blazing now like a furnace. I put the file in the left luggage office at the bus station and went to the Salvation Army.

Next day I returned to the *Echo*.

'Here, kid.' One of the reporters gave me a cup of coffee. 'Sit down and wait over there. We've heard about you.' He came back later and gave me a packet of fags.

At two o'clock a lady came to see me. She was nice-looking in a short-haired, efficient way.

'Mr Gaskin? I'm Lynne May. Come along to my office and we'll talk.' When we were seated she said, 'Tell me about your life.'

'Me life? All of it? Where do I start, like?'

'At the beginning. What do you know about your parents?'

By four o'clock Vincent Kelly was there too. He silently handed me a packet of fags, then sat down to listen.

'Well,' Lynne May said at the end, 'it's one hell of a story, Graham. One thing, though. Why should anyone believe it?'

'It's true,' I said. 'That's why. An' I've got me file to prove it.'

They went out to talk, but were back in a minute.

'Will you let us photocopy it, Graham?' Lynne May said.

'Yeh. O' course. I want yer to.'

She called a taxi and took me to the bus station to pick it up. While we were there she bought me a packet of fags, which I put in my pocket with the others.

'Er, d'yer mind if I let me cat 'ave a little walk, like? She 'ates bein' stuck inside all the time.'

Vincent Kelly had a spread laid out for me when we got back to the *Echo*, pies, cakes and coffee. While I was eating a junior reporter took my file away to be photocopied. Later Kelly pulled me to one side.

'Look, Graham. Now that we have a copy you'd better give that file back. Technically, you've committed theft.'

'Yeh, I've been thinkin' about that. D'yer think I should ring social services first an' get 'em to give me a letter sayin' I won't be prosecuted? Then I could swop it for the file, like.'

'Yes.' He nodded. 'That should cover you.'

'An' I'll get 'em to promise they won't discipline Wendy at the same time, eh?'

'Good idea, Graham. That idea does you credit.'

He gave me my entrance fee into the Salvation Army again.

Drring, drring. Drring, drr . . .

'Social services department,' a honeyed voice answered. 'I'm afraid there's a dispute on today, no social workers are available.'

'I don't want one,' I said. 'I want one o' the chiefs. Tell 'im it's Graham Gaskin.'

Silence. After a minute a man's voice came over the line. 'Dave Davis here.' He was one of the social workers who knew me. 'Is that you, Graham? Look, what d'you think you're playing at? You can't steal from us any more than you can from anyone else, you know. We could call the police.'

'Yeh?' My contemptuous tone let him know how much that scared me. 'Look, I'll get to the point. D'yer want it back?'

'Yes, we do, and you'd better get it here double quick.'

'Hmm. I want a written assurance first, see, statin' two things. First that I'll be safe from prosecution for pinchin' it, an' second that Wendy won't be got at. 'Ow does that grab yer?'

There was a pause. 'Who've you been talking to, Graham? Have you shown it to anyone?'

'Never mind that. Do I get me written assurance, or what?'

'*I* can't do it,' he said, 'I'll have to talk with the Director. Ring back in half an hour.'

When I phoned he hadn't found the Director, but agreed to bring my letter himself.

'Stand outside the office at four o'clock,' he said, 'and I'll bring it out to you. When you've read it you can hand me the file.'

'Okay. I won't 'ave the file on me, though. It'll be with a mate around the corner.'

This was bluff, but you can't be too careful.

At the appointed hour I stood in blustery Dale Street. Dave Davis came out and gave me the note, which said exactly what I had demanded. I pulled the file from the back of my trousers and handed it over. He didn't say anything and neither did I.

My mistake at this point was thinking things would change, quickly. I was eighteen, and therefore impatient. Nothing really changed, though I was materially better off for a time. Social services suddenly decided they could pay me £2 a night for the Salvation Army, and for a time Kelly paid it as well. My weekly Giros still came so I had some lavish evenings in the pub with

Jed, my Halfway House friend. After a week or two everything dried up.

For my cat and myself things went on as before. In the evenings we alternated between Arden House and The Crypt, and in the daytime she peeped from my pocket while I trudged town or stood in the stores to keep warm.

Many of the phone box windows were smashed, and a bitter wind streamed through.

'Is that the *Echo*? Can I speak to Vincent Kelly? It's Graham Gaskin.'

After a couple of minutes he came on to the line.

'Hello? Graham?'

'Er, yeh.'

'What can I do for you?'

'Well, I've got nowhere to stay, like. I'm on the street.'

'Whereabouts are you, Graham?'

'In Victoria Street, by the New Court Bar.'

'Wait there,' he said.

Vincent Kelly is a good man. Ten minutes later he arrived in his car and took me to his house in Hightown. He and his wife were due to go out to a party, but he let me have a bath and even gave me some of his old clothes. His wife opened a tin of food for my cat, and I spent some time talking to her.

A day or two later social services decided they could afford to put me in a hotel. It was a place for distressed families and was clean and comfortable, but there was nothing whatever to do there, not even a television. The fact that still nothing had changed got me down. I began popping valium again in earnest, and drifted back to The Crypt.

John Rossington had become a true friend by that time. How he coped with my havoc I cannot say, it is a testament to his patience and humanity that he did. Once I went off my head for three days, popping valium and artane. On the second night I cracked up completely in The Crypt, tore my clothes into shreds and lay naked on the couch in the office. John took me to hospital, where they put me to bed. My rags were in the bedside locker with more capsules hidden in them, and next morning I awoke very early, dressed swiftly, popped a few and left without anyone knowing. When my binge was over I woke up in The Crypt again, with John at my bedside. He told me the following story.

The previous afternoon I had tottered into the Day Centre, shouting. He had bought me a meal and tried to talk to me, but I had thrown it at him and the Day Centre staff had phoned the police. They had taken me to the Bridewell and he had followed, getting them to promise to release me when I had slept it off. Last night I had staggered into The Crypt and fallen asleep on the floor. As he told me this story pieces of it started to come together, like fragments of a jigsaw dream.

'Colin, this is Graham, the lad I told you about.'

Colin Oxenforth was a small, Mephistophelean-looking guy, the vicar of St Margaret's on Princes Road, and a good friend of John's. We shook hands.

'Where's your bag?' he asked.

'Bag? I 'aven't got no bag. On'y a cat.'

'You'd better bring it in, then,' he said.

With that I left the world of dosshouses and valium behind me, I hope forever. Colin's was a nice house, clean and brightly furnished, and I could take a bath whenever I wanted. John came to see me often, and our friendship grew. He took me to see Rex Makin, who is just about the best lawyer in Liverpool, and an action for damages against social services was begun. This is still going on now, three and a half years later, the main wrangle being that they won't release my original file for evidence. John Rossington was Chairman of Liverpool Liberal Party then. He took me to see David Alton, the M.P. for Liverpool Edge Hill, who was very interested in my story. In December of that year, 1978, John took me to London for my nineteenth birthday, and we visited the Liberal Club.

'I've another surprise for you,' he said as we drove back into Liverpool.

'Ah, 'ey John. I think yer've done enough, lar.'

'This one didn't cost me anything.' He grinned. 'You might say you're about to take your rightful place in society.'

We drove towards our unknown destination, and to my surprise were soon in the Rice Lane area of Walton, where I should have lived as a kid. We stopped outside a big, recently refurbished house with a sign outside.

LIVERPOOL IMPROVED HOUSES

FLATS TO BE LET AT FAIR RENTS

John pulled a key from his pocket and dangled it.

'It's yours, Graham,' he said.

He hadn't quite been telling the truth when he said it hadn't cost him anything. There was a brand-new carpet on the living room floor. He took me to Colin Oxenforth's for that night, but told me to be at the flat next day. He wouldn't say why.

At three o'clock next afternoon a van pulled up outside my flat and two men started unloading second-hand furniture. I ran down.

'Graham Gaskin?' one of them asked.

'Yeh.'

'This lot's for you, then. Some of the reporters at the *Echo* have collected it for you.'

Everything was soon inside, and I waved goodbye to the men and closed my front door, then sat on a rolled-up carpet looking at the stuff they had brought. There was even a fridge.

'Come on, puss.'

She lay in my lap purring for all she was worth. I stroked her soft fur and felt again her delicate bones. As it grew dark I went over to the window and stood looking out. Lights were on in some of the houses, individual squares that shone here and there. What the future might hold for me I could not tell, and fear at this thought tightened my chest for a moment. I looked out at the city to calm myself. More lights had come on, and I told myself that I was like one of the people in those rooms now, that I could turn on my light and add my symbol of warmth to theirs whenever I chose. Yet my fear stayed with me. None of my life so far had been normal, and I had had no training to prepare me for the usual life that people lead. How would I survive out there, in that abnormal world which was normal to everyone else? It seemed probable that I would fail, but if I did I would try again, and never give up trying until I managed to snatch some happiness for myself.

My cat miaowed and began to paddle restlessly with her paws, so I put her down. She scampered into the kitchen and I turned away from the world outside and followed her. For the moment, at least, I was an outsider no longer.